Afro ⚜ Texans

SERIES EDITORS: WILL GUZMÁN, KIMBERLY D. HILL, AND WILLIAM T. HOSTON

Also in the series:

Emmett J. Scott: Power Broker of the Tuskegee Machine
by Maceo C. Dailey Jr.; edited by Will Guzmán and David H. Jackson Jr.

Images in the River: The Life and Work of Waring Cuney
by Cynthia Davis and Verner D. Mitchell

Their Stories, Our Stories: Four Presidents of Huston-Tillotson University
by Rosalee Martin

THE WATER CRIES

UNCOVERING THE SLAVE AUCTION HOUSES OF GALVESTON, TEXAS

ANTHONY PAUL GRIFFIN

TEXAS TECH UNIVERSITY PRESS

Copyright © 2025 by Anthony Paul Griffin

All rights reserved. No portion of this book may be reproduced in any form or by any means, including electronic storage and retrieval systems, except by explicit prior written permission of the publisher. Brief passages excerpted for review and critical purposes are excepted.

This book is typeset in EB Garamond. The paper used in this book meets the minimum requirements of ANSI/NISO Z39.48-1992 (R1997). ♾

Designed by Hannah Gaskamp
Cover design by Hannah Gaskamp
Cover art by Rachel Maynard

Library of Congress Cataloging-in-Publication Data

Names: Griffin, Anthony P., author. Title: The Water Cries: Uncovering the Slave Auction Houses of Galveston, Texas / Anthony Paul Griffin. Description: Lubbock, Texas: Texas Tech University Press, [2025] | Series: Afro-Texans | Includes bibliographical references and index. |
Summary: "Searching for the true location of Galveston's long-mythologized slave auction houses using historical documentation and family archives"—Provided by publisher.
Identifiers: LCCN 2024017002 (print) | LCCN 2024017003 (ebook) |
ISBN 978-1-68283-199-1 (paperback) | ISBN 978-1-68283-198-4 (ebook)
Subjects: LCSH: Slave auctions—Texas—Galveston—History. | Slave trade—Texas—Galveston—History. | African Americans—Texas—Galveston—History. | Historic sites—Texas—Galveston.
Classification: LCC E445.T47 G75 2024 (print) | LCC E445.T47 (ebook) |
DDC 363.6/909764139—dc23/eng/20240612
LC record available at https://lccn.loc.gov/2024017002
LC ebook record available at https://lccn.loc.gov/2024017003

25 26 27 28 29 30 31 32 33 / 9 8 7 6 5 4 3 2 1

Texas Tech University Press
Box 41037
Lubbock, Texas 79409-1037 USA
800.832.4042
ttup@ttu.edu
www.ttupress.org

To Albert and Lillian Wright, who have always been my guiding light. To those who stood by the water hearing strange fruit call them by something other than their names and surely not their original names. This includes Susan (about 24), Fanny (about 21), Susan (about 50), Elvira (about 15), Tamer (about 16), Eliza (about 16), Lucy Ann (about 18), Winnie (about 18), Isiah (about 6 months), Rueben (about 21), George (about 20), Bennett (about 21), Mason (about 18), William (about 21), Henry (about 10), Charles (about 16), Sam (about 16), Jack (about 15), Harrison (about 17), Nathan (about 17), Robert (about 13), Rachael (about 14), Charles (about 31), Jacob (about 30), Toney and family: Toney (about 48), Mary (about 28), Alfred (about 12), Eliza (about 10), Ann (about 7), Rufus (about 3), Melinda (about 5 months)—all auctioned in conjunction with seven or eight large American mules, two horses and wagons—and the millions of souls who traveled through the port of Galveston and other fraught designations.

CONTENTS

ILLUSTRATIONS		IX
ACKNOWLEDGMENTS		XI
CHAPTER 1:	Why Search?	3
CHAPTER 2:	Working Against and with Our Shared Duality	17
CHAPTER 3:	Letting You Hear Me Scream!	21
CHAPTER 4:	Things of Value	29
CHAPTER 5:	Much Like Water	39
CHAPTER 6:	Their Cries Remain Audible	59
CHAPTER 7:	Why Is the Truth Important?	79
CHAPTER 8:	We Must Say Their Names and More	89
CHAPTER 9:	For History's Sake	93
CHAPTER 10:	Maybe the Negroes Went Too Fast	107
CHAPTER 11:	History's Voices Continue to Circle	149
CHAPTER 12:	Above and Circling, Always Present	161
CHAPTER 13:	Epilogue	169
NOTES		175
INDEX		253

ILLUSTRATIONS

5	Fig. 1: Chesterana Demus Wright
22	Fig. 2: Middle Passage plaque
33	Fig. 3: Brooks & Dobbins ad, *Civilian and Galveston City Gazette*
34	Fig. 4: New Orleans commission ads, *Civilian and Galveston Gazette*
41	Fig. 5: Juneteenth plaque
46	Fig. 6: William H. Jones & family
47	Fig. 7: Galveston College Board of Regents
66	Fig. 8: Plantation ads, *Galveston Daily Civilian*
67	Fig. 9: New Orleans, Galveston & Velasco ad, *Civilian and Galveston Gazette*
95	Fig. 10: Construction of seawall
98	Fig. 11: Wedding portrait of Charles Aaron and Willa A. Bruce
100	Fig. 12: Beachgoers
103	Fig. 13: Pair at the beach
106	Fig. 14: Old Hospitals, University of Texas Medical Branch, Galveston
110	Fig. 15: Dock workers
114	Fig. 16: Ads for Pope's Bath House and rooms for rent
120	Fig. 17: Klan Parade, Waco
125	Fig. 18: Central High School faculty
128	Fig. 19: Marimba
129	Fig. 20: *The Day that I'll Always Remember*, musicians
130	Fig. 21: Florence Fedford (Henderson) and Izola Fedford (Collins)
131	Fig. 22: Izola and Roy Lester Collins Sr.
133	Fig. 23: Idle Wyle's annual picnic
135	Fig. 24: Working Girls' Social Club
136	Fig. 25: Hutchings, Sealy, etc. ads, *City Times* (Galveston)
137	Fig. 26: F. E. Stewart, Mrs. J. Mouton's restaurant & Mrs. N. C. Washington ads, *City Times* (Galveston)
138	Fig. 27: Galveston chapter of the Circle-lets
139	Fig. 28: Rachel Pope
141	Fig. 29: Marie Harderman's class, Booker T. Washington Elementary

ILLUSTRATIONS

- 142 Fig. 30: Segregated restroom sign
- 158 Fig. 31: Sharon Baldridge Lewis, Ellis Bernard Baldridge, Dorothy Corine Baldridge
- 159 Fig. 32: Poll tax, Chesterana Wright
- 162 Fig. 33: Dr. I. L. Jones ad, *City Times* (Galveston)
- 163 Fig. 34: Idle Wyle's Club ad, *City Times* (Galveston)
- 164 Fig. 35: Group at Live Oak Missionary Baptist Church
- 165 Fig. 36: Reedy Chapel Church group, Galveston
- 172 Fig. 37: Joyce Finch Landry

ACKNOWLEDGMENTS

This work would have never seen the light of day without the help of a disparate and diverse group of people: Travis Snyder with Texas Tech University Press for saying yes and recognizing this story as one that should be told. To my oldest daughter, Rachel Maynard, for delivering the cover art on a timely basis, even though she was struggling with her health. To Ellyn Julia Clevenger, Esq., who I believe is nothing more than an internet spy masquerading as a lawyer. She sat in the office listening to me scream, moan, and protest much too much before getting involved, using her skills to find invaluable information, information that helps make this book work.

To the women who shared their family's histories: Penny Pope, Starita Smith, Eddie Bernice Johnson, and Izola Collins. Izola, I know you stayed on me to write this work years ago. Although you are no longer with us, thank you for being a friend over the years. And one more thank you. Heber Taylor retired from the *Galveston Daily News* around the same time I stopped practicing law. Heber served the newspaper as the managing editor and enjoyed his work as much as I enjoyed mine. Heber, thank you for reading—your suggestions, persuasion, prodding, and yes, contributions to the Fourth Estate.

Absolutely I have been a pest. This pest thanks each of you.

THE WATER CRIES

CHAPTER 1

WHY SEARCH?

It Happened So Long Ago...

It was a summer day. The wind was silent, stagnant—hers an unknown presence—permitting the sun to enhance her God-like characteristics. The sun positioned herself directly overhead, staring, controlling, supreme. I arrived consumed in thought. My goal was simple: clean one or two lots and leave. A limited goal, but still taxing; her—the sun's stare served as a constant reminder of what awaited. Our persistent coastal weather pattern invited others (heat and humidity) to join. This was the anointed committee.

I was here yesterday. I just cleaned this area yesterday. The weeds remained content, undisturbed by my lament. I am sure they heard every thought. I swear I heard laughter. It had to be *their* laughter, not the multitudes dispatched from below. They had greater numbers, but they were silent. A silent movement, a seemingly disjointed unity—outward, forward, upward. Immediate and magical, triggered by my transgression, the disturbance of their peace. When I did notice them, I didn't initially say anything. I was lost in thought.

Unimaginable swiftness was theirs; a brilliant, unrelenting attack followed—immediate and silent efficiency. They couldn't care less about my thoughts, any subsequent plea for mercy, or why I dared return. The seagulls circled in a slow flight pattern, squawking. These reddish brown creatures ignored the noise coming from above.

Maybe they too are part of the committee.

I saw indications of their presence the day before: small, shattered mounds on this and other lots, but not the massive mound now in place. I admit I was first to act. The day before, I tried to kill all of them. Their numbers told me they knew my intentions. Today they seemed full of hate, angry. I guess my actions were pure and utter folly.

Maybe I should sue the manufacturer of the ant poison. They seem so healthy.

I had never bothered to learn their scientific name (*Solenopsis*). Perhaps this was the insult, not bothering to know anything about them, never knowing there were two hundred different species, and knowing little about how they have adapted. I knew them as fire ants, invasive pests that appeared to grow in number every year. This day, that day, their numbers seemed disproportionate to my recent attack on them.

They immediately covered the top and sides of my right boot. I stepped out of the weeds, retreating, back onto the concrete. A pointless act. At the time I did not have occasion to think any of this, my movement was more instinctive reaction if anything, survival.

The sun continued to stare. The seagulls continued to squawk—shrill, frantic. Their sound could have well been them saying "we tried to warn you earlier, fool." My movements were now crooked, angled, none too graceful, backward, awkward. *Lord, I hope no one is looking.*

Reinforcements seemed to flow from everywhere. Over the concrete's edge, circling—both sides, the rear—preventing their prey's escape. Someone may have been hastening the second hand, time was now moving faster. *Oh no, they are inside my pants legs!*

The buildings that previously occupied this portion of the land had long been demolished; the vibrancy of the area was now generations past. The neighborhood, Old Central Carver Park, was in full transition towards a slow painful death. I have lamented over the years about the city's neglect of its residents and infrastructure—providing little in social services and funding. Every time funding was promised, the funds were diverted to other areas. Small acts that did take place were minuscule in the scope of the community's problems. Even the non-official description of the area seemed tainted: The Jungle. On that day, though, the absence of people provided me an advantage—there were no witnesses to my cowardice.

I pulled off both gloves, struggling, jerking, making use of teeth, and threw them as far away as I could. I tugged at the right boot, the sock, leaving them on their own, both now covered. My decisions were acts of a desperate man. This did not stop the unrelenting attack. The appearance of the additional forces persuaded me to quicken my escape.

Some of their masses were now in new positions: a perfect circle around my right ankle, ensconced between each toe, on the top of the foot. I had no one to consult with or provide me with directions, comfort, or aid. My mind was an active participant in the conspiracy, it reminded me of those I flung away with the

Figure 1: Chesterana Demus Wright.

shoe and sock. *They are probably dismounting and coming back for you.* Oh my, I was the epitome of manhood, bravery, and unimaginable courage.

I moved as fast as a one-legged man could move. With one leg lifted, I hopped and jumped toward the van. I lifted the rear door, took a seat, and began picking, swatting, and pinching even those who were burrowed deep. One of their number was halfway up my thigh. I didn't discover this until it bit me. I assume he/she/it received a mystical command. I can now imagine a scientist who has dedicated his/

CHAPTER I

her life to studying these creatures wanting to explain to me what was occurring. I frankly wouldn't care to have this discussion—then or now!

My maternal grandparents, Louis (Daddy Louis) and Chesterana (Muh Chest), lived in a small African American farming community. The land was situated in both Freestone and Limestone Counties. The only Whites I saw on the farm were few and far between: the water-well men who showed up looking for water to dig a new well; the White man who visited the land across the road from their farm. He would pull up in a white truck, get out and open the gate, drive his truck back on the land, move toward oil/gas equipment located towards the rear of the property, and leave. The land was wooded and fenced and extended for miles and miles. I never climbed the fence to explore. The signs said "Keep Out." I wasn't worried about the signs, I was told by my grandparents "no." No explanation, no reason, "no!"

Their farming community was in one of Texas's agricultural belts. The soil was a sandy loam, which contributed to bountiful crops. My grandfather's church was approximately a mile north of the farm. Daddy Louis was a member of Gibson Chapel, an African Methodist Episcopal (AME) congregation. Muh Chest was Baptist. To get to her church from Gibson Chapel, I remember you made a right turn out of the church's parking lot and walked/drove no more than fifty yards before making a left, then proceeded approximately another one hundred yards before making another right. There were no stop signs, street signs, or streetlights. The roads were of compacted red clay with rocks lining the edge on both sides. When making the turn onto the new road, the land the White man visited was on the left side, and on the right were houses and my grandparents' land, a small farm. Cousin Evaline's house occupied the corner portion of the land, a small plot fenced off on the property. I never remembered which side she was on—a Demus, a Wright—or how she was a cousin. She got tired of telling me and just welcomed me into her home. She always had peppermints in a glass bowl, which was on the coffee table when you entered. My grandparents' farm was next, then Uncle Sanford (Daddy Louis's brother) and Aunt Margaret's house/farm next. As a child I thought Uncle Sanford was mean; I didn't like the way he treated Daddy Louis. I liked Aunt Margaret; she remembered our names with joy and ushered us into the room to see our great-grandparents. "How old? How tall? What do you want to do when you're grown?" I told them I was five. I watched and listened to them: their skin tones, their size. They both had gray eyes. I never asked how long they had been blind. I don't ever remember having any conversation past their brief inquiries. They asked me how momma was, little else.

Honestly, I thought too much as a child. I kept my head down, worried. I don't know why I worried so much as a child, I just did. At five I didn't have the vocabulary to explain. At nighttime there was a void—nightmares; suspended in space, dangling; worried I was going to drop. I can't explain this sensation any better. Screaming as I cried, "Air, air!" I didn't need air; I was afraid of the air. I was falling. I can't go any further, trust me.

My great-grandparents, Albert and Lillian Wright, lived with Uncle Sanford and Aunt Margaret. There was another piece of land owned by my grandparents, it was four, five, ten miles away from the main house. The other field was located in a different county, Limestone. It seemed a long way by wagon. We would jump on and off the wagon and run with the dogs as we traveled. Always, when we arrived, I was astonished by the other field. Rows and rows of freshly burrowed land initially, then magically, the next time we visited, there were rows and rows of peas.

Daddy Louis guided the mules to the edge of the fence line. He would unhitch them from the wagon and tie them to the fence under a shade tree. Muh Chest would make sure our hats were in place and instructed us on what we were doing that day. Picking peas involved working both sides of the row using both hands. The unshelled peas were deposited in a large croker sack attached to your body, draped crosswise. An experienced picker was able to manage two bags at a time. We were not experienced pickers. The bag was bigger than us. We dragged the bag through the sand as we inched along, leaning.

At harvest time, others came to help reap the other crops surrounding the farmhouse: cotton, corn, and potatoes. Grown men with knives and guns appeared on the farm when large animals were slaughtered. I now assume on this occasion the families took a portion of the slaughter. Large trailers were backed into the entrance to load cattle and pigs, the stock going to market. We went by wagon to the cotton gin to get supplies not produced on the farm. I didn't like those people at the cotton gin.

During winter your work in the fields would reappear as part of dinner, in that a portion of the summer crops were preserved. Our portion of the slaughtered animals and birds were pressure-cooked and also preserved. I discovered this when Muh Chest asked me to hand her turkey from the pantry. I looked around, confused. "Where?" She smiled and pointed, "From the pantry." I had never opened the door she pointed to. I was amazed at what I saw: from top to bottom, glass bottles containing fruits, vegetables, and poultry. I did as I was told but peeked again before fully closing the door.

As we picked, the sun was always there, staring, providing an unbearable and intense heat, searing memories. *"Roll your sleeves down! Put your hat back on!"* The crickets cried in the distance. We inched along on hands, knees, bowed backs, picking. Muh Chest was always present. Other than the birds fluttering and singing in the tree line, her low, faithful humming was the only sound. I thought we would never finish, but we always finished what she said we were going to do that day.

CHAPTER I

"Do I pick this little baby pea?" My sun-browned hand held high.

"You already have, baby; put it in the bag."

Muh Chest slowed her pace to keep sight of us. She gave instructions about how to work faster and how to conserve our backs. She forever told us to stay covered and keep our hats on.

"Keep up."

I remember her laughing once when lapping us. I suspect she laughed at her wonderful summer helpers, her filling three to four times our pitiful contributions no matter how hard we tried.

Muh Chest was Baptist. I remember going to Muh Chest's church more than Daddy Louis's—Wednesdays and Sundays. There was a once-a-year pilgrimage to the farm by her church members. Slowly moving across the land, not at all rushed—a sea of different shades of brown people draped in white against a backdrop of blue and greens—to conduct baptisms. This was pretty to me—the colors, the sun, the same faithful hum done in unison.

It was a tree-lined tank, the trees situated roughly fifty yards away; they surrounded the westerly portion of the tank. It was the largest tank on their land—twenty feet upward to get to the top. Once on top—always, always—greeted by the wind's welcoming breath, a peaceful oasis. I understood why her church members came every year. The water was magical. Men and women prayed, sang, and fanned out—first during the journey from the front of the farm, then again when they reached the water's edge.

The tank was on the back side of the farm, the northwest edge. Five or six people carried tambourines, the others' voices served as their instruments. I don't remember many people who were my size among their numbers.

I still can see my mother's (Georgia Ann) honey-brown skin in the distance, walking toward us in a flowing dress. She came to see if her babies were ready to come home (to Fort Worth). I was the only one who elected to stay. She showed up a week later and required me to come home "just for a short time." She let me come back a week later. My siblings fled as rapidly as they could back to the city. I don't remember any of them wishing me off. To me, the days were not long enough. I was there for another year and saw the pilgrimage return. The group seemed smaller. During the year, men and women visited Muh Chest when death neared—days for some, weeks for others. They always occupied the extra bedroom. She cared for her neighbors, fellow farmers, and church members. She bathed and prayed over at least ten of them that summer. They came to die.

"Everyone is dying, why?" The next morning, she had me help.

"Baby, we shouldn't fear death. It is a natural process. Put your hand on his chest."

Even though Daddy Louis and Muh Chest attended different congregations, they reconciled the difference by nightly prayer service. This came after dinner and baths; the prayer service was one to two hours. Prayer was followed by the radio coming on the first time, with the voice of what sounded like a White man. He introduced himself as "Reverend A. A. Allen." We never went to bed prior to A. A. Allen anointing us—except for the time Muh Chest got sick, and the nightly routine changed.

Apparently, there was no one to bathe and pray for her as she had done for others. She and Daddy Louis were brought to the city to live with Uncle Warren and Aunt Mildred. To this day, I still cry over the voidness in her eyes, wondering whether the small room made her sadder. When she later transitioned to the hospital I could see the buzzards circling. I wanted her to tell me to go check on the animals. I wanted her to remind me to go into the barn and look for eggs and snakes. I wanted to see her bend over laughing when she saw the fear in my eyes when I saw a snake in the middle of the chickens. She told me to kill it! I missed wildly, swinging the hoe repeatedly! I never touched it! I never touched it! The snake was surrounded by indentures in the soil while Muh Chest, bent over laughing, grabbed the hoe and swiftly executed the largest snake I had ever seen. With these memories, I just wanted her to tell me anything.

Every night we tested the strength and construction of the human body, praying on our knees with hands extended outward while Daddy Louis and Muh Chest took turns serving as our prayer leaders. Light shone from a single bulb positioned in the corner. The cord ran along the wall, attached to an extension cord, hanging on a small nail driven in the wall. The overhead light remained off throughout the session.

The chickens were in coops (some in the barn at the top), a few settled in the outdoor toilet, quietly seated around the edge. They were all quiet by this time. I knew their location because my job in the morning was to check for eggs.

Roughly three dozen turkeys were located behind the house, to the right. They too were settled. The cattle, the one horse (sometimes two), and two mules were in the barn area—long settled and quiet. The pigs, roughly one hundred of them, were located further out in a fenced-in area near the second tank. They settled mostly along the fence line, some on the water's edge, peaceful. Even the large mean boar, who lowered his head before charging, was peaceful. He pretended to be invisible. He was not. I always watched for him.

I never knew where the dogs bedded or whether they spent the night roaming the land. I would guess the latter. Chesterana had no qualms about telling everyone their roles. At the nightly prayer service, no man, woman, child, or creature disturbed Muh Chest as she sang and paid homage. We always ended each prayer session in song, no matter how tired any of us were.

My siblings and I complained of our knees hurting more than once—to each other only. Remember, we too were quiet like everyone else.

My grandparents were dedicated to their faiths. I also noticed something as a child: they honored Mother Nature with equal reverence. Mother Nature probably helped them reconcile any differences between their faiths. An *Old Farmer's Almanac* calendar hung on the wainscoted western wall in the kitchen. They forever used "she" or "her" in referencing any part of Mother Nature.

With a rain bonnet over her head, Muh Chest lingered, the rainwater coating her almond-colored skin. I never asked what she was doing. She permitted me to stand next to her, looking upward, watching.

I once complained about a headache when we were sitting on the porch. Muh Chest told me to sit between her legs. "Look at the clouds, study them, watch their movement." I did, while pointing out the differences. She applied pressure to my head.

"I feel the pain's movement... better?"

She rubbed both of her hands together and went back to doing what she had been doing before I disturbed her. She was right, the headache was no more.

She walked the land with a stick looking for water after three men told her there was not any place on the front part of the farm in which to dig a new well. I watched her walk the four corners of the fenced portion, talking to herself, praying. Her hands trembled. She stopped and told them to dig.

"Ma'am, we have walked this area three times; there is no water there."

"Dig! There is water here. Dig."

She turned and went back into the house. The men told her again, "There is no water. This will be extra!" They didn't dig long before one in their ranks called out in excitement. Muh Chest returned and smiled faintly. She dusted her hands on her apron and turned and walked back into the house.

We would sit on the porch in total darkness. Muh Chest instructed me to look at the sky; I saw stars. I don't believe I ever saw what she saw. Contours, connecting lines—what she wanted me to see—pointing out the Milky Way, the North Star, constellations. I looked again and saw nothing but bright lights shining from afar. To me, that was enough. She continued to look upward, studying, marveling, before predicting when we would see rain again. This was her habit.

She placed her nose into the wind and would forecast the weather for two or three days forward. We suffered an extended drought during the spring and summer of 1962. She prayed and walked more. She prayed for rain that night and the next. Chesterana Wright knew the moon's phases, as a mother knows when her daughter is in menses or pregnant. She applied different meanings to each. She and Daddy Louis would use what they saw and smelled to identify when to plant. She forever looked at the sky, upward—always upward—and gave thanks.

I don't ever remember the county's agricultural extension agent visiting their farm. They didn't own a truck. They didn't own combines, tractors, or expensive implements. Daddy Louis walked behind a plow, pulled by a mule, until he was in his eighties. Daddy Louis came back to the land after Muh Chest's death. He kept a small garden until his death, a few months after his one-hundredth birthday.

We went to market in a wagon pulled by mules or sometimes a horse. Muh Chest slaughtered chickens for the winter, done with unimaginable and incredible quickness—fifty to sixty at a time. The farmland was always plentiful because of what Daddy Louis and Muh Chest saw, smelled, and touched. I tell this story to say—please provide me the privilege of personifying the elements in this book, the same way as my elders did; it is my way of paying homage to them and to her.

Our minds are amazing. On the day I stood on the edge of the lot—on the concrete—retreating to the van, I was thinking about other matters. There was a small army of invasive creatures in pursuit. I moved backwards because of them. I danced the dance of anguish, turning in place, swiping, not at all being silent, at times now squawking because of them, for some reason thinking at the same time: *where were the slave auction houses in this city?* This was a fleeting thought initially, but a persistent, lingering thought seconds later as the ants charged, scaling the walls, demonstrating amazing persistence while they attacked. I recognize theirs was a battle of survival, sacrificing a few for the benefit of the whole, executed perfectly while their clumsy enemy retreated cravenly in another direction for another day.

The attempt to clean the land took place at a now recognizable time: the beginning of the pandemic. Remember, the worldwide pandemic altered our movement, including our sense of time and place. Local, state, and federal governments adjusted their operations and functions. Small and large businesses and corporations were compelled to modify, change, and deviate from their prior practices. The courts shut down. No matter how important we thought ourselves, Mother Nature presented a greater threat, what appears to some to be a Hobson's choice. Most of us felt we had no other choice. And although some complained ferociously, alter most of us did—for our collective survival.

I didn't understand how the unified attack would affect my thoughts. I didn't foresee how an initial tangential thought would become a persistent nagging worry, a long-term project. I never predicted that I would find myself writing this book to address the pain.

CHAPTER I

I found myself calling the Rosenberg Library's History Center a day later. Rosenberg is Texas's oldest continuously operating public library. When standing on the lot, I was a mere four or five blocks away—but practically a world away, if that makes sense. When I sat in my office calling, I was five or six blocks away. I inquired of a historian whether the library was permitting visits to the building. She answered my question with a question: "Why?" I told her what I wanted to find out, "I want to know where the slave auction houses were located."

She said, "There were none."

"That doesn't make sense to me."

"Because of the pandemic, I am willing to do your research for you." I refused her offer. "You cannot readily say there were none and then do my research for me."

"I understand," she replied and began to tell me the conditions for visiting: masking, gloves, shortened visits, no pens, pencils, or equipment. "We will provide the paper, pencils, and the gloves—and social distancing, sir. You will be permitted to visit only an hour at a time."

All seemed eminently reasonable and painless to me. I wrote down the time of the first appointment. When I visited the History Center the first time, the historian's answer changed slightly. "There may have been one at 22nd and Strand."

"Do you know the address?"

"I don't know the exact address."

I didn't tell her I had already seen this reference in a small book I had recently read. I wasn't satisfied with the author's assessment nor hers. Ours was a brief exchange. I was consumed with why I was here, with what happened days before, the sounds that invaded the inside of my head at the time, and why I was in this much-too-cold room on the upper floor of the library. A Black male employee remained in place listening to our exchange. He served as the library's sentry of sorts, sitting behind a desk, watching my actions, reminding me how to handle the materials. At times, his grunts were sufficient to alter any wayward behavior on my part.

This book is academically driven. In a subject as fraught as the enslavement and sale of humans, documentation seems indispensable.

An admission is in order: this book contains the author's history, musings, and emotions—the overwrought anguish of an African American male. I was born in the apartheid conditions of the American South and thus am a byproduct of the stained institution of slavery. Any analysis on my part will be influenced by this history. Why is this admission necessary? My maternal great-grandparents were formerly enslaved in rural Central Texas and were still alive during my childhood. Albert and Lillian Wright were enslaved until the ages of thirteen (Albert) and fifteen (Lillian). There is no way possible this history will not shape, mold, and contour the search and findings. Their physical presence and spirit can never be extinguished from the core of my existence.

I was born the year *Brown v. Board of Education* (1954) was decided by the United States Supreme Court. This heir grew up during the milieu of the second civil rights struggle. We were the generation of children who were the test students, bused from one location to another into unwelcoming places. They were scared. We were too.

One last admission: Initially, this book's sole focus was to document the location of slave auction houses in the city of Galveston, Texas. Meaning? The auction houses themselves and their locations were the author's concerns—setting out the evidence to establish the where and when but not necessarily the how. At least, that's what I thought; at least, that was the plan. The initial focus and intent of the book absolutely remained in place throughout, but additional concerns arose with each additional discovery. The historical myths were gnawing. The reminders, the words used to describe the enslaved remain bothersome: assigned names, in some cases no names, rarely a last name—being described the same as animals, by color and size, while culling and assigning animalistic roles: bucks. These facts compelled this work. I still see Albert's and Lillian's eyes. I still feel their touch. My initial focus proved to be much too narrow.

I spent practically a lifetime practicing law in this community—thirty-seven years. Maybe leaving the practice is one of the reasons I was able to ponder on matters other than law, matters that have nagged me for far too long. When practicing law, though, one truth was always clear—whether trying cases in other cities or states, I never had to explain where Galveston was; it seemed everyone knew something about Galveston. I may have been required to remind them Galveston is an island city. A few asked, "Near where?" I never mentioned the 1900 storm, a hurricane comprehending the nation's deadliest natural disaster. Perhaps this is because of effective mythical telling of the city's history through song, literature, stories littering the landscape. Galvestonians' actions—good and bad—have left indelible footprints in the sand. The point is, those in other places knew the name.

I will admit to once listening to a lawyer err in final argument about Galveston. He referred to Galveston as the big city and to me as a big city lawyer. Let's be clear, Galveston is a small city, although at one time it was Texas's largest city. This fact is no more.

Sitting in a small rural county seat (Austin County), in a town of perhaps 3,000 to 4,000 people (Bellville), while fewer than 30,000 occupied the county, I could see why he could say it was a larger city, but big city and big city lawyer seemed a bit much. Laughter slowly invaded the courtroom. I smirked. The judge smirked. Those in attendance giggled, then laughed. We then shared a communal laugh, participating in the theatre of the absurd. The country lawyer looked around the courtroom perplexed why everyone was in on the joke and he excluded. He wasn't excluded, he just overreached. No comment on my part was sufficient, our laughter was good common-sense. Everyone knew something about Galveston, a small city whose reach extended across the state of Texas. The initial railroad depots were now towns. More than one of these places was named after Galvestonians along the railroad route, which extended hundreds and hundreds of miles into the interior of Texas, while Galvestonians deposited the enslaved to tend to land, crops, and animals.

The position that there were no slave houses in Galveston—or perhaps one—was a continuation of the position that Galveston was different from other Southern cities and slavery was not an economic driving force in the city or state. This never made sense to me in the past nor when I stood in place in Rosenberg Library asking to look at the personal papers of some of Galveston's founding members.[1] The myths of Galveston's history and founding still have support in academia and provide resonance and comfort for some. These myths allow the institution of slavery to overlay a stain on America's and Texas's historical legacy, preventing an honest discussion of the institution's legacy and truths.

Before beginning the search for the slave auction houses, this author posited that Galveston's practice—in the context of slavery—would not be particularly unique from that of other cities. My assumption seems logical: any such slaves' houses/blocks would have adopted the procedure and practices of other locales, migrating with the people and purveyors of the trade.[2]

An inquisitive child was I, forever Georgia and Leon's third child. Muh Chest would nod and remain silent as I repeatedly peppered her with questions. She forever appeared to ignore me, humming a hymn, nodding, displaying a faint smile, answering every now and then, while continuing to do what she was doing. She always listened, though. Mama's physical manner was much the same, although she differed slightly in her approach. She encouraged exploration, doubt, questioning, and permitted me to challenge authority. When she answered, she answered with a question, another, and another. She too seemingly never answered, but she did. Her answer came after I figured it out. She would then give her thoughts. Dancing on the head of a pin was her wont—except she always made the impossible possible. She was also a good and beautiful dancer.

I said only one more admission earlier; well, I have another. Occasionally, Georgia was required to pull me back from the edge if I stepped dangerously too close. Honestly, I do not know where Doubting Thomas lived, or his people, or even whether he was a real person. I must readily admit, we may be closely related.[3]

The historical and societal myths and the effective whitewashing of history are

WHY SEARCH?

what this book is partly designed to address. Merriam-Webster defines a myth as "a usually traditional story of ostensibly historical events that serves to unfold part of the world view of a people or explain a practice, belief, or natural phenomenon."[4] The traditional story of ostensible historical events told with respect to Galveston's role in slavery are the myths told and the supporting reasons for slavery. Implicit in any such discussion about Texas's role in the slave trade, particularly Galveston's outsize role during the period Texas transitioned from a slave territory/republic/state, is the story of how slavery has been explained, particularly the practice, and the beliefs surrounding the enslavement of human beings.

So, bear with me; the structure of this book is societally driven. Embedded in stories, the writing of novelists and historians, our faiths, the words we use in expressing our views of history, and the arts. Our nation has worked arduously to create and protect these conditions and in the context of the discussion of slavery and slave auction houses, it would be naïveté displayed in its rawest form to ignore this. The path of the search and my findings are documented in chapters 1 through 7. Chapters 8 and 9 address the additional questions compelled by my abject curiosity and anxieties. What did these men and women face and accomplish once freed? What happened in Galveston and throughout Texas between the period of 1865 and 1950?

Previously, historians and storytellers told stories of Galveston's development that seemed glamorized to me, stories that fit perfectly. I always wondered whether we were being told the truth. If the city was societally and economically advanced during this time, was it a comforting place for Negroes? I had seen references in the newspapers as to Galveston being the Wall Street of the Southwest. Was this a true recounting of wealth's accumulation? I went past the search for slave auction houses because this previously told and untold history made me uncomfortable.

I will admit the little boy in me resurfaced throughout this project—pulling my grandmother's apron, talking too much while Muh Chest continued to peel potatoes, nodding, a faint smile intact, twirling a small piece of the tree branch from a tree out front. The tree stood to the left of the gate when entering the property. She taught me to break a small piece off the end of the branch and chew one end to cause it to fray like a toothbrush. The twig was pliable. It worked better than the real toothbrush. She placed the frayed end in her mouth daily. I did too. Her teeth remained immaculate up until her death. I still see the men who came to her farm to be noisy, asking her about herbs, plants, and remedies. Until recently, I never understood why she told them anything. Muh Chest walked them around the farm, taking cuttings, telling them what cured what. And Georgia? She remains forever the listener, compelling me to ask question after question and then research. She forced me to work through the contradictions and mistruths.

This book has caused me to scream internally and at others for unknown reasons; I still hear the voices of men, women, and children crying. I share this work so that you see and hear the same. Part of this work also caused me to smile, laugh, and exude pride. I share these findings also.

Criticizing without proposing solutions is untenable—so I have learned throughout life. Chapters 10 and 11 are the byproduct of the student in all of us. Chapter 11 is a bit unorthodox, but we should all remember our communities share commonalities as we struggle with the historical legacy of slavery. We grappled with a persistent and stained color line while insisting nothing of the sort existed, then and now. Chapter 12 sets out recommendations for the creation of a historic district. The proposed district lines are based upon the findings in this book referencing locations, people, and places as related to the colored population between 1905 and 1920.

Slavery was too long ago, one may say. I still remember the voices and touch of my great-grandparents. They—former human chattel—sat and rocked together as the wind gently cooled. The crickets sang in the distance, the sun touched each of us as we sat under the porch's awning. They rocked and talked. I did what children do. I sat next to them, under them, listening. Oh no, to the contrary, it has not been too long.

CHAPTER 2

WORKING AGAINST AND WITH OUR SHARED DUALITY

"After the Civil War, most former auction sites quietly blended into the main streets of today. Except for the occasional marker or museum, there was no record of the horror of separation suffered by many black families. The emphasis on national unity and reconstruction created a desire to paper over the atrocities of the past and many of these sites were forgotten."[1] Galveston is one of those cities which has effectively papered over this history by applying both an invisible and visible veneer, hiding its role in the slave trade. Contrary to the librarian's first and second assertions, I learned slaves were actively sold at several different sites. The byproduct of this book is clear: Galveston's deafening historical chant—*them not us*[2]—should be discarded and silenced.

Years ago, a close friend invited me to attend Dickens on the Strand.[3] Dickens is an annual Christmas festival held by the Galveston Historical Foundation (GHF) during the first weekend of December. This friend, Gwen, was an employee of GHF and a Yale-educated architect. Gwen was proud of her work for the organization and did what friends do: She extended an invitation to attend Dickens. I don't believe she saw the detour we were about to take. "I'm Black, Gwen. I can't, Gwen. I can't."

At the time of the invitation, Dickens was in its infancy; we were too, in a sense. Young professionals, youthful in appearance, with our invisible/visible naïveté in place. Naïveté, as used in this context, is not wielded as criticism. The word is used to explain how it serves the young well—creativity and seemingly the absence of fear. The young are sometimes remiss and do not know one should be fearful, compelling them to step forward, while the wary elder cautiously moves away, backward, sometimes even screaming for the fearless to stop. On this occasion, though, I had none of this. I belied my age and the characteristic of youth: I cloistered my thoughts and turned inward. Gwen never gave any indication, one way or the other, what she thought about my protestation.

The movement inward was because of my disdain for all things Victorian. This disdain first arose in high school, in English classes to be exact. Every sentence was tainted, the characters disjointed, a perverse sickness embedded every line, paragraph, and story, a palpable disconnect from humanity was the tales' tale. This historical film aptly remained in place no matter the authors' topic, covering every book, both hands, the desks/table/grass on which the book lay and clouding minds, thoughts, beliefs. There was simply nothing romantic about slavery.

I have never been able to rid myself of this internal rage. I am the byproduct of the transatlantic slave trade—simplistically defined as the period in which Africans were enslaved by Europeans and transported to the New World. This trade can never be deemed transient, remaining in place from 1480 to 1888, institutionalized in both worlds.[4] My understanding of this history reached out and grabbed my chin first, forcing it downward against my chest wall, then grabbed my vocal cords, causing them to constrict—a faint whisper followed, dribbling downward, outward, causing me to repeat the same words again: "I can't, Gwen."

Charles Dickens was a British novelist who published works from 1836 (*Oliver Twist*) until 1861 (*Great Expectations*).[5] At the time of Gwen's invitation, I was intellectually incapable of distinguishing between historical injustices and individuals. My bent was to create a mental stew, combining everything in the same pot, incapable of nuance and never appreciating Dickens's previous documented criticism of the institution of slavery—thus my reaction and misguided response.[6]

My inability to participate in a festival named after Charles Dickens is symbolic of the duality in which people who look like me have had to balance every day, deciphering reality from fiction, a dance done on the proverbial pin, in real time. This duality is expressed best by Dr. W. E. B. Du Bois. Dr. Du Bois ultimately concluded the challenge for the United States in the twentieth century was the color line.[7] It seems Du Bois's observation remains in place a century later—heirs of the institution existing in a unique pathos.

Societal nonacceptance of the lost war, statues erected cherishing and enshrining those Southern warriors, stories of honor on both sides of the Mason–Dixon Line. Washing history while ignoring the war was about slavery, always about slavery. Extended fists—actual and proverbial—hateful words shouted, outward and wayward. The reality: these men were insurrectionists, fighting to preserve slavery. Meanwhile, our existence was a different reality—walking on the side of the roadway in a segregated and hostile world, Whites drove past laughing and shouting. Most of time, their words were mangled by Mother Nature and technology—I didn't hear what they said when they passed. Hearing was not necessary. I knew exactly what they, female and male voices, said. I was forever grateful they never stopped, even those at whom I yelled back.

Seeing the police before they saw us, moving behind anything, wanting to be invisible, joking when teens, "Three indeed is a crowd, four surely represents probable cause." Our words were never intended to be funny. In hindsight, we never laughed. Indeed, a fraught, troublesome history. Constant confusion was our daily existence; ours was an everyday attempt to make sense of a world. In hindsight, seeing and hearing the voices and the *oh so creative* use of the language—Dutch, English, French, Portuguese, Spanish words—told in tales, religious parables, songs, symbols—all to effectuate a negative color divide worldwide.

Persistent and sustained anger—on both sides—was always present, while our respective families strove to survive in an apartheid America. One should be clear: This duality should not be defined as exclusively Southern. Ironically, a duality which seems to leave little room for one to be proudly Southern—but we were, in food, language, mores and traditions, song, and dance.

W. E. B. Du Bois's description of this duality—the color line—always seemed more complicated, when experienced live and not on the black and white pages of a book. Doing the dance, through all phases of our life cycle, was an act of survival in a hostile America. With my past experiences and history, I knew proceeding forward, no matter what I discovered, the findings would always involve working against and with this shared duality.

CHAPTER 3

LETTING YOU HEAR ME SCREAM!

Professor Jonathan Daniel Wells provides an apt description of the transatlantic slave trade:

> During the four centuries of the trade, from around 1500 to about 1900, captives mostly came from West Central Africa, the Bight of Biafra, and the Gold Coast. But virtually all people throughout the continent were vulnerable, and the slave trade ensnared those from Senegambia in the northwestern region to Madagascar off the southeastern coast. Following the northeast and southeast trade winds, and the westerlies that circulated back to Africa, slavers could cross the ocean in a matter of weeks. About two-thirds of the captives were men, and about 20 percent were children. On some voyages, such as the Middle Passage between the Bight of Biafra and the Caribbean, mortality rates averaged 30 percent, so on a trip with six hundred captives, almost two hundred would perish from disease.[1]

Currently situated on Galveston's waterfront is a plaque which seemingly pays homage to the horrors of the Middle Passage. The plaque is located at 22nd and Wharf in the Strand Historical District. A careful examination reveals none of the arrows point to Galveston. New York, Richmond, Charleston, New Orleans, but not Galveston. The arrow closest to Galveston's location is directed at New Orleans. The plaque ignores that Galveston was one of the designated ports in which the slave traders' human cargo was deposited.

CHAPTER 3

Figure 2: Middle Passage plaque, 20th and Wharf.

A mere two blocks away from the plaque slaves were auctioned (20th and Wharf).[2] A block away additional auction houses were located. I did not know at the time of my initial study of the plaque, only during the search did it become clear, hallowed sites were located in all directions and the plaque was a misdirection. However, on my first view, something seemed historically amiss.

Can one honestly take the position Galveston is uniquely different from other Southern port cities and did not participate in the buying and selling of slaves? I do not know whether it is proper to answer a question with a series of questions, but I will. Weren't Galvestonians some of the largest slave and plantation owners in Texas? The practices in other Southern states would have easily migrated to Texas—the people, methods, and practices simply moved from one location to another. Doesn't this make sense—Galveston was no different from the state, territories, and countries in which slavery was well entrenched.

James M. Schmidt described 1800 Galveston as home to the largest slave market west of New Orleans. "A number of merchants regularly bought and sold slaves on the streets and in the auction houses of Galveston, including J. Castanie & Co., T. H. McMahan & Gilbert, John O. & H. M. Trueheart and Colonel John S. Sydnor."[3] Schmidt provided little documentation of this assessment. Whether or not his assessment was correct, Schmidt's lack of documentation meant I had to tread carefully and not make the same historical mistake as others: assuming any and every historical assertion is correct; this author believes any such assumptions are dangerous and irresponsible. Our history has been bastardized and laden with false assertions of facts far too long.

Earl Wesley Fornell's writing provides the structural support for the complained-of myths: "By the very nature of their station the fifteen hundred slaves living on Galveston Island ought to have been considered the least privileged group residing in the city; yet, for many points of view, this was not the case, for the actual privileges enjoyed by a vast number of the more fortunate slaves on the Island were many indeed. The Negroes loved the Island life and were always loathe to leave it."[4] Fornell identified C. L. McCarty and Colonel John S. Sydnor as well-known slave dealers—McCarty being an additional name, Sydnor previously referenced by Schmidt.

Fornell also boldly claimed Sydnor would "drown out the bid of an undesirable buyer who sought to purchase a Galveston slave of long and respectable residence. . . . Among the leading citizens on the Island it was considered to be a mark of gentility not only to take good care of one's Negroes but also to allow them to indulge their love for 'fancy clothes.'"[5]

> A visiting British colonel, in 1863, was amazed as he observed the behavior of the whites and the blacks on a festive occasion to see innumberable [sic] Negroes and Negresses parading about the streets in the most outrageously grand costumes—silks, satins, crinolines, hats with feathers, lace, mantles, &c., forming an absurd contrast to the simple dresses of their mistresses. Many were driving about in their master's carriages or riding on horses which are often lent to them on Sunday afternoons. All seemed intensely happy and satisfied with themselves.[6]

Fornell's description is the myth of the happy, happy "Negroes and Negresses" and served a purpose—creating an illusion, while ignoring these mythical happy souls were actually, factually enslaved. This myth was designed to soothe and comfort others, the good and beneficial trade bestowed happiness and a wonderful life on these poor souls. Fornell does not question the supposed extraordinary love slaves possessed for Galveston. His argument—*a fact is a fact*—seems a bit specious in context of the evidence remaining with us.

> While the mercantile families were certainly not accustomed to deprive themselves of luxuries nor to live the puritan's life, they nevertheless seemed to derive pleasures and prestige by permitting their slaves to enjoy the fruits of occasional carefree excursions. Perhaps they indulged in these contradictions to the customary non-Southerner's vision of the "slave system" in order to confound the traveling traders from New England who often visited the Island, or perhaps they treated their Island Negroes well in order to show their disdain for some of the crude planters on the mainland; they might also have indulged their servants because they knew that some of their own class were in the African slave trade. They may have felt a need to demonstrate the benefits which might someday await the progeny of the unfortunate passengers arriving along the coast via the clandestine slavers' ships. In any case, there were good reasons why the position of the Galveston "city Negroes" was envied by the slaves in the interior.[7]

Fornell was correct in his assessment that McCarty was a slave trader. In 1858, McCarty informed the public he was opening a new auction house and requested the public's patronage.[8]

> C. L. McCarty will attend to usual business as salesman in real estate and Negroes, public and private, when called upon.
> Office on Centre Street.[9]

In 1860 McCarty was elected the Sheriff of Galveston County. His office was two doors down from his auction house on Centre Street.[10]

The meaning of the happy, happy "Negroes and Negresses" remains the same, even if told in different forms. In the book *Oleander Odyssey: The Kempners of Galveston, Texas, 1854–1880s*, the author Harold M. Hyman addressed Harris Kempner's view on race: "Ike never abandoned the conviction that 'many of those who had been slaves found sudden freedom a great disappointment,' a judgment that is susceptible to considerable disproof. But it is undoubtable that in the 1870s and 1880s 'a plethora of servants sought positions, but above all maintenance of themselves and their children.' Black women servants earned ten dollars a month, and men, fifteen dollars. All servants were 'bountifully fed,' Ike recalled, and 'their numerous children, whether legitimate or "source unknown," crowded into the quarters assigned their mothers and were fed by our household without question.'"[11]

Without addressing these previous historical conclusions, one's search would be tainted, preventing one from ever believing certain locations were fraught places for Negroes, including those enslaved, purportedly free during slavery's existence, or for those freed after emancipation. With an actual accounting of societal conditions and attitudes, any such research permits one to question previous findings that serve as the structural supports for the previously mentioned myths.

An additional explanation is necessary: The search for slave auction houses in Galveston was undertaken to challenge the untruth I was initially told, that these structures and places in which slaves were sold did not exist. If these places did exist, it is indeed false to contend otherwise to this day. Stories of the Lone Ranger, Tarzan, superhero sagas have been set out in books, scripts, television shows, films, all providing a backdrop for the goodness of the American people, the American psyche. Good against evil, conquest over adversity, helping and conquering primitives—for the greater good.

A myth, in the author's mind, is when a pebble of the truth is used to support the lie or distorted position a person, organization, or society desires to articulate. Although the position may be indeed mythological and false, contrary findings are readily rejected—the greater good. In my childhood, these heroes were painted white; "Oh the color of the character doesn't matter, irrelevant, just to tell the story, nothing else," always, always the explanation. And always I was the incredulous child, questioning and repeating over and over in my head, "It doesn't matter?"

This author does not ignore the limited time period in which slaves were traded in Texas in the context of the four hundred years in which the transatlantic slave trade existed.[12] During the formation of the original colonies, Texas was part of Mexico, which opposed the colonist slave trade. Mexico began to restrict slavery as early as 1820 and abolished it in 1829.[13] Prior to the Republic of Texas becoming part of the United States, and after it joined the Union, Texans came into the Union as a slave state. This author posits the short time frame is irrelevant. This is so because this author views history through a different prism—hearing the familiar historical chant in one ear: cotton was king[14]—while a different and more oppressive chant rings in the other: no, slavery was.[15]

Seeing clearly my maternal great-grandparents' hands extend out, touching my face when I visited, tracing and outlining the contours—nose, lips, eyes—running their hands over each of our heads, sensing who was who, saying our names. Even though both were blind, their condition blessed them with additional and enhanced senses—magical powers—layered with doses of kindness, while both still somehow were able to tolerate the heat-induced and red dirt smells we emitted. Absolutely, I trust their touch more than the historical writings and tales about them told by others. I can still hear and see the lecturers, standing in the front of the room, telling the same familiar false tales. Something always did not make sense.

"By the 1830s, nearly three million southern slaves, toiling in fields from Texas to Virginia, picked cotton under the threat of the lash.... Millions of bales passed from the fields to southern ports like New Orleans, Savannah, and Norfolk, bales destined for the North or the United Kingdom."[16] Insurance companies also profited from slavery, "modeling themselves after eighteenth-century Dutch insurance institutions that had helped to protect the slave trade. In fact, American insurance companies helped to underwrite slavery by taking on slaves as collateral as well as by insuring ships destined for the illegal transatlantic slave trade. The profits of banks, insurance companies, and the Stock Exchange helped make Wall Street synonymous with high rates of return."[17] The American writer and abolitionist Theodore Weld explained,

> Enslaving men is reducing them to articles of property—making free agents chattels—converting *persons* into *things*. A slave is one held in this condition. In law, "he owns nothing, and can acquire nothing," His right to himself is abrogated. If he say, *my* hands, *my* body, *myself*; they are figures of speech. To use *himself* for his own good, is a *crime*. To keep what he earns is *stealing*. To take his body into his own keeping is *insurrection*. In a word, the profit of his masters is made the end of his being, and he is a mere means to that end—a mere means to an end until which his interests do not enter, of which they constitute no portion.[18]

One meaning of the term looking through a prism is "a medium that distorts, slants, or colors whatever is viewed through" it.[19] To be clear, this definition is not my intended meaning. Mine is founded on a lifelong distrust of what we were told about our ancestors, including those who had survived the Middle Passage; others who were born into bondage on these shores; and the oft-times historically ignored—those who were free, kidnapped, and then enslaved.[20]

Supposed facts are not necessarily true facts, in that supposed truisms are oft-times used to misdirect and deceive. Supposed facts are never facts when placed in an improper context. This is one of the foundational bases of this book, discussing the facts in context of my fundamental cultural mistrust. We have never been deemed as smart, talented—nary successful—implying as much on some occasions, on most occasions stated as unabashed assertion of facts. Fornell did write, "[I]t was considered to be a mark of gentility not only to take good care of one's Negroes, but also allow them to indulge their love for 'fancy clothes,'" didn't he?[21] We must proceed carefully through this briar patch of knowns and unknowns. Failing in this regard means this book would be the same as those who have auspiciously painted a false and distorted history.

CHAPTER 4

THINGS OF VALUE

Slaves were considered property, which could be transferred in a variety of ways and manners, the same as other real or personal property: in exchange for other things of value, gifted, sold, for good and valuable consideration.[1] And, so they were—gifted and sold, the seller binding [him/herself/themselves] and agreeing to forever defend the title to the enslaved against any, all, every person, or persons whatsoever. Illustrations of this foundation are reflected in the Deed Records of Galveston County, Texas:

- Deed of Trust dated May 21, 1840, William L. Morgan & A. J. Cody signed a joint note to John S. Sydnor for the sum of one thousand eight hundred and forty dollars for the sale of negro slaves: two female slaves, Harriet age twenty and Emily aged fifteen; Tom aged sixteen years.[2] In addition, two female slaves—Patsy, thirty-one; Sally, fifteen; and a boy named Shade, fourteen, were included in the transaction. The deed of trust conveyed Patsy, Sally and the boy Shade to P. Edmond, trustee on the joint note, to have and hold on behalf of P. Edmond.

- Bill of Sale dated June 19, 1840, Brushrad B. Wilkins for the sum of eleven hundred dollars paid for two negro slaves named Jennings, age twenty-eight, and his wife, Hannah, about twenty-six; sale by A. J. Cody.[3]

- Bill of Sale dated August 24, 1840, Abner Cody sale to John S. Sydnor; sale of the following negro slaves: Cornelius aged about thirty-five; Susan about age twenty-four; Clarissa about twelve, Hiram about ten; Littleton about five; Francis about three; and Little Buck, an infant, about four months.[4]

CHAPTER 4

- Bill of Sale dated October 6, 1840, William L. Morgan & A. J. Cody for the sum of two thousand thirty-six dollars paid by John S. Sydnor for the sale of the following negro slaves: Harriet about twenty-one years of age; Emily aged about fifteen; Tom aged about sixteen years old, and three others—Dolly, twenty-four, and daughters Caroline and Sally, about sixteen.[5]

- Bill of Sale dated February 16, 1841,[6] transaction between Dr. O. P. Kelton and John Sydnor, for the sum of eight hundred dollars, sale of a dark-complexioned negro boy about sixteen, named Washington.[7]

They—no, may I say, we—were also the subject of litigation.

- In 1845 in *Settle v. Jones*, the Sheriff of Galveston County, Henry M. Smyth, with the execution of bond by Settle, said Negro Catherine "levied on this 11th day of June 1844 & claim bond filed on the 13th June 1844 with the Sheriff by H. W. Smyth by John A. Settle, [Attorney] for Fred Settle . . . sufficient amount to cover value of the negro & any damages" incurring thereof /s/ Benj. C. Franklin, [Plaintiff's Attorney].[8]

- In 1849 in *Clara White v. Archibald A. Moffatt,* the sale of Negro woman Ellen was voided after a jury trial verdict entered, "We the jury find for Plaintiff the amount of seven hundred and fifty dollars ($750) . . . and it is ordered and adjudged that the sale of the negro woman Ellen . . . be, the same be hereby set aside and annulled."[9]

- On April 28, 1845, a jury entered its finding related to the mortgage of two Negro slaves: "a jury-to-wit: Samuel M. Williams, Joseph Osterman, Israel L. Hasbrook, John S. Sydnor, William M. Cook, Isaac B. Bailey, John L. Darragh, William M. McCutchan, John Heply, J. E. Rump, Edward Kaufman and C. Tschudy, good and lawful men," voided a mortgage related to three Negro slaves, "Celia, a negro girl of black complexion aged fourteen or fifteen years & her sister Betsey or Elisabeth of dark complexion aged about 8 or 9 years & both slaves for life, sound in mind & body."[10]

In 1856, the law of the land was affirmed by the United States Supreme Court in *Dred Scott v. Sandford.*[11] Dred Scott, a slave, was born in Virginia and owned by a Dr. Emerson and his wife. Harriet was Dred Scott's wife. She too was born a slave and belonged to a Major Taliaferro. Harriet was purchased by Dr. Emerson in 1835; he held her in slavery until 1838. In the year 1836 Dred and Harriet married with the consent of Dr. Emerson. Dred and Harriet sued for their freedom.[12] The Supreme Court ruled the Scotts had no standing in federal court because they lacked US citizenship, even after they were freed. The Court reversed the lower court's judgment freeing Dred and Harriett. In actuality, the Supreme Court affirmed its previous decisions and found the Scotts had no title to freedom by being taken by their owner from Rock Island in Illinois (a free state), and back to Missouri (a slave state).[13] The Court's reversal made it clear the enslaved African race was not intended to be included in the broad and sweeping language of the Declaration of Independence.[14]

> **They had, for more than a century before been regarded as beings of an inferior order, and altogether unfit to associate with the white race either in social or political relations, and so far inferior that they had no rights which the white man was bound to respect, and that the negro might just and lawfully be reduced to slavery for his benefit.** He was bought and sold and treated as an ordinary article of merchandise and traffic whenever a profit could be made by it. This opinion was at that time fixed and universal in the civilized portion of the white race. It was regarded as an axiom in morals as well as in politics, which no one thought of disputing or supposed to be open to dispute, and men in every grade and position in society daily and habitually acted upon it in their private pursuits, as well as in the matter of public concern, without doubting for a moment the correctness of this opinion. [*Dred Scott* at 408, emphasis added.][15]

We were mortgaged, traded, and exchanged, the same as chattel.[16]

Samuel May Williams (October 4, 1795–September 13, 1858), considered one of Galveston's founders and a close associate of Stephen F. Austin, was an Anglo-American colonizer of Mexican Texas. Williams's papers illustrated the duplicitous nature of the institution of slavery:

> Correspondence inquiring of Williams as to what to do with "negress" and the children [the children were by the master], after the death of the master [23-01109 | 1828]; letter informing Williams of the arrival of sixty negroes from Savannah, Georgia [23-1531 | 1831]; letter providing introduction to Colonel Fannin who is interested in negro speculation [23-1119 | 1833]; purchase of negro boy, Dick 23-1354 | 1834]; correspondence in papers, Foley to Austin— inquiring about the conditions for bringing slaves into country (reference is to Mexico's laws prohibiting slavery) [23-1370 | 1834]; Williams's purchase of plantation [23-1883 | 1840]; Williams's bill of sale of a negro and his wife and three

CHAPTER 4

children [23-2180 ¦ 1849]; documentation of Williams's hiring of negroes, and presumably hiring of other slaves for work in Galveston [23-2351 ¦1850; 23-2383 ¦2850; 23-2391 ¦1840; 23-2448 ¦1851; 23-2450 ¦ 23- 2451¦ 1851]; correspondence from Thomas Baird announcing his anticipated move to Texas and bringing slaves [23-2519 ¦1852]; Williams's sale of two negroes [23-3182; 2304318 ¦ 1855]; copy of correspondence—Wood of New Orleans to Jenkins, President of N. O. Gas and Light Company; in pursuit of runaway slave [23-4003 ¦ 1858]; copy of list of negroes owned by Shaw, James [23-4055 ¦ 1858].[17]

A valuable commodity, we were—if commodity is the proper noun:

- In Williams's inventory setting out the property he owned, land holdings and slaves were his most valuable assets [23-2265 ¦ 1849 (inventory of San Bernard Plantation]; 23-2333 ¦ 1849 (tax assessment for Galveston County, taxes on land, Negroes, horses, cattle).[18]

- In 1838, W. H. Grimes, New York, affirmed a five-million-dollar loan to back Williams [23-1566 ¦ 1838].[19] The backing of Wall Street to propel Texas's independence from Mexico, which had banned slavery, is one possible reason for the loan. Another may have been a regular business transaction (banking) to continue the support of the various aspects of the Galveston enterprise, including cotton brokerage, land sales, and slaves. The document is unclear as to the actual purpose of the loan. What is clear, however, is the importance of slavery and support of the enterprise by the northern states.

As an additional aside, $5 million in 1838 is the equivalent of $165,414,516.13 in 2023.[20]

Author Earl Wesley Fornell said: "It was notorious, said this observer, that the slave trade had existed on the Texas coast for years. It was also notorious that the trade was carried on chiefly by Northern citizens; the vessels engaged in the traffic were fitted out in New York, Boston, and Portland. Between 1840 and 1859 over fifty slavers had been captured and brought into the port of New York, nearly all of which were fitted out with Northern capital. Yet the number of vessels captured were but a small number of those fitted out in Northern ports."[21] Without anything else, one could readily assume the ships moving into the South were primarily a northern problem—they were not. "The slave fleet which leaves New York, Boston and other seaports, in a single year consists of about forty vessels of various sizes, ranging from four to six hundred slaves each. The whole capital invested was not more than four million dollars upon which 'a profit of

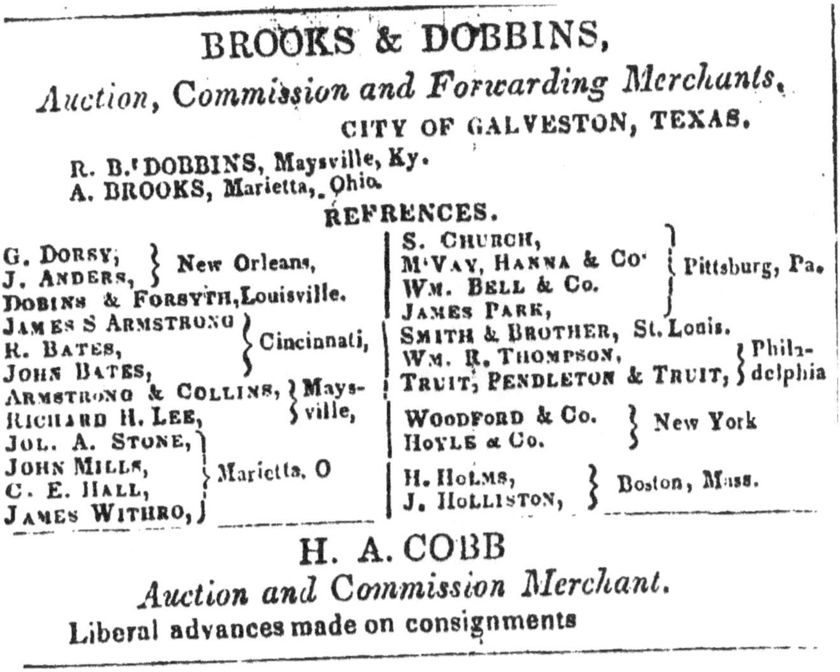

> **BROOKS & DOBBINS,**
> *Auction, Commission and Forwarding Merchants,*
> CITY OF GALVESTON, TEXAS.
>
> R. B. DOBBINS, Maysville, Ky.
> A. BROOKS, Marietta, Ohio.
>
> REFERENCES.
>
> G. DORSY, J. ANDERS, } New Orleans,
> DOBINS & FORSYTH, Louisville.
> JAMES S ARMSTRONG, R. BATES, JOHN BATES, } Cincinnati,
> ARMSTRONG & COLLINS, RICHARD H. LEE, } Maysville,
> JUL. A. STONE, JOHN MILLS, C. E. HALL, JAMES WITHRO, } Marietta, O
>
> S. CHURCH, M'VAY, HANNA & CO. WM. BELL & Co. } Pittsburg, Pa.
> JAMES PARK,
> SMITH & BROTHER, St. Louis.
> WM. R. THOMPSON, TRUIT, PENDLETON & TRUIT, } Philadelphia
> WOODFORD & CO. HOYLE & CO. } New York
> H. HOLMS, J. HOLLISTON, } Boston, Mass.
>
> **H. A. COBB**
> *Auction and Commission Merchant.*
> Liberal advances made on consignments

Figure 3: Brooks & Dobbins ad, *Civilian and Galveston City Gazette*, January 28, 1843, 8.

something like eleven million dollars is realized annually.'"[22] Eleven million dollars in 1850 is equivalent to $433,895,000 in 2023.[23]

Traded, hunted, hired out, desired—the enslaved African was part of the socioeconomic structure of the city and state (as in other regions of the country), an interconnected web in place to support the production of resources, goods, and the construction/development of infrastructure. Property—things of value, no different than a buggy—but clearly an exceedingly more valuable commodity.

Other examples: H. A. Cobb, in his work as a commission agent and auctioneer, valued the Negro. He placed advertisements related to the sale of a "fine light Buggy" and his search for "a smart, active Negro girl." Whether Cobb's desire for "a smart, active Negro girl" was sexual or only for labor is unknown. Either speculation, of course, would not be outside the realm of historically verifiable truths. Cobb's advertisements were posted in the *Civilian and Galveston City Gazette* in the year 1843.[24] Cobb's advertisements were not out of the ordinary. In the capacity of the roles mentioned above he regularly bought and sold slaves. He also hired out his Negroes.[25] Cobb's auction house at the time was in the same general area as John Sydnor's (Tremont, 23rd Street, and Custom House).[26]

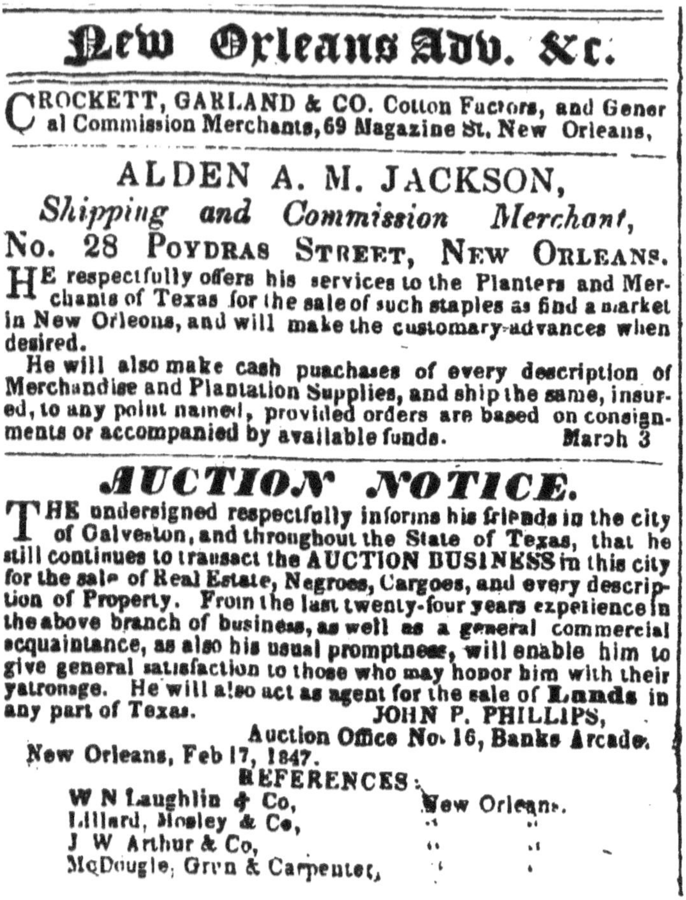

> **New Orleans Adv. &c.**
>
> CROCKETT, GARLAND & CO. Cotton Factors, and General Commission Merchants, 69 Magazine St., New Orleans.
>
> **ALDEN A. M. JACKSON,**
> *Shipping and Commission Merchant,*
> No. 28 POYDRAS STREET, NEW ORLEANS.
>
> HE respectfully offers his services to the Planters and Merchants of Texas for the sale of such staples as find a market in New Orleons, and will make the customary advances when desired.
>
> He will also make cash puachases of every description of Merchandise and Plantation Supplies, and ship the same, insured, to any point named, provided orders are based on consignments or accompanied by available funds. March 3
>
> **AUCTION NOTICE.**
>
> THE undersigned respectfully informs his friends in the city of Galveston, and throughout the State of Texas, that he still continues to transact the AUCTION BUSINESS in this city for the sale of Real Estate, Negroes, Cargoes, and every description of Property. From the last twenty-four years experience in the above branch of business, as well as a general commercial acquaintance, as also his usual promptness, will enable him to give general satisfaction to those who may honor him with their patronage. He will also act as agent for the sale of **Lands** in any part of Texas. JOHN P. PHILLIPS,
> Auction Office No. 16, Banks Arcade.
> New Orleans, Feb 17, 1847.
>
> REFERENCES:
> W N Laughlin & Co,   New Orleans.
> Lillard, Mosley & Co,
> J W Arthur & Co,
> McDougle, Gren & Carpenter,

Figure 4: New Orleans commission ads, *Civilian and Galveston Gazette*, June 8, 1848, 4.

On January 28, 1843, Cobb placed another advertisement.[27] The advertisements reflected either Cobb's connection to the other concerns or Galveston's connection to slave trading entities and concerns in other parts of the country: Maysville, Kentucky; Marietta, Ohio; Louisville, Kentucky; Cincinnati, Ohio; New Orleans, Louisiana; Pittsburgh and Philadelphia, Pennsylvania; New York, New York; and Boston, Massachusetts. Other auctioneers who advertised in 1843 included George B. Innes (referencing his location at the Auction Room in Haskin's building adjoining the Merchants Exchange; Innes advertised his connection to the largest auction house in United States, no reference to the sale of Negroes), E. O. Lynch, A. F. James (reference to sale or barter of Negroes), C. L. McCarty (location on Centre, Office at Washington Hotel, reference to selling and hiring Negroes).[28]

We were the subject of foreclosures at sheriffs' sales for debt(s) due and owing.[29]

The institution by its nature begot deviant behavior: theft and immoral acts directed against a people; kidnapping; acquisition by trick and device;[30] the institutionalization and protection (by laws, cities, and states) by the enactment of ordinances, codes, and laws to protect the continuation of the debasement.[31] Of course, when viewed in a different light—from the eyes of the owners—all of this was designed to protect the owners' interest in their chattel. This was in the textbooks we were taught in school, wasn't it? There is nothing wrong with the protection of a man's property, is there?

The 1859 Galveston city directory is a good source to track Galveston's birth and development. "There have been five different acts of incorporation of Galveston, the first in January, 1839, the second in February, 1840, which repealed the first, the third in February, 1844, which amended and in part repealed the previous charter; and the fourth in February, 1845, which amended and in part replaced the one of the year previous, and the fifth in August, 1856, which embraced many provisions of the previous charters and super[s]eded them all, and is now in force."[32] Voting in city elections was restricted to "[a]ll white males . . . who are twenty-one years old, and who have resided one year in the city, and who have paid all the taxes assessed against them."[33]

Condensed ordinances related to slavery were also provided in the 1859 city directory:[34]

> The salary of the Harbor Master is $500 and 2 1/2 per cent on all the dues collected.
>
> THE SEARCHES OF VESSELS is required to search all vessels bound to all ports other than those of slave States, to see if any slaves may be concealed on board, and for each vessel searched he receives $3. He is also required to search vessels bound for Brazos Santiago or mouth of the Rio Grande, and from such vessels he received but $1. Any captain neglecting to report other Searcher for inspection as required, is liable to a fine of not less than $25, nor more than $100. . . . SLAVE—No person is allowed to buy or to *receive* from any slave any goods or ware whatever, without the written consent of the owner; and every offence against this ordinance is subject to a fine of $100, or imprisonment for fifteen days. Nor is any person allowed to sell or to *give* any intoxicating drinks to a slave without the owner's written consent, and an offence against this regulation is subject to a like penalty. Any person engaged in retailing intoxicating drinks is forbidden to allow slaves to congregate at or around his or her premises under a penalty of $50, or imprisonment for fifteen days. Slaves are not allowed to rent houses and hire apart from their owners or persons having legal control

of them, nor are they allowed to hire their time, nor can their owners give them *general* written permits to seek employment for a longer period than one week. Any slave found in a place where liquors are retailed without a written permit from his or her owner, is liable to be taken up and receive thirty-nine lashes, unless his or her owner interpose by paying a fine not exceeding $25. No slave found or free person of color is allowed to have any fire-arms or other deadly weapons, or powder or shot. The city bell is rung every night at 9 o'clock, from April 1st to October 1st, during the balance of the year at 8 o'clock, and every slave or free person of color found in the street or away from home, after such ring of the bell, without proper pass or permit, shall be liable to be taken up and kept in custody till morning when the owner is notified and required to pay costs, for the regulars in full in regard to slaves.[35]

Galveston thus was a well-regulated society, supporting the slave infrastructure and the owners' rights to their chattel; requiring vessels to be searched to avoid escape to free states or to Mexico; establishing apartheid conditions, including prohibiting the slave from contracting, owning property, or imbibing intoxicating liquors; and prohibiting any other person from assisting the enslaved.

Slaves were not permitted to rent homes, apart from the slaveholder, or to hire "their time" out, apart from the master. Conditions established to prevent those of like kind from gathering seemed to remain in place in this author's youth (policing the congregation of Black youth and criminalizing the same). These restrictions also included the establishment of night-time curfews and the requirement "every slave or free person of color" shall be off the streets after a certain time—a reflection of how communities of color are policed, making mere presence a crime or at minimum a justification to stop and search (stated differently, providing probable cause for law enforcement).[36]

The ordinances purported to treat free persons of color differently than slaves, but a careful reading reveals they were not. The practical effect was to enslave all persons of African blood, even if this meant converting a free person of color to chattel and selling them on the auction block.

Why do we continue to hide the places in which these untenable bargains and exchanges took place? Men, women, and children standing before others who bartered over their servitude and enslavement, a most untenable bargain and exchange indeed.[37] This is the reason for the search: identifying the locations humans were sold as chattel and not making the fatal mistake of pretending no such acts took place—not in Galveston—indeed not, not in Galveston. By our failure to document and tell the truth, we ignore history's lessons, permitting history to repeat itself. Meaning? By pretending these acts never occurred, we continue to tarnish the deaths of humans whom we stripped of families, culture, history—and something as simple/complex as a name. Tribes, civilizations, countries of origin have disappeared, thus reducing the continent of Africa to a monolith, wiping out distinctions, completing the process of dehumanization.

Reduced to Négresses and Nègres.[38]

Kraków-Płaszów concentration camp in Poland was a Nazi concentration camp in the southern suburb of Kraków. The camp was initially a labor camp but was ultimately the site of executions. Even though the camp was demolished when the Allies approached (leaving an empty and burnt-out field), the site remains hallowed ground, recognizing the death of Polish and Hungarian Jewish victims and non-Jewish victims who died unjustly.[39] "French police rounded up 13,000 people on two terrifying days in July 1942, wresting children from their mothers' arms and dispatching everyone to Nazi death camps. France honored those victims this weekend, as it tries to keep their memory alive.... A week of ceremonies marking 80 years since the Vel d'Hiv police roundup on July 16–17, 1942, culminated Sunday with an event led by [Emmanuel] Macron, who pledged that wouldn't happen ever again."[40] Attempts to scrub history clean have been rejected in this context and others. The same position is required to be taken in context of African slaves and their heirs. If we don't succeed, we are forever condemned—all of us—to the historical cycle of forgetting—instead of never forgetting—thus permitting history's well-respected tenet to occur: history repeating itself.

The abolitionist Frederick Douglass, born into slavery in 1818, on July 5, 1852, gave a speech to the Rochester Ladies Anti-Slavery Society titled, "What to the Slave is the 4th of July?" Douglass's speech was initially the expected ordinary historical pablum, until it wasn't. Turning his words from the wonders of the American experiment to the plight of the enslaved—stored in holes, sold, kidnapped, killed, and placed on auction blocks. Standing before a receptive audience, he delivered the unexpected, speaking through his eyes and the eyes of those who looked like him.

Before proceeding, it will be helpful to stop and pause—just briefly to adjust the prism—and listen to Douglass's words spoken (see endnote for links). Please note, it won't take long to do so. First, by the award-winning actor, James Earl Jones, who breathes life into the black and white text normally provided.[41] Secondly, continue the pause and listen to Douglass's descendants. Their voices, faces, and our history remind us of the importance of Kraków-Płaszów and other hallowed sites. One more clarification: *no, no, no,* even though I professed this manuscript was academically driven, I *never, never, never* said the approach was a traditional one.[42] How could it be?

CHAPTER 5

MUCH LIKE WATER

In December 1836, Col. M. B. Menard purchased from the Republic of Texas for the sum of fifty thousand dollars "one league and labor of land" on the east end of Galveston Island, the site of the present city of Galveston. He associated with him several others, they formed themselves into a stock company and through their Trustees, Dr. Levi Jones, Wm. R. Johnson, and Thomas Green issued stock in the number of one thousand shares, estimated, nominally, at $1,000 each. The company was known as the Galveston City Company, which held its first meeting for organization on the 18th day of April 1838.[1]

The Galveston City Company was incorporated by an Act of Congress of the late Republic on February 5, 1841.[2]

> Laying out the city with streets and avenues and alleys, on no niggardly scale, it left every tenth block in one of the central ranges of block for a PUBLIC SQUARE; it gave three separate sites within the corporate limits for PUBLIC MARKETS; it set apart an entire block for a COLLEGE; three eligible and valuable lots for a FEMALE SEMINARY, and an area of several blocks for a PARK, and gave to every denomination of Christians, large and convenient and valuable sites for their CHURCHES.[3]

The first settlers were granted "wharf privileges, for the sole consideration of constructing them, so that a man, by merely building a wharf, acquired a property, securing a fortune in the future for himself and his family."[4]

On January 21, 1843, E. G. Phipps and J. S. Sydnor placed an advertisement announcing their business venture.[5] The advertisement may have been sufficient

CHAPTER 5

in its day in providing a location; however, 181 years later, the advertisement is deficient in providing a precise location of the Messieurs Phipps and Sydnor's auction house.

The Texas State Historical Association (TSHA) has posted online a drawing of Sydnor's 22nd and Strand location. TSHA attributes the image to the Galveston Historical Foundation. The artist is not identified. The drawing depicts a building labeled "Auction & Commission House." There is no address listed on the building.[6]

"The National Gallery of Art, founded as a gift to the nation, serves as a center of visual art, education, and culture."[7] The National Gallery, with respect to modern photography, explains:

> Photography was introduced to the world in 1839. When the new medium arrived in the United States that year, it first established itself in major cities in the East. Photographers based in Philadelphia, New York, and Boston recorded the scenic vistas of tourist destinations such as the White Mountains and Niagara Falls, first photographed by Hugh Lee Pattinson in April 1840. Many early practitioners came to the medium from scientific or mechanical backgrounds, drawn to its seemingly magical ability to reproduce nature. And most—including Pattinson—adopted the daguerreotype, named after its French creator Louis-Jacques-Mandé Daguerre. This process fixed an image onto a silver-coated copperplate. Characterized by a mirrorlike surface and precise detail, the daguerreotype dominated photography in the United States for the next decade and a half.[8]

Sydnor's advertisement was placed in 1843, so one can understand photography was in its infancy and a picture of the location would not be available or not easily available. But wait, there is more.

What to make of the GHF's image? Does the sketch derive from another drawing or from the newspaper or magazine? One can readily assign the building to 22nd and Strand, but after that—where on the block? The corner, the middle of the block, next to what? The Strand runs east to west. The buildings face north or south. Phipps and Sydnor's advertisement does not specify which. The William L. Moody building was not in existence in 1843.[9]

A parking lot across the street from the W. L. Moody Building represents the previous location of the Osterman building. A Juneteenth plaque is currently situated on the site, located off the sidewalk, facing north.[10] In the summer of 2021, a Juneteenth mural was painted on the wall, which previously featured the signage "Old Galveston Square."

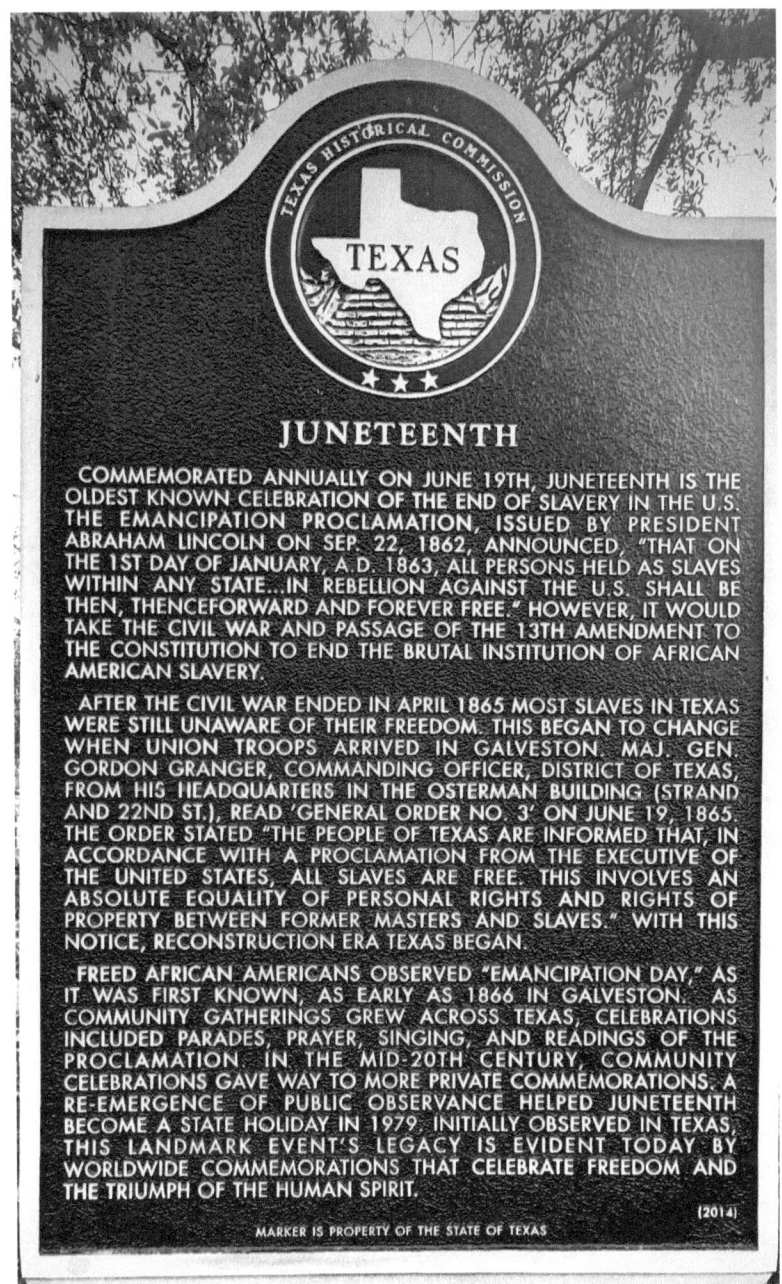

Figure 5: Juneteenth plaque put in place at 22nd and Strand by the Texas Historical Commission. (Photo by author.)

J. Osterman took out an advertisement in 1843 with H. A. Cobb, who was previously introduced as a person active in the buying and selling of slaves. The advertisement contained the following language: "The highest premium paid." In 1843 "the highest premium paid" had a particularized meaning. The language meant that J. Osterman was financing any such transaction.[11] Cobb's advertisement ran on multiple occasions.[12]

M. Garcia & Co also ran an advertisement that read as follows:

> **NEGRO WOMAN FOR SALE.**
> For sale low for cash or cotton, a good negro woman about 24 years of age, a good cook, washer, and Ironer, and good house servant in every particular, well known.[13]

On October 7, 1843, Cobb placed an advertisement informing others that he and his brother John A. Cobb "will continue to transact a general AUCTION AND COMMISSION BUSINESS under the style H. A. Cobb & Brother."[14] These advertisements were not isolated. See those by J. O. and H. M. Trueheart: "Wanted to buy. A Likely NEGRO GIRL about ten or eleven years old"; "For sale, A Likely Yellow Woman and Child; she is a No. 1 House servant and seamstress; C. L. McCarty"; "Wanted to Purchase, A Wet Nurse—say in the age from 14 to 20 years—in perfect health. For further particulars, call the Red Flag Agency Office, Market Street, C. L. McCarty."[15]

May I digress for a brief moment? H. A. Cobb's search for "an active Negro girl" is perhaps a meaningless phrase. Perhaps more an American tradition, where history continues to spill out in public view at family events, on the death beds of loved ones, through DNA results, through storytelling. Sometimes our/their cups runneth over, permitting the teller to tell, refusing to remain complicit in the lies.

> Thirty percent of our fathers were white men. They were slave ship crew members, overseers, slave traders, or slaveholders. They were history's largest aggregate of absentee fathers. We began to have a tradition in our families of "parental events." In other words, for the sake of family stability, we began to claim fictive kin as real. Truths about blood became buried, and with that, our trees became adulterated with white lies. Black folks picked up where white folks left off and continued to amend family records to mask adoptions, episodes of abuse and impropriety, and emotional lament.[16]

The above quote is from Michael Twitty's book *The Cooking Gene*. Twitty's assessment and calculations are consistent with others' findings.[17] For those who loudly proclaim heresy, they should reference other previously published historical tattletale events. The heirs of Thomas Jefferson, a president;[18] Aaron Burr, a vice-president;[19] and Strom Thurmond, a United States senator from the great state of South Carolina and an avowed segregationist, can attest to this truth. Listen carefully to family histories; read between the lines. This will help in controlling any incredulity resulting from Twitty's and others' assessments.[20] One author confidently wrote: "Certainly, no evidence remains to suggest that interracial sexual relations occurred beyond the walls of brothels."[21] The author would be somewhat accurate in his writing "no evidence remains," in that the institution was designed to destroy all evidence—capturing and enslaving humans, while never accurately documenting real names and ages; passing laws which made clear the enslaved had no rights; stripping memories, names, places of origin, and, more importantly, hope.

Destroying families, claiming ownership of the female and male bodies to appease the deviant sexual pleasures of those designated as White, and making clear a White person is free to take the life of an enslaved with impunity. Yes, yes, the author's assessment is pretty accurate, except when memories and tongues are not completely severed.

Oh, sure, we exist in a society that has loudly preached against miscegenation. This never meant the loudest voices were not taking full advantage of the benefits of property ownership and supposed superiority. Would restating this differently help?

If the woman is not permitted to say no (she being enslaved), why do we wrongfully conceptualize she has the power to willingly say yes? Having the gift of gab, the ability to weave prose, the capability to interpret and recite biblical edicts, matters not. The fact remains: bargaining with a gun, a whip against a woman's head or a threat against the life of her child or any other loved one can never be considered a reasonable free bargain and exchange. Do you feel comforted? My cup runneth over indeed. Clearly love has nothing to do with it. Somehow, we have permitted the illegitimate institution of slavery to taint our views of the integrity of the enslaved bodies, which explains the tainted legacy of society's views of the bodies of men and women of color.

Do not hear this author to say that we should not love the children of these illicit unions. If nothing else, historical records have proven we have. These heirs are part of the veritable rainbow. History also tells us some children have been placed in an untenable position of not being loved by any one group—this too is a byproduct of slavery. However, it is beyond dispute these children have been a part of our communities and the distinction haunts us even today (the one single drop of Negro blood, the artificial construct that has been used to distinguish, differentiate).[22] The point: we should no longer be silenced. This, too, should be part of the process of reconciliation and willingness to tell the truth. Consider the

CHAPTER 5

previously unknown kin of William Pitt Ballinger.

In discussing the yellow fever season that occurred in Galveston in 1858, Earl Wesley Fornell explained, "The seriousness of the epidemics may be seen in the fact that in the seven-week 'fever season' in 1858 at Galveston took 373 lives. Other 'fever seasons' took numerous lives as well: 400 persons died of yellow fever in Galveston in 1844 and 535 in 1853. The personal aspect of these statistics may be seen in the fact that E. H. Cushing lost his wife and son during one epidemic; William Pitt Ballinger, the prominent Galveston jurist, lost four of his children to the fever; and the German editor in Galveston, Ferdinand Flake, lost five children during various epidemics."[23] William Pitt Ballinger was born September 25, 1825, and he passed on January 20, 1888.[24]

Death certificates do not have a box for "untold." It would seem inserting "untold" would properly capture the secrets/non-secrets of our untenable institution.

According to Penny L. Pope, the missing link in her family tree is William Pitt Ballinger:

> He was the father of William H. Jones—born to a slave, Lucy Dowdy. William Pitt Ballinger was grandfather to Charles Scott Jones, Harold S. Jones, and Anita Jones Barksdale [William H. Jones's children]. William H. Jones [William Pitt Ballinger's son] had a sister named Olive Dean, who lived in Galveston. I do not know whether Ballinger was her father or whether she was fathered by another man. William S. Jones [Pitt Ballinger's grandson] retired from the Galveston Wharves and during breaks or after work would go to the Mills Shirley law firm to rest and visit. They called him "Uncle Goodie" at the firm.[25]

There is no need to be shocked, dismayed, or accusatory. This was and remains the previously unspoken family lore: "Lucy Dowdy was one of three or four sisters brought from Africa; Lucy Dowdy had children by William Pitt Ballinger."[26] I suspect those cousins—Charles Scott Jones and Ballinger Mills—knew this as they performed their civic duty on the Galveston College Board.

William Pitt Ballinger was a prominent jurist who owned slaves. His daughter Lucy married into one of Texas's richest families. The Mills family was the owner of some of the largest plantations in the state and were reported to own the largest number of slaves within it.[27] From the Mills and Ballinger union Ballinger Mills was born, who also became a prominent jurist.[28]

The Mills' family genealogy is as follows: Adam Mills was born in 1755 in Ireland. He married his first wife, Jennett Graham, in Chester District, South Carolina. Jennett Graham was born in 1777 and died in 1817 in Christian, Kentucky. Adam and Jennett had seven children: William Mills (born 1800),

Hannah Nancy Mills (1803), Andrew Granville Mills (1805), Robert Mills (1809), David Graham Mills (1812), Janet McKee Mills (1815), and Mary Margaret Mills (1815). Janet and Mary were twins.[29]

Adam's oldest son William had three children during his first marriage: Samuel D. Mills, Green R. Mills, and John Mills. William married a second time to Minerva Hill. They had two children: Andrew Graham Mills[30] and David Graham Mills.[31]

Andrew Graham Mills and Lucy Ballinger (William Pitt Ballinger's daughter) married in Galveston, Texas, on February 13, 1878.[32] Ballinger Mills was born of the union of Andrew Graham Mills and Lucy Ballinger in 1879.[33]

The Mills side of the family were extensive land and slave owners, exceptionally wealthy for their day:

> According to the 1850 Agricultural Census, David G. Mills had 850 improved acres, with another 100,000 acres unimproved, and $25,000 worth of farm machinery. He had 10 horses, 50 mules, 25 milch cows, 25 work oxen, 300 head of cattle, and 200 swine. His plantations produced 6500 bushels of Indian corn, 1000 of Irish potatoes, 2000 of sweet potatoes, 350 pounds of butter, 4 tons of hay, 656 hogsheads of sugar, and 40,000 gallons of molasses. The 1850 Federal Slave Census Lists R. & D. G. Mills with 235 slaves.[34]

By 1860, "the Mills brothers [Andrew Graham Mills and David Graham Mills] owned over 300 slaves in Brazoria County alone, with 20,189 acres of land according to the 1860 tax record. David G. Mills reported his real estate value at $364,234 and value of his personal estate at $250,000."[35]

The 1860 Census lists Robert Mills as living in Galveston. He valued his real estate at $700,000 and his personal estate at $9,000. According to the 1860 Slave Census, Robert Mills held eight slaves as his own property.[36]

William H. Jones, according to the 1940 Census, was born in 1884 (listed as colored), but according to his death certificate he was approximately 82 years old when he died in 1961, which would put his date of birth as 1879.[37] His death certificate lists his mother as Lucy Dowdy (she too is listed as colored). His father is listed as "unknown." William H. Jones lived in Galveston with his wife, Bessie Elizabeth Scott Jones.[38] William H. Jones and Bessie Elizabeth had three children, Charles Scott Jones, Anita Elizabeth Jones, and Harold S. Jones.[39] William H. Jones's daughter, Anita Elizabeth Jones Barksdale, was born in 1903 and died in 1980, at the age of 77, at St. Mary's Hospital in Galveston.[40] She was a retired Galveston Independent School District teacher and a member of the National Association of Retired Teachers. Her obituary did not mention her parents or

Figure 6: William H. Jones & family. William H. Jones is standing, back row, far right; to his right are his wife, Bessie Scott Jones, Anita Jones Barksdale (sister), and Lena Verdell Pendergraff. Sitting, R–L: Lynne Nita Barksdale Pope, Leonard N. Barksdale II, Leonard N. Barksdale III, Joan Pendergraff Barksdale, Beverly W. Pendergraff. (By permission of Penny Pope.)

her date of birth, only her surviving heirs, referencing two brothers, Harold S. Jones of San Antonio and Charles Scott Jones of Galveston.[41]

William H. Jones's son Charles Scott Jones was born on October 4, 1904, and died in 1983. Charles Scott Jones retired after working for forty-five years at Interfirst Bank (later known as First Hutchins Sealy). His obituary does not identify his parents,[42] but does identify his wife, Minerva Jackson Jones, and his "niece, Lynnita Pope."[43] On Charles Scott Jones's death, the publisher for *Galveston Daily News*, Les Daughtry, wrote, "Charles Scott Jones's recent death ended a lifelong record of service to his community. Jones was instrumental in establishing Galveston's first junior college, now known as Galveston College. He was appointed to the original college Board of Regents in 1966 and subsequently won election to that office. He served 14 years as board vice president and at the time of his death was secretary of the board."[44] Charles Scott Jones served on the board for the Community Action Council and was also a member of the St. Paul United Methodist Church in Galveston, serving as a lay leader from 1934 to his death.[45]

Charles Scott Jones finished fifth in one regents' election when citizens were not

Figure 7: Galveston College Board of Regents. (Public domain.)

able to cast a vote for his election: "Mechanical problems with voting machines the morning of April 5 prevented voters from casting ballots in certain combinations. The machines would accept only the first two choices in these cases."[46] The news article identified Scott as the only minority board member and explained he intended to file suit. His lawyer was identified as John Eckel, with the Mills Shirley law firm—which was known then as Mills, Shirley, Eckel & Bassett.[47] At one time, Charles Scott Jones and the firm's partner, Ballinger Mills, served on Galveston College's Board of Regents together.[48] On Charles S. Scott's death, Janice Stanton filled Mr. Scott's unexpired board position with Galveston College.[49]

Lynne Nita Pope was the oldest child of Leonard N. Barksdale and Anita Jones Barksdale. She was born in Washington, DC, on October 9, 1925. She attended public schools in Galveston and was a member of St. Paul United Methodist

CHAPTER 5

Church.[50] Lynne Nita was a longtime teacher in Galveston. She and Reginald B. Pope married and remained married for 47 years.[51] She is the granddaughter of William H. Jones Jr. She and Reginald Pope had three children: Penny L. Pope, Reggy Nelle Pope Knowles, and Reginald William Pope.

In trying to untangle history's secrets, I realized this story is no different than the stories of many families in cities and rural areas. Traveling to the cotton gin in a mule/horse-drawn wagon, seeing the same person who introduced himself at a family event, "I'm your cousin." Of course, not now—in mixed company, his previous acknowledgment now muted, restricted, contorted. These are some of the reasons the tracing of heritage and lineage between the two distinct societies remains problematic. Slave manifests contained made-up names, no last name, no accurate age and/or date of birth (age listed as "about"). The documents also contain a vague description of these human souls and little or no information about lineage. Time's unkindness—as related to memories—obfuscates and misdirects, even amongst the well-intended; tracing becomes problematic, almost impossible. This may be one of the reasons Alex Haley resorted to fact/fiction in his telling the story *Roots*.[52] One more fact, in context of Lucy Dowdy: the name "Lucy" was a common name.[53]

I hear the screams! This means little or nothing in context of tracing, particularly when documents exist showing the Mills side of the family was the largest slaveholder in the state. A brief search reveals they owned a slave assigned the name Lucy on October 21, 1837, a little under twenty years before Robert and David G. Mills purchased Bynum Plantation. Again, no last name, no social security number (social security didn't exist at the time) or other identifying traceable numbers, or family documents.[54] Again, the slave's age was always recorded as "about." All this represents the success of the institution of slavery in the dehumanizing of these human souls and even the benefactors, hiding the unspeakable.

The process of enslaving was designed to avoid the type of birth heritage afforded to those of other races. Remember, less than human, accorded little or no rights, things of value. The inability to track and affirm was by design. Thomas Jefferson's heirs screamed bloody murder when the Hemings family told what had been verbalized for generations.[55] Galveston, like other slave societies, still retains unexpected stories, untold truths, all buried in plain view. Yes, yes, I know, to contend something is buried in plain view is nonsensical.

Generation after generation, Penny Pope's forebears have conveyed to her the "untold," connecting the lineage chain. They knew. Enough evidence remains to support these oral historians. "William Pitt Ballinger was William Henry Jones's father." Heresy—no, no, this is the duplicity of the institution of slavery, the origins of Du Bois's observation.

One more example: She, Starita Smith, told me she was the descendant of a "Henry A.Wise, who was the Governor of Virginia, a congressman, and an ambassador to Brazil. Wise signed the execution papers for John Brown and attended his hanging. Brown's raid and death predated Virginia leaving the union and the start of the Civil War." When Starita called I was in bed. When this information was given, I returned to a prone postion, I rolled, rolled again, before rolling back in place. I was trying to clear my head to talk.

"Can I call you in a couple of days? I need to think."

"Oh, sure!"

I went to bed early because I was anguished. My mind was muddled. I was one possessed with an indescribable speech pattern and tone. Whether sleep was a tonic for my maladies, I don't know. At the time, the call disturbed me, adding another layer of worry. I had yet to fall asleep. I actually misspoke/misdirected when I told Starita Smith I needed to think. I should have said I was thinking too much.

Who was John Brown? What other information can be discerned about Henry A. Wise?

On October 16–18, 1859, John Brown led twenty-one men on a raid of a federal arsenal at Harper's Ferry, Virginia.[56] The twenty-one men consisted of five Blacks and sixteen Whites. He planned to arm slaves with weapons seized from the arsenal. Brown was an abolitionist, an evangelical Christian with strong religious beliefs who expounded on the evils of slavery. For his actions, Brown was tried for treason, convicted, and hanged on December 2, 1859.[57] The historian Mary Frances Berry explained "although this affray was clearly of little military signifigance, it provided the southerners with comforting evidence of the continued government willingness to respond swiftly when the South was threatened."[58] The incident became a cause célèbre in the South, and provided additional propaganda surrounding the need to protect the institution.

"Henry A. Wise was a lawyer, a member of the U.S. House of Representatives (1832–1844), U.S. minister to Brazil (1844–1847), and governor of Virginia (1856–1860) during John Brown's raid on Harpers Ferry, and a brigadier general in the Confederate army during the American Civil War (1861–1865)." Wise led Virginia into secession and into the Civil War.[59]

I called Starita Smith back a week later.

Henry A. Wise's story is the American tale normally told. Stories similar to Starita Smith's history represent the stories needed to be told to unpackage America's history.

Wise is listed as having three wives and fourteen children, four children from his first wife (Ann), ten from his second wife (Sarah). Sarah died during childbirth. In addition, only three of their children survived infancy. Starita explained the historical records did not reveal Henry A. Wise fathered additional children with one of his slaves—one for sure, perhaps two. "He is my great-great-great-grandfather. The slave, Elizabeth Grey, is my great-great-great-grandmother. Their son was named William Henry Grey. Wise freed Elizabeth Grey, the only slave he is listed to have freed, and sent her and their son to Washington, DC, to live as free Negroes."[60] I saw Penny Pope's firm cheeks when she elected to tell me her families' story. I realized we all have a story to tell, to share.

"William Henry Grey worked as a page for Henry Wise." Starita didn't provide a year but explained they had another child—a girl—but she hasn't been able to find any records on this. After the Civil War, William Henry Grey and his wife, Henrietta Winslow, moved to Arkansas. He ran for legislature during Reconstruction. He was among the first six African American legislators to serve in the Arkansas House. He also served as the Clerk and Recorder of Deeds in 1870.[61]

"My family settled in Helena, Arkansas. William Henry Grey's birth records revealed who his mother was but do not reveal the father."[62] I saw Penny Pope nodding and intermittently chuckling.

The *Encyclopedia of Arkansas* affirms Starita's information and fills in additional blanks, albeit referencing William Grey's work for Congressman Wise as that of a "servant" and not a page:

> William Grey was born in Washington, DC, on December 22, 1829, as a free man. His parents' names remain unknown, although he is recorded in census records as a "mulatto," indicating that one of his parents, most likely his father, was white. He attended the "pay school" of John F. Cook while in Washington. He was also a servant to Congressman Henry A. Wise of Virginia, who affiliated alternatively with the Democratic and Whig parties as a member of the House of Representatives (1833–1844).[63]

The State of Arkansas' records provide other answers:

> Around 1840, Grey's family moved to Pittsburgh, Pennsylvania, and then to Cincinnati, Ohio. After his parents (most likely his mother and stepfather) died during a cholera epidemic in 1852, Grey moved to St. Louis, Missouri, and was employed as a cook on steamboats traversing the Ohio and Mississippi rivers. In 1854, he married Henrietta Winslow; together they had eight children. In the 1850s, he became a member of the African Methodist Episcopal Church, serving as a minister. By 1865, Grey had relocated to Helena, founding a grocery and bakery, with Oliver Winslow and H. B. Robinson as his business partners.[64]

I wrote out this history by hand, trying to keep up, praying I would be able to read my handwriting later.

"I'm confused, how does this connect to you?"

"William and Henrietta had children, eight in fact, one of these children was Nancy Grey who has a child with James Carter; James and Nancy moved to Cincinnati and had William H. Carter. James E. Carter my grandfather, his child Velma is my mother. Velma married Charles Smith."[65]

I finally got it and responded not as a wordsmith but as a listener: "Wow!"

The ever-foreboding anguish caused me to talk to the point of rambling, interspersing questions on top of questions, until this former journalist, now doctorate-bestowed sociology professor and mother, did what teachers and mothers do. She told me to take a deep breath and let her answer just one of the many questions flowing out of my mouth much like water.

> Where is the hope in these stories, was one of the questions you asked.
>
> Hope is sometimes hard to find when the discoveries evolve out of horrific findings. Slavery affected so much of our lives, from life to death, and we have to individually and collectively figure out what we will work on daily to challenge and change this history. And my sense of history tells me we did this in the past and are doing the same now.

• • •

> I will attempt to give an accurate account of the language and ceremony of a slave auction as I possibly can. "Gentlemen, here is a likely boy; how much? He is sold for no fault; the owner wants money. His age is forty. Three hundred dollars is all that I am offered for him. Please to examine him; he is warranted sound. Boy, pull off your shirt – roll up your pants – for we want to see if you have been whipped." If they discover any scars, they will not buy, saying that the nigger is a bad one. The auctioneer seeing this, cries, "Three hundred dollars, gentlemen, three hundred dollars. Shall I sell him for three hundred dollars? I have just been informed by his master, that he is an honest boy, and belongs to the same church that he does." This turns the tide frequently, and the bids go up fast; and he is knocked off for a good sum.[66]

• • •

Let me digress. Remember, E. G. Phipps and J. S. Sydnor's initial advertisement placed their auction house at Strand, corner of 22nd street. The Galveston

Historical Foundation has previously posted online an image of the Osterman Building.[67]

One could readily speculate the Osterman Building may be the same building depicted in the drawing of Sydnor's Auction House. Any such speculation is not supported by the evidence. Existing contemporary evidence places Sydnor's Auction House elsewhere on the Strand.[68]

> A two-story white frame building on the corner, partially occupied by Andrews and Grover, then Ball, Hutchins & Co, then Sydnor's Auction House, adjoining a building occupied by Wallis Landes and Company at the end of the block at 23rd Street (Tremont) was E. L. Ufford's Auction House.

The *Galveston Daily News* article cited above referenced a sketch, but a sketch does not appear in the electronically saved article. The absence of the drawing does not negate the article's value: the Osterman Building is referenced as being situated across the street, "which replaced a building occupied by Lepart & Dyer."

Sydnor's introduction to Galveston (in advertisements) appeared initially in 1843. Even if Sydnor's Auction House was located on the northern portion of the block (with the building facing south), this only means that Sydnor's business was not in the Osterman Building. Sydnor and Ufford's auction houses were separate buildings located between 22nd and 23rd Street on the Strand. They were on the same side of the street, while on the other side of the street were competing slave traders.

The torture and execution of a slave provides additional evidence. The enslaved soul was tortured at length and then hung by a mob. The news article explained he was confined in a building/jail. On careful reading, the location was either Sydnor or Ufford's auction house. The offending events took place on July 6, 1844, and printed on February 13, 1870—twenty-six years later.[69] The newspaper article read:

> On the 6th day of July 1844, a black man, the slave of Mr. R. P. Jones, an Englishman living on the riverfront, was hung for attempted rape on the person of Mrs. Helfenstein. He had been sent to the house of the lady to deliver wood, and while there attempted the outrage, choking her. She succeeded in escaping and told her husband. As there was a very imperfect organization of courts, a jury of twelve of the most respectable citizens were extemporized to try the offender. Mr. James P. Cole was assigned to his defence, and the trial was conducted with all the decency and decorum of a regular court. They adjudged him guilty and sentenced him to be hung the next day. In the meantime, he was confined in a frame building on the corner of Strand and 22nd Street. In the

afternoon, Henry C. Potter made a speech at the Tremont House, in which he denounced the proceeding as mob law and induced some of the people to release the man. Thereupon, the citizens assembled and arrested the man a second time and confined him to the hour of execution. A rope was then put around his neck, and he was brought down the stairs, the husband of the injured woman leading him not so very tenderly. Once to the street, the rope was fastened to a dray, and accompanied by the mob, started down Market street. The mob followed, hooting, and hallooing and throwing stones. At one place the man was much cut by a drunken man. When near Labadie's corner, the rope was so tight he was choking, and to keep him alive until he was hung it became necessary to slack up. He was then taken to Sylvester bar room bout where Schott's drugstore now stands, in the back yard which a demolished a ten-pin alley, from one of the beams which how he was hanged. The body was then taken out to the northwest corner of the town and the head cut off by Dr. Weschester. The mob took it and used it as sort of a football, throwing and kicking it about. The next morning it was found stuck on a pole near the markethouse, a grining [sic] warning to all negroes. The skull was afterwards removed by Dr. [Nicholas D.] Labadie and may be in the collection he left when he died.[70] The body, however, was refused burial by the Negroes and laid in the prairie until it became offensive. It was thrown into the bay. After a few days, Mr. Jones, the old master found it floating in front of his house. He had it buried in Saparac, where it was years afterwards found by boys who were playing. This was rough and certainly not refined justice, but it answered the purpose and prevented a repetition of the crime.[71]

No name was attributed to the man, a slave. In that this event occurred in 1844, there was no trial accorded slaves under law. What is styled as an extemporized jury consisted of White men (extemporized, meaning assigned off the street with no procedures in place for a fair trial). The enslaved person was tried on the same day. There is a reference to the imperfect organization of the courts, which does not mean the court system was not in place, but this should be read in the context of the law that didn't permit the enslaved access to the court system and surely the enslaved was not permitted to testify against a White person. May I use another analogy to be clear: cooking on an Easy Bake Oven would not and does not mean one is cooking. Absolutely, there was no transcript of these proceedings. And if one sought to examine the evidence, any evidence would be long ago buried, secreted. The building in which the enslaved person was placed—we now know—was located in the block of 22nd and Strand and was Sydnor's or Ufford's Auction House.

The above lynching was retold in an article written years later, titled "Capital Convictions in Galveston." The article recounts an execution under the civil laws,

CHAPTER 5

one of Charles Heminger who was hung in 1842, who lived down the island, who killed a neighbor in "a quarrel about some sweet potatoes." There is no mention of the race of the condemned. The second hanging was that of the enslaved man mentioned above on July 5, 1844. The third was the hanging of John Henry Schultz, who was hanged in 1854 for killing two men at Virginia Point, thirteen years prior. The next was the execution of another enslaved person—a Negro woman—in 1857. The enslaved woman's name was not given; she allegedly killed her owner, Mrs. Doherty, and afterward threw her body down the well. The enslaved woman was executed. Two years prior to the freeing of slaves in Texas (1863), a Negro man was hung on the corner of 20th and Winnie "to a lamppost by the mob." He was accused of rape and was in the hands of the Confederate military. "It was said Dan Gallagher was the most active in this execution." Gallagher was also later accused of killing a Negro sergeant after the war. It appears the sergeant was with the Union forces. Gallagher was sentenced to death; his conviction was reversed.[72] Galveston was a fraught place for the enslaved and not a place for the mythically happy Negroes mentioned and clearly not a place where "Galveston 'city Negroes' w[ere] envied by the slaves in the interior."[73]

Other examples: *The Galveston Daily News* reported on the first executions in Austin, Texas. Each example is more and more disturbing. Most of the persons reported were either enslaved or persons who attempted to help the enslaved. This reporting appeared in the August 23, 1879, edition of the news: "The first person hanged in Austin was unlucky slave named Lucky, who killed old man Baker and his wife in escaping, having been taken in by Sterling Robertson as a runaway slave. . . . A jury appointed by judge Lynch condemned him. A mob executed him."[74]

The next was also a slave, belonging to Mr. Lowt, who killed an old German. He was hung according to the law. The next was a White man named Prestage, who organized a band of slaves during the war to steal horses and make their way to Mexico. He was executed by the citizens.

The next were two Mexicans, who suffered in the same way.[75]

An 1890 advertisement identified the location of the Osterman Building's location as 2207 Strand.[76] In an advertisement dated July 16, 1897 (remember this is after emancipation), Osterman sought tenants for available spaces (large airy offices on second and third floor). The designated rental agent was L. Lovenberg.[77] A similar advertisement was taken out on February 12, 1890 (again, after emancipation), seeking a tenant for the entire third floor.[78] It is clear any reference by the auctioneers to 22nd and Osterman Building is not the same reference made in Sydnor's advertisements also referencing 22nd and Strand. As seen in the advertisement above, H. A. Cobb and J. Osterman had a business relationship. Each had a vested interest in slave trade and the ownership of human chattel. In 1860, Joseph Osterman is listed in the Slaver Register as owning five female slaves in the city, one that was labelled as mulatto; John S. Sydnor had fourteen.[79]

This interconnection is further documented in the County Clerk's records.[80] On April 24, 1844, John S. Sydnor's father—Edward G. Sydnor of Henrico County, Virginia—lent the sum of $5,795.00 (equivalent to $209,369.62 in today's dollars) to John S. Sydnor and Henry A. Cobb.[81] The loan was to be paid back in three annual installments, with the final payment due and owing in 1847. John S. Sydnor and Henry A. Cobb were able to repay Edward Sydnor just one year later.[82]

One last point: The actual locations of Sydnor's and other auction houses seems not to matter because of a more salient point: the Strand was a Slave Business District between the period of 1840 and 1865.[83]

On August 28, 1857, an auction notice was placed in the *Galveston Daily Civilian* providing a new location for Sydnor's business: the corner of Strand and Market Place, opposite the Brick Wharf.[84] The term "the Brick Wharf" is not used today. The 1859 city directory explained the Brick Wharf was located at the "Foot of 20th Street, built in 1845, by John S. Sydnor and now owned by the Galveston Wharf Company, has a front of 380 feet."[85]

In the same period, an advertisement by the firm McMurry & Winstead told of an impending sale of "a large lot of young and likely Virginia and North Carolina Negroes." The sale/auction location? Leonard's Hall on Church Street.[86] Charles H. Leonard served as Galveston's mayor from 1864 to 1867 and 1879 to 1880. He also served as the tax assessor collector for the city from 1872 to 1875 and as a Galveston alderman from 1858 to 1861.[87] Leonard was born March 23, 1813, in the south of Ireland. He immigrated to the United States in the spring of 1834, and after a short period in Washington, DC, New Orleans, and Victoria, Texas (fighting in different conflicts), he came to Galveston. He married Adeline D. Reilley of Galveston on January 1, 1853.[88]

In 2019, the City of Galveston entered a Development and License to Use (LTU) Agreement with the American National Insurance Company for the construction and operation of a raised pedestrian bridge and grade level pedestrian streetscape within the right-of-way of 20th Street between Mechanic and Market Street. In a letter addressed to the city manager, the mayor, and city council members on August 14, 2019, the City of Galveston's Development Services Department wrote:

> Historical Considerations: Historic District or Potentially Eligible Historic District. The subject site was the location of both Galveston's first and second

CHAPTER 5

City Halls. The first City Hall is the subject of a Texas Historical Commission plaque installed at the site in 2014. The text of the plaque is as follows:

> During the 1830s, an informal, outdoor market started in the half-block north of Market Street between 20th and 21st streets. In 1846, mayor John Sydnor hired Ives and Crow to build a 250-foot-long structure in the center of 20th Street between Mechanic (C) and Market (D) streets to serve both as a produce market and as the city hall. The Colonial style white frame building had four dormer windows and a roof cupola. The ground originally housed 34 meat, vegetable, and coffee stalls, with the city offices, including the police department and a large public meeting hall located on the second floor. A fish market operated across the street. Galvestonians celebrated the building's opening with a grand ball. The market stalls were stocked with produce, meat, fish, and other goods brought in from the bay area on cat boards and landed at the nearby Brick and Kuhn's Wharves. Before the Civil War, annual stall rents ranged from a high of $100 (meat) to a low of $35 (fish) and the city added a 100-foot extension to meet the demand for stalls. On October 7, 1862, Galvestonians gathered in the market and voted to peacefully accept Union occupation. Having escaped damage during the Civil War, the market house survived serious threats from fire in 1865 and again in 1885. Installed in 1867, a bell in the cupola rang to tell the time of day. After the Civil War, critics found the market house run-down, but expense deterred renovation. One of the last improvements occurred in 1874 when the city installed pavers. An attempt to use the attic as a holding cell in the 1870s ended when a woman prisoner broke through the roof. In 1888, a new three-story stone building replaced the 1846 frame structure.[89]

What is missing from the city's staff report? Sydnor's advertisement revealed he was auctioning slaves in the marketplace. What is the evidence supporting this position? First, Sydnor makes clear in his advertisement his location was opposite the Brick Wharf. Second, additional extrinsic evidence reveals on January 12, 1846, Sydnor transferred Sydnor's Wharf to E. Martin and Henry A. Cobb. Then in 1848 Martin and Cobb filed for bankruptcy.[90] On May 15, 1848, a new document was signed wherein the parties agreed to cancel the promissory note, which was entered on January 12, 1846, and to transfer the Brick Wharf back to Sydnor.[91] The City's Report and the Texas Historical Commission's signage mentions none of this. The Historical Commission engages in a bit of diversionary telling of this history. Sydnor was the mayor of the city at the time. The city readily admits Sydnor built City Hall.

Of equal concern, the bell mentioned on the plaque is not and was not the Liberty Bell. The Liberty Bell has always represented a symbol of liberty. The Liberty Bell was celebrated during the post–Revolutionary War period, then adopted by abolitionists fighting to abolish slavery.[92] Let's not glamorize Galveston's disdainful bell.

The condensed slave ordinances found in the 1859 city directory identify the purpose of the bell:

> The city bell is rung every night at 9 o'clock, from April 1st to October 1st, during the balance of the year at 8 o'clock, and every slave or free person of color found in the street or away from home, after such ring of the bell, without proper pass or permit, shall be liable to be taken up and kept in custody till morning when the owner is notified and required to pay costs, for the regulars in full in regard to slaves.[93]

The State of Texas's historical plaque is partly true and partly false—inherently the definition of a myth. There was a bell, true; however, the rest is whitewashing, papering over, and lying. John S. Sydnor built the building for the city, advertised his auctions at the location, and was mayor of the city for more than one term. The bell was rung every night at 9 o'clock. The bell's purpose is engrafted in the city's ordinances; nothing in the ordinance mentions its use was to tell the time of day. Anyone viewing this official State of Texas plaque over the years would never know how the story has been changed or retold falsely. We should never glamorize Galveston's use of the bell; it was a method of controlling Galveston's slaves and colored population.

In addition, the discontinued use of the slave trader's (John S. Sydnor) building may well have been because the condition of the building could have deteriorated or because slavery had come to end in 1865, two years after the Emancipation Proclamation news finally reached the island. Federal troops came onto the island. Absolutely no evidence exists supporting this untruth: "Galvestonians gathered in the market and voted to peacefully accept Union occupation." The South surrendered, United States troops marched onto the island, and General Gordon Granger read his imperfect order. The signage should honestly recount history and identify the location as one of the places John S. Sydnor sold human chattels and a bell hung from the cupola, ringing every night to ensure Galveston's slave population and free persons of color were regulated. The ringing of the bell was required by the city's code and ordinances, which were passed in 1859, while the

CHAPTER 5

plaque by the State of Texas purports the bell was not put in place until 1867, two years after June 1865.

My, my, what a circuitous route.

There were at least five slave auction house locations discovered to have been in existence between the period of 1840 to 1850: the 22nd and Strand (location of Ufford and Sydnor's auction houses); Leonard's Hall on Church Street; George B. Innes was located at the Auction Room in Haskin's building adjoining the Merchants Exchange; and 20th and Wharf, the reference to E. G. Phipps and J. S. Sydnor's advertisement which places them in business together. There is little—no, let me correct this misstatement—there was no reference to these auction houses in any previously published works.

In my search I located another site referenced as an auction house. The site belonged to Edmund Joseph Cordray, a pharmacist. The *Galveston Daily News* on March 19, 1967, reported a historic plaque was to be installed in front of Cordray Drugstore at 1501 Postoffice. The plaque read as follows: "'Cordray Drugstore. On site of the busy slave market. Nearby cottage built 1866. Cordray pharmacy here since 1918.' John S. Sydnor, one of Galveston's early mayors, reportedly traded in slaves and auctioned them on the site. A carpenter's shop and grocery store occupied the ground in the years following, using the cement auction block as a foundation."[94]

The current plaque located at the address has now been changed and does not reference an auction house.[95] Whether the post office address represented a slave auction site remains unclear to this author. In my search, the purported source of this information surrounding this site was the *Galveston Daily News*. The story explained the source: "reprinted from August 13, 1963, *Galveston News* article." After pulling the cited reference, the information provided was of no worth, "according to local historians."[96] No dates of sale, court filings, transfer documents, and/or any other supporting documentation. No reference to the name of the local historians so that the historians' work(s) can be reviewed and studied. In other words, further research is necessary with respect to this location.

CHAPTER 6

THEIR CRIES REMAIN AUDIBLE

The Water Always Cries

They stood in place, silent, as a strange, possessed man screamed – rapidly –
in a language they did not understand.
A language they did not want to understand.

For some, the first time.
others, a second.

. . . a third.
a fourth.
a fifth.

No longer wishing death.
Never, never understanding. "Mbona! Mbona!"

Looking hither. Looking yonder.
He, the sixth time.
He was an exception; grown old, still strong.

a seventh.

―――――

She too was silent – above, flowing –
Hovering near a different water this time.
Different from the one she, he, they knew.

CHAPTER 6

Over, around, over again.

The birds flowed, trashed, disturbed.
The water was told to join, and she did,
flowing, trashing, disturbing.

No – names, new – names, insulting – names –
Priced.

They stood in place listening, not listening.

She was pushed forward.
He too later.

She – no longer for him.
He – no longer for her.

Rapture!

Their young child wailed.
She was there. She was always there –
Hers a silent voice.
Filling small spaces, large rooms –
Docksides.

Above – around – about – harrowing places –
Always near water.
Always near the water.

Over, around, over again -
Unseen – always unseen.
Distilling an unextinguishable flame.

"You live."
"You live."
"You live!"
"Live!"

She replaced one fire with another –

THEIR CRIES REMAIN AUDIBLE

This one different.
Incapable of being quelled,
not by disease,
not inhuman conditions.
Surviving holes, shackles,
beatings –
rape –

The possessed man was indeed strange fruit.
He continued to scream and count.
Few saw . . . or heard her voice.
No one bothered to look up.

The strange fruit continued to squeal –
"*A good strong buck!*"

Near the waters, counting, pinching, pointing.
Teeth, tongues, eyes, skin.
Inserting fingers where they should not be – writing.

He was pleased.

She was not; over, over, around.
Her voice remained constant – otherworldly –
circling, circling, circling.

Moving over, and around, over, back, around.

Hers – the same voice – remaining in place for generations later –
Curing, blessing, protecting.

They picked and pulled on a young active girl.
Lucy was her fourth name.
She was only 25.

Pulling, striking, pushing –
You will be . . . "*Hiawatha.*"

. . . his sixth . . .

CHAPTER 6

Always near the water –

She was sold.
He was sold.
The child was sold.

The voice? The same voice indeed –
Not to be quenched.

Hovering, pointing, over, above, around – to the water.
Directing generations to hallowed sites.
. . . flowing, trashing, disturbing.

She – he, walked out one door.
The strange fruit smiled, he out the other.

The water cries –
The water always cries.[1]

When E. G. Phipps and J. S. Sydnor took out their advertisement in January 1843 they announced to the world they were opening a General Commission and Auction Business, including the auctioning of "Real Estate, Negroes, etc." The location listed was "Office Strand corner of 22nd Street." In 1859, the city directory gives no indication of E. G. Phipps residing in the city. The directory does note Sydnor—John S –: "auctioneer and commission merchant. Strand between 22nd and 23rd Streets—residence corner av I & 16th st."[2]

The 1859 directory also lists businesses such as commission merchants,[3] exchange brokers, cotton factors, and collecting agents.[4]

Austin, W. T., commission merchant, Strand, between 21st and 22nd Streets.

Ball, Hutchings & Co., cotton factors, commission merchants and exchange brokers, corner Strand and 24th Street.

Bolling & Sayre, auctioneers, Strand, between 22nd and 23rd streets.[5]

After they had been at St. Louis a few weeks, another cargo of human flesh was made up. There were amongst the lot several old men and women, some of whom had gray locks. On their way down to New Orleans, William had to prepare the old slaves for market. He was ordered to shave off the old men's whiskers and to pluck out the gray hairs where they were not too numerous; where they were, he colored them with a preparation of blacking with a blacking-brush. After having gone through the blacking process, they looked ten or fifteen years younger. William, though not well skilled in the use of scissors and razor, performed the office of the barber tolerably. After the sale of this gang of Negroes, they returned to St. Louis and a second cargo was made up. In this lot was a woman who had a child at the breast yet was compelled to travel through the interior of the country on foot with the other slaves. In a published memoir of his life, William says, "The child cried during most of the day, which displeased Mr. Walker, and he told the mother that if her child did not stop crying he would stop its mouth. After a long and weary journey under a burning sun, we put up for the night at a country inn. The following morning, just as they were about to start, the child again commenced crying. Walker stepped up to her and told her to give the child to him. The mother tremblingly obeyed. He took the child by one arm, as any one would a cat by the leg, and walked into the house where they had been staying, and said to the lady, 'Madam, I will make you a present of this little nigger; it keeps making such a noise that I can't bear it.' 'Thank you, sir,' said the lady. The mother, as soon as she saw that the child was to be left, ran up to Mr. Walker, and, falling on her knees, begged of him, in an agony of despair, to let her have her child. She clung round his legs so closely that for some time he could not kick her off; and she cried, 'O my child, my child! Master, do let me have my dear, dear child! O! do, do! I will stop its crying, and love you forever, if you will only let me have my child again.'" But her prayers were not heeded; they passed on, and the mother was separated from her child forever.[6]

Carnes & Trabue, commission merchants and cotton factors, Strand, between 23rd and 24th streets.
Darragh, J. L., office Strand, between 24th Street and Bath Avenue.[7]
Hendley, W. & Co., commission merchants, corner of Strand and 21st.
Heydecker, Adolphus, commission merchant, corner of Strand and 21st street, upstairs.
Kaufman & Klaener, grocers and commission merchants, 22nd street, between Strand and [A]venue C.

Kuhn, J. C., grocer, and commission merchant, corner of Strand and 22nd street.
Le Pert & Deadrick, commission merchants, Strand, between 22nd and 23rd streets.
Lynn & Williams, cotton factors and commission merchants, corner of Strand and 24th Street.
Mather, Hughes & Saunders, commission merchants, foot of the Brick Wharf.
McCarty, C. L., general agent and auctioneer, 21st street, between avenues C and D.[8]
McKean, J. L. & A. C., cotton factors and commission merchants, Strand.
McMahan, G. W. & Co., commission merchants, corner of Strand and 21st Street, upstairs.
McMahan & Gilbert, cotton factors, commission merchants, and exchange brokers, Strand, between 23rd and 24th streets.
Miller, Montgomery & Co., commission merchants and collecting agents, Strand, corner of 23rd street, upstairs.
Mills, R. & D. G., cotton factors, commission merchants, and exchange brokers, corner of Strand and 23rd street, upstairs.
Nichols, E. B. & Co., commission merchants, 20th Street, foot of Brick Wharf.
Parsons, B. S., commission, and lumber merchant, foot of Brick Wharf.
Ruthven, A. S., commission merchant, Strand, corner of 22nd street.
Shackelford, John, commission merchant, Strand, between 22nd and 23rd streets.
Sydnor, John S, auctioneer and commission merchant, Strand between 22nd and 23rd Streets.
Trueheart, J. O., agent, office Avenue D, between 21st and 22nd street.
H. M. Trueheart, assessor and collector, Avenue D, between 21st and 22nd Street.
Ufford, E. L., auctioneer, corner of Avenue C and 23rd Street.[9]
Wagner, Theo, commission merchant, corner of Strand and 21st Street.
Wilder, Geo. H., commission merchant, corner of Strand and 21st Street.
Wood & Power, cotton factors and commission merchants, corner of Strand and 21st Street.[10]

There were four businesses/individuals listed as auctioneers in 1859 (Sydnor, John S.; Bolling & Sayre; McCarty, C. L.; and Ufford, E. L.).[11] Their locations: Sydnor—Strand, between 22nd and 23rd Streets; Bolling & Sayre—Strand, between 22nd and 23rd streets; McCarty, C. L.—21st, between Avenue C & D; Ufford, E. L.—Avenue C and 23rd Street. There were twenty-six entities/persons who were identified as commission merchants; three previously mentioned took out advertisements that advertised slaves for sale. These individuals or companies are listed as agents or in a different profession. One company named A. Cameron

& Co. identified itself as auctioneers, "Will attend to Selling at Auction in Every part of the City."[12] In 1852, P. G. Merritt self-identified as an agent when placing for sale "A Negro Male 28 years old, warranted in every particulars for sale."[13] The Truehearts—father and son—also should be included among those who were engaged in the business of selling the enslaved.[14] If one referenced only the city directory, one would never know their involvement. One particular transaction is of note: J. L. Darragh was listed as having an office located on the Strand, between 24th Street and Bath Avenue (25th Street). Darragh was engaged in a large sale of slaves in 1854. The sale involved fifty-six men, women, and children.[15]

> As it is hard to tell the ages of slaves, they look in their mouths at their teeth, and prick up the skin on the back of their hands, and if the person is very far advanced in life, when the skin is pricked up, the pucker will stand so many seconds on the back of the hand.
>
> But the most rigorous examinations of slaves by those slave inspectors is on the mental capacity. If they are found to be very intelligent, this is pronounced the most objectionable of all other qualities connected with the life of a slave. In fact, it undermines the whole fabric of his chattelhood; it prepares for what slaveholders are pleased to pronounce the unpardonable sin when committed by a slave. It lays the foundation for running away and going to Canada. They also see in it a love for freedom, patriotism, insurrection, bloodshed, and exterminating war against American slavery.[16]

Words such as "slave" and "enslaved" seem to continue history's litany of dehumanizing a human being. The deprivation of a person's culture, connection to family, clan, tribe, or country seems equally compounded by the initial stripping of the person's name. My grandparents hated and always corrected their grandchildren when you called another sibling out of their name. Maybe this was their teaching manners. Perhaps it is their recognition of the societal hostility and lack of respect that is accorded to people of color. Called out of your name, referenced by racial epithets—boy, girl, them people, those people—but never by your name. My mother hated nicknames, viewing them as a continuation of the racist insult.

My generation participated in the fight over names also: we were no longer Negroes or colored, now Black, before seeking a greater connection to a lost history and heritage—no longer referenced as boy or girl—no matter one's age, status, familiar history. A cultural fight waged daily: demanding our elders be respected and called by formal titles, not "Mary" or "Frank." This seed was planted by our forebears. Over and around, over, back, around.

Legal documents are part and parcel of history's visible tracks: deeds and contracts provide a method of documenting parties' intent, particularly related to things of

CHAPTER 6

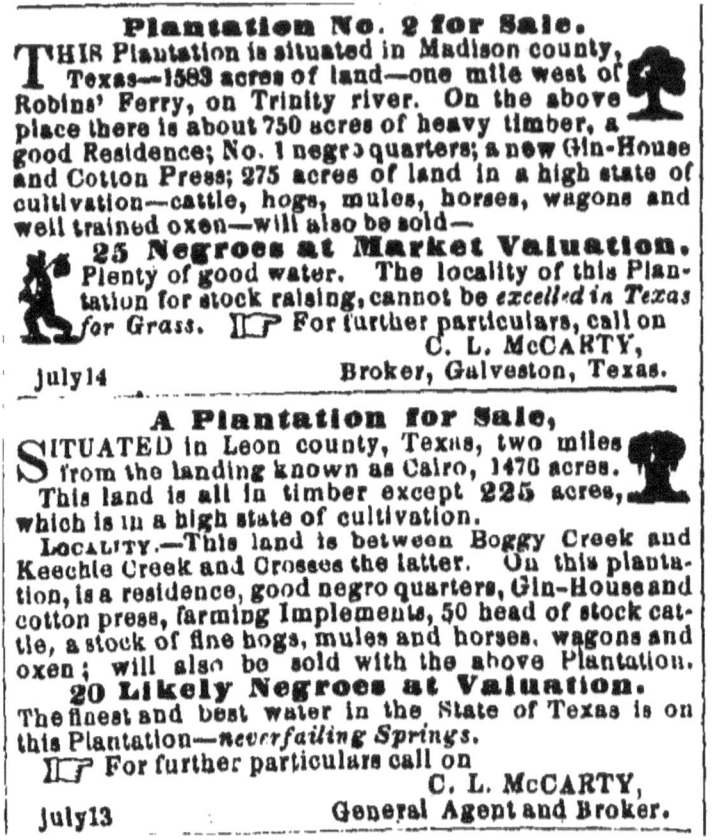

Figure 8: Plantation ads, *Galveston Daily Civilian*, August 28, 1857, 3.

value. They also provide additional proof of the dehumanization process, particularly when assigned no name or first name only. My maternal grandfather named his mule Elick. He never named two of the three dogs that roamed the farm. With respect to these fifty-six human souls sold and exchanged in the Darragh transaction, I have attempted to interpret the handwriting found on the sale documents. Their names:

> Candie, Daniel, Emma, Stephen, Mary, Harriet, Joe, Isaac, Ben, Anthony, a Carpiton; Cornelius, Marcia, Martha, and her three children: Rose, Austin, and Betsy; Elijah, Patsy, London, Hannah, Im[a], Maxwell, Amanda and her two children, to-wit: William and Carolina; John, George, Few, Elliott, Bertha, Rose and her two children, to-wit: Frank & Isaac; Sally, Mary Ann; Violet and her three children, to-wit: George, Harriett, and infant Moses; Grace and her four children, to-wit: Wilson, Sam, Ely and infant Moses; Kitty, George,

> **NEW COMMUNICATION BETWEEN**
> # N. Orleans, Galveston & Velasco
> *Connecting with the new light draught steamer ELITE, running from Velasco to Washington and intermediate Landings.*
>
> THE well known and substantial Steam Ship **MARIA BURT**, Capt. Emmerson, will leave New Orleans on Wednesday 31st July at 5 o'clock P M. positively, to arrive at Galveston on Saturday 3d August—leaving Galveston for Velasco on Sunday August 4th. at 8 o'clock A M, and arrive at Velasco same day, and connect with steamer Elite for Washington and all intermediate landings on the Brazos river.
>
> Will leave Velasco on Tuesday 6th, and Galveston the 7th at 4 o'clock, P M, for New Orleans.
>
> From and after this date she will make regular trips as above every fourteen days. Shippers and passengers by this line are assured that punctuality and despatch may be depended upon
>
> For freight or passage, having superior accommodations a low rates, apply on board or to
> HARRISON & STEWART agents Quintana
> GREEN, HARDING & CO., agents,
> Aug 2   6m   66 Poydras st, New Orleans

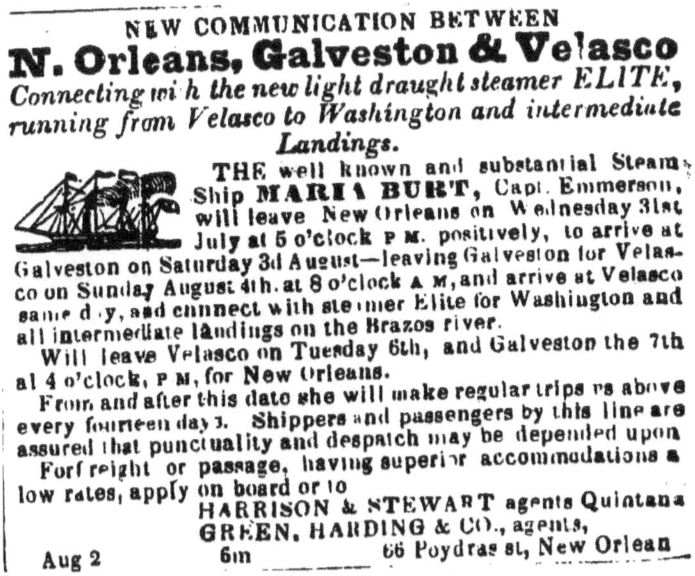

Figure 9: New Orleans, Galveston & Velasco ad, *Civilian and Galveston Gazette*, January 24, 1851, 3. (Public domain).

Charlotte, Charity, Ralph, Anthony, Rachel and her two children: Priscilla, Andrew; Priscilla, and Orange.

It can be argued that deciphering the handwritten text is an act of futility. I submit not.

Darragh was the trustee on the sale, the party in the second part. The transaction took place on March 1, 1854.[17] William Maner of the county of Brazoria is listed as the party in the first part. Maner purchased the slaves and agreed to indebt himself in the sum of $14,400.00 to Richard B. Doswell, trading under the firm of Doswell, Hill and Co. The sale took place in the offices of Doswell, Hill and Company. The firm's name is listed in the 1859 city directory; R. B. Doswell's address in 1859 was on 23rd Street in Heller's *Galveston Directory*; after the Civil War—1886-1877—the name of the firm had changed to Arnold, Menard & Co., with an address of 120 E. Strand, 2nd Floor.[18] Darragh was the president of the Galveston Wharf Company in 1886. His residence was listed in the 1859 city directory to be at the corner of Avenue F and 17th Street. He ultimately built a new home at 1519 15th Street.[19] Darragh served as alderman in the years 1848-1849 and 1856.

The previous reference to the United States census is important in another context: the advice the government tendered its data collectors. The census takers were instructed not to accept how the citizens categorized their work if evidence existed as to other employment. In Darragh's case, the historical records reveal the wisdom of the government. He was actively involved in the business of slave trading and auctioneering—not of mice but of Negroes and Negresses.[20] Darragh was the owner of Texas General Agency Office, formed in 1842. In 1868, Darragh was listed as: president of National Bank of Texas (located on Strand Street, at the corner of 22nd Street); board of director for the Houston & Galveston Wharf and Press Company; a stockholder with Galveston City Company.[21]

E. O. Lynch's advertisements revealed he was an auction and commission merchant located on Strand in Galveston.[22] The same applies to an entity named Harrison and Stewart (below). Lynch, like others, was an auctioneer; Harrison and Stewart self-identified as an entity willing to service plantations.[23] Since slaves were considered property, those involved in the sale of property would properly include real estate agents and lawyers. From time immemorial, lawyers have been involved in business transactions, contracts, protecting the status quo. In an advertisement found in the *Galveston Daily Civilian*, an advertisement concerned the sale of two plantations, one located in Leon County, Texas, 1,476 acres and "20 Likely Negroes at Valuation," the other in Madison County, Texas—1,583 acres of land, "25 Negroes at Market Valuation."[24]

In assessing the economic force of slavery in Galveston at the time, the role of lawyers in the South cannot be ignored. Slavery contributed to lawyers' wealth, the same as other professions. As mentioned earlier, one of a lawyer's most important roles throughout history is the protection of the status quo. The Atticus Finches (*To Kill a Mockingbird*) of the world remain few and far between. And, of course, Atticus Finch is a fictional character.

The wealth from slavery proved to be generational, and at the same time lawyering was an attractive profession for subsequent generations to enter. In this context, Galveston was a recently formed city of immigrants who brought with them their institutions—including slavery—and other same or similar professions they left when moving from other states or countries, this coupled with a firm belief in the doctrine of manifest destiny.[25]

One way of explaining better is to trace one such family:
Archibald Rowland Campbell Sr., 1841–1920, was born in Georgia. Some record his birth as being in the state of Alabama. His father was John Wesley Campbell (1794), his mother Ann Williamson Clark (1801). The 1850 census revealed Ann Williamson Campbell was in DeSoto Parish, Louisiana; other members of the household included Archibald Rowland, Edwin Eliza Campbell, Douglas McQueen Campbell, Frances Rebecca Campbell, and Samuel D. Campbell. When the 1860 census was taken, John Wesley Campbell is noted to have a household of Archibald Rowland Campbell, Ann Williamson Clark, Douglas McQueen

Campbell, and Frances Rebecca Campbell. "[John Wesley] J. W. Campbell is listed in the 1860 Slave Schedule with 40 slaves (11 of whom were age 10 and younger, and 3 of whom were age 60 and older) and 8 slave houses."[26] Archibald Rowland Campbell married Alice Lee Matthews in Galveston County in 1869. According to the 1880 census, Archibald was listed as a lawyer. Other members of the household included Alice Lee Campbell, Flora McQueen Campbell, Bessie Clark Campbell, Maud M. Campbell, Sarah Wiggins Campbell, and Samuel Williams Campbell.[27] In 1900 Archibald and Alice were located at 1515 Broadway.[28] Archibald died in Galveston on May 1, 1920, at the age of 78.[29]

Archibald Rowland Campbell, the son of Archibald Rowland Campbell and Ann Williamson Campbell, was born in 1888. This Archibald is properly a junior, but another individual is listed as junior in the record. His obituary of December 16, 1985, revealed he served as the vice president of T.T.T. Ship Agencies.[30] In addition, "[d]uring his lifetime he also served as chairman of the board of the Galveston Wharf Co., was president of the Galveston Cotton Exchange and on its board of trustees, and served for more than 20 years on the Galveston draft board."[31] His survivors on death included two sons: Archibald R. Campbell and Chesley R. Campbell, both of Galveston; four daughters: Katherine Oliver of Waco, Texas, Mary Lee Davis of Dickinson, Texas, Alice Gaughan of Leawood, Kansas, and Nancy Martin of Galveston.[32]

The person who is referenced as junior in the historical records, Archibald Rowland Campbell Jr., was "born in Galveston on May 24, 1917, to Archibald R. and Kate Rountree Campbell." He passed on December 11, 1994. His father died in 1985; his mother Katherine Wilson Rountree died in 1984.[33] He was survived by his wife Eugenia Harris Campbell, his daughter Eugenia H. Campbell, and two sons—Archibald R. Campbell III[34] and John Harris Campbell. Archibald Rowland Campbell III retired in 1980 from American Indemnity Insurance Company, where he was senior vice president. He was a lifelong member of Trinity Episcopal Church and served on the board of trustees for the Rosenberg Library.[35] One of the sons (John Harris Campbell)[36] became a licensed lawyer, specializing in estate planning and tax law; the other (Archibald R. Campbell)[37] appears to be in the oil and gas industry, handling trusts and the family's wealth.

John William Campbell (1866–1940) was the son of Marcus Campbell and Caroline Lucy Williams, the daughter of Samuel May Williams. Marcus L. Campbell is Archibald's son—this is the Archibald Rowland Sr. born in 1841. Caroline was the daughter of William Pitt Ballinger. John William married Mary Virginia Stowe, daughter of J. H. Stowe, in 1894 in Galveston, Texas, at St. John's Church. John William Campbell and Mary Virginia Stowe appeared in the 1900 census in Galveston, Texas, living at 3218 Avenue O; other members of the household included Wesley Neal

Campbell and Marcus A. Campbell. John William Campbell was employed as a lawyer according to the 1900 census. He served as the county judge in 1900, one year as the tax assessor in 1904, and as a state representative (representing Galveston) in 1910.[38]

What is the point of this recital? The wealth bequeathed by the institution of slavery courses through the veins of the Southern milieu. Human chattel was more valuable than the land on which those enslaved toiled, creating generational wealth for families and institutions and allotting privilege based on race.

In the Galveston city directory of 1859, there were twenty-five to twenty-seven attorneys. This number represents an estimate, in that this author attempts to exclude the judiciary but include names of persons seen elsewhere, but not in the city directory.[39]

The 1850 U.S. federal census of slave schedules in Galveston lists William Pitt Ballinger as having seven slaves; James P. Cole as having seven; Benjamin C. Franklin as having five; John Jones as having four; and Hugh McLeod as having nine—all those named were lawyers.[40]

Before going on, in the 1860 U.S. federal census of slave schedules in Galveston, another Campbell is found—John C. Campbell owned fifteen slaves.[41] He was the son of John Wesley Campbell (1794–1850) and Ann Williamson Clark (1805–1885) and is identified as a physician.[42]

When Georgetown University (located in Washington, DC) admitted its survival as an institution was assured by its ownership of plantations and slaves, this admission drew a straight line between slavery, land, and wealth.

> In 1838, to save Georgetown University from financial ruin, the Society of Jesus sold more than 272 enslaved people from their five Maryland plantations. Some of these enslaved individuals—women, men, child, and infants—were torn from their families and sold to plantation owners in southern Louisiana and held as collateral by Citizens Bank of New Orleans between 1838 and 1865. Citizens Bank has since been acquired by JPMorgan Chase.[43]

Between the sixteenth and eighteenth centuries, the Jesuits and the Catholic Church were some of the largest slave-holding institutions in North America.[44] An opposite description (opposite of Fornell and other historians) of Galveston came from a journalist, John Coulter, in 1900. Coulter provided the following:

> This settler stock of Galveston Island was of queer characteristics. The island settlement was of a sort of Captain Streeter origin. The only variation was that the Colonel Menard who founded it brought the island and established a town-site company to attract immigration. The mainland, as flat and desolate as the island,

was three miles away. But deep water was there and to the north was an agricultural country that one day would have cotton to export. So the settlers waited. They held to their sand lots and traded with the "mosquito fleet" which sailed up and down the coast from Corpus Christi to New Orleans. This mosquito fleet was the only means for bringing outside traders to the town. As it grew it developed that the city's export trade was all it had. It did a wholesale business that was to its retail business in the proportion of 100 to 1!

In this way Galveston developed in-growing propensities. It scoffed at the mainland for years after the gulf shore began to be peopled. It was satisfied with its railroad "bridges," which were mere trestlework mounted on piling driven into the shallow water of the bay. If the mainland wished to reach the city let it row out or sail out; the city would not go to the expense of a wagon bridge....

As a result, Galveston was the most somnolent city in Texas, save on the wharves where tramp and coastwise ships and steamers loaded. When the market house closed by law at 10 o'clock in the morning, and when Galveston's own local population had in its supplies for a midday dinner and for supper and breakfast, Strand street took a nap.[45]

William Pitt Ballinger was the founder of Texas's oldest continuous law firm (see Mills Shirley).[46] William Pitt Ballinger's papers reveal the prevalence of the institution of slavery.

> [71-0328]—letter dated December 21, 1829, proposed sale of El[li]ck & George; [71-0337]—letter dated November 13, 1862 written to "My Darling Wife"; slave John, slave of Ballinger pp. 3–4; [71-0341]—letter to wife, writing from Houston in 1862; reference to Sydnor having left for New Orleans, either to go on to Virginia . . . ; [71-0349]—to "Darling Wife," hired out Dave for $12.50 a day . . . signed "Devoted Husband"; [71-0350]—letter dated November 26, 1864; "My Darling Wife"; discussion of Dave & Ellick; discussed theft by Dave, helped himself; reference to stealing by Dave, must sell; called police, proposed sending him to penitentiary to work as convict labor; Ellick promises me faithfully to report if see him; [71-0357]—purchase of slave Agnes by Ballinger; [71-0351]; [71-0082; 71-0092]—Letter to H. M. Trueheart and Co.—mortgage on slave George.[47]

Fornell identified Agnes as a house servant for Ballinger's wife; she particularly "liked her face."[48] Ballinger purchased her for $1,050—at a reduced price because she was already "in a family way." In 1863—during the Civil War—"Ballinger sold Agnes and her children to Aaron F. Coffee for $2,000 in gold."[49] With regards to slave Dave, Fornell's explanation of the events paint a disturbing picture. Dave

CHAPTER 6

kept running off after Ballinger hired him out to Aaron Coffee on the Halcyon plantation. Halcyon was in Brazoria County.[50] After voiding the contract, Ballinger brought Dave back to Galveston and hired him out in Galveston.

> I called him in and charged him. Ballinger wrote in his diary. At first, he denied it. I tied him and stripped him and was about to commence on him when he said he would tell all. He confessed to opening the trunk four times. Took sums of .50 [cents], $2.50, and $2.25 in specie. He used pieces of wire to take off the hinges which served as well as if he had possessed a key.[51]

Fornell's position that Ballinger was a moderate as compared to others is disturbing. William Pitt Ballinger was ensconced in the slave trade: buying, selling, and hiring out and subjecting human souls to inhuman treatment. Human bondage can never be considered a moderate position. When Dave disappeared for a period of time, Ballinger worried whether he was attempting to flee to the enemy, the Yankees.[52]

May I be Southern for a bit? William Pitt Ballinger's peoples are from Kentucky. "He was born in Barbourville, Kentucky on September 25, 1825, the son of James Franklin and Olivia (Adams) Ballinger."[53] He moved to Galveston in 1843.[54] The historical record touts Ballinger as a statesman, jurist, and family man.[55] One historian described him as a "reluctant rebel," meaning he voted against secession because of business considerations, but once the war was started, he did everything possible to succeed in the battle, including purchasing arms.[56] Another author attributed the following quote to Ballinger, with regard to President Lincoln's death: "With my whole soul, I regard the effort to overrun, subdue and govern the South to have in it every quality of tyranny. I regard Mr. Lincoln as a fanatic in that design—as the most formidable of all our oppressors, and I feel that his fate is the deserved fate of tyrants."[57] Historians have failed to recognize the duplicity and complicity caused by a morally corrupt institution (slavery). This failure of an honest assessment continues, "yesterday, tomorrow and forever."[58] The continued attempt to nuance the institution, mythically propping up and outsizing the personalities, to justify the institution and its participants' behaviors, should not be tolerated by historians and the rest of us—but it has, but we have. The town of Ballinger in Runnels County, Texas is named in honor of William Pitt Ballinger, who was a stockholder in the Gulf, Colorado and Santa Fe Railway.[59]

On January 13, 1857, C. L. McCarty, general agent and broker, placed an advertisement for the sale of "twelve likely men, House Servants and field hands; a likely negro, a Brick-layer and Plaster Do-A boy, Three smart negro boys, fit for house or out service."[60] In context of extrinsic evidence of other professions aiding in the business of slavery, James E. Preston in the *Galveston Daily Civilian* newspaper identified his business as a custom house broker, stating it "Will Makes Entries of Merchandise, enter and clear vessels, Slaves.... Office of F. Gonzales, Kuhn's Building, Strand, Galveston."[61] In the same newspaper, T. B. Stubbs and J. S. Sydnor advertised their business of T. B. Stubbs & Co., located next to Sydnor's auction house. In the Sydnor advertisement, Mondays, Wednesdays, Thursdays, and Saturdays are identified as the days in which private sales of Negroes and real estate occurred, always with fifteen to twenty Negroes available.[62] Ball, Hutchins & Co.—an entity consisting of G. Ball, J. H. Hutchins, and John Sealy—identified itself as being cotton factors and commission merchants.[63]

The market was bountiful! In this vein, the reference to Galveston being the Wall Street of the Southwest is accurate, in that Galveston was no different from Wall Street itself: built on the sale, kidnapping, and profits associated with the exchange of slaves in both the South and North. The Strand was our active marketplace—with businesses related to the exchange and sale of human bodies—running from 20th to 25th Street (running north and south), from Wharf to Church Street (running east and west); auctioneers, commission houses, realtors, and, ah, of course, attorneys were abundant.[64] By the 1850s, Sydnor had created the City Marketplace; prior to this move, Sydnor and two other slave traders were doing business at 20th and Wharf, with the Osterman and Kuhn Buildings housing other slave traders.

Other examples are in order. In an earlier documented advertisement, John O. and H. M. Trueheart held themselves as auctioneers in the selling of Negroes. This was in 1850. In 1972, when the historical application for the Trueheart-Adriance Building was submitted to place a historical marker on the front of the building, the following information was set out in the application:

[Historic Marker Application: Trueheart-Adriance Building] Page: 1 of 20
   TSJSC Staff (JS), 9/22/72
   Medallion w/16" x 12" Interpretive Plate w/post Galveston (Order #4726).
Location: 212 Twenty-second Street, Galveston
   TRUEHEART-ADRIANCE BUILDING
   DESIGNED IN NEO-RENAISSANCE,
   HIGH VICTORIAN STYLE BY NICHOLAS
   J. CLAYTON, NOTED ARCHITECT, FOR H. M.
   TRUEHEART & CO., FIRST CHARTERED
   REALTY FIRM IN TEXAS, FOUNDED BY
   JOHN O. TRUEHEART IN 1857.
   H. M. TRUEHEART JOINED HIS FATHER

CHAPTER 6

IN 1866, ADMITTED JOHN ADRIANCE AS
A PARTNER IN 1872.
AFTER H. M. TRUEHEAERT RETIRED IN
1906, THE FIRM CONTINUED THROUGH
1953 AS JOHN ADRIANCE & SONS.
RECORDED TEXAS HISTORIC LANDMARK—1873.
INCISE ON BASE: RESTORED BY THE JUNIOR LEAGUE OF
GALVESTON.[65]

The history of the father and son business as auctioneers/slave traders would be unknown by reference to the application only. The celebration of being the first chartered realty firm in Texas is commendable; however, the failure to provide a full account of these historical figures represents the fatal lie. The application compounds the problem. H. M. Trueheart did not join his father in 1866—he joined him as early as 1850. This inconvenient truth is inconsistent with the application. The Truehearts' advertisements ran multiple times during this period. They were active slave traders. By historians' concentrating on the period after 1865 (after the Emancipation Proclamation), this works to bury/hide/obscure the truth.

The reference to the concept of a fatal lie is a term that has been stolen, borrowed, lifted from the great Texan, Bill Moyers. Moyers, in a speech to the Texas Historical Association, explained:

> Sometimes ignoring the stories of those who have been less visible can lead to some pure and nearly eternal lies—even fatal lies. . . . It's not only that the depiction of slavery was just prettied up, it was flat out deceitful. Any youngster reading *Texas History Movies* could have reasonably concluded that Black people enjoyed being owned body and soul by a master. Of course, it was some of the masters—or some of their children and grandchildren—who were telling those tales. Not until many years later did it occur to me to wonder how these stories would have sounded had they been written by children and grandchildren of the slaves. . . . As schoolchildren we read—and this is a direct quote—that "Any man who inherited slaves were bound to free one-tenth of the number." That was a lie; slaves were legally designated chattel, not flesh and blood, and any man who inherited slaves was no more bound to free a single one of them than he was obligated to liberate a portion of his cotton fields, his pigs, or his grandmother's silver. . . . "Slaves could change masters at will," we read. Another lie. And we read, "The law provided for the education of Negroes even while they were slaves,"—this we read under the picture of a little barefoot Black child in a shabby schoolroom spelling "K-A-T." In truth, the law provided for the severe

punishment of any slaves caught educating themselves, but many Black children and adults who, in their hunger for knowledge, accepted the terrible risk, learned to spell a heck of a lot better than that.[66]

John S. Sydnor was a Virginian before moving to Galveston; his father, Edward G. Sydnor, remained in Virginia. In 1853, Edward G. Sydnor recorded an excerpt from his last will and testament with the Galveston County Clerk's Office, devising to his grandchildren—John S. Sydnor's children—certain properties. The will set out Edward G. Sydnor's statement that because he was "desirous to advance his legacy" he was leasing to his son, John S. Sydnor of Galveston, Texas, the following slaves:[67] "to-wit Eliza and infant named Westley[,] Henrietta[,] Martha[,] and Powhatan appraised and valued as per statement annexed."[68] He gave as a gift a Negro he called Martha, whom he valued at $373.00, to his granddaughter Columbia Sydnor.[69]

Powhatan, listed as one of the slaves gifted by Edward Sydnor to his grandchildren, was also the name John S. Sydnor bestowed on the home he built on 21st Street in Galveston. According to the Galveston Garden Club, housed in the original building that is now located at 3427 Avenue O, John Sydnor built the house in 1847 and named it "after the Indian tribes in his native Virginia."[70] Although there may be little question as to when the house was built, it is not so clear whether its name was assigned before or after the slave Powhatan was transported from Virginia to Texas.[71] There is no reference to Edward Sydnor's will and his gift of Powhatan by the Galveston Garden Club. Creating myths by omission may have been of better service to the organization.

In February 1861, Texans voted overwhelmingly for secession, 46,697 for secession and 14,747 against.[72] In Galveston, the vote was 765 for secession and only 33 opposed.[73] South Carolina was the first state to secede from the Union on December 20, 1860.[74] Mississippi, Florida, Alabama, Georgia, and Louisiana seceded in January 1861.[75] Texas officially seceded from the Union on March 5, 1861.[76]

In the 1860 U.S. federal census of slave schedules in Galveston, John S. Sydnor is listed as having fourteen slaves in the city.[77] During the period of time leading up to the start of the Civil War (April 12, 1861) to the war's termination (May 9, 1865),[78] John Seabrook Sydnor and his son, John B. Sydnor, remained active in the buying and selling of slaves.[79] In the [Houston] *Tri-Weekly News*, April 30, 1863, p. 2 an advertisement saying, "Have large Auction Sales every Tuesday"—none of the 1863 advertisements include the physical location of the auctions—"And from this date, in the absence of a Chamber of Commerce to regulate commissions, our charges *will be as follows*: Negroes and Real Estate, 4 1/2 percent . . ."

was posted—and again in the [Houston] *Tri-Weekly News*, January 10, 1863, p. 1: advertisement by J. S. & J. B. Sydnor that they were conducting auctions in both Houston and Galveston—auction sales in Houston every Tuesday, at 10 a.m. On December 8, 1860, in the *Galveston Daily Civilian*, J. S. & J. B. Sydnor advertised their conducting auctions "every Tuesday and Friday at ten o'clock, a.m."[80]

In April 1863, the Sydnors were fully functioning and engaging in increasingly larger sales of human stock, as you can see from these advertisements: [Houston] *Tri-Weekly Telegraph*, April 15, 1863, p. 2, c. 2, "A large auction sale of sixty . . . negroes, men, women and children." "They were sold in lots of families, and brought $105,000.00, or about $1750 each. From a casual glance at the catalogue, we should judge this would give an average of about $2250 for good field hands, which may be regarded about their price. The negroes were a good lot, though there were many children among them"; [Houston] *Tri-Weekly Telegraph*, April 29, 1863, p. 2, c. 2, "Sale of Negroes.—Yesterday the sale of negroes belonging to Gen. H. P. Bee, took place at the auction rooms of Col. J. S. Sydnor, and the price ranged beyond those paid a week or two since. The number sold was 31, and the amount of the sale was between eighty-five and eight-six thousand dollars. Women from 18 to 20 years of age, sold for $4000 to $4500. One woman with two children sold for $5,700. Ordinary negro men brought over $4000. The lot was not an extraordinarily good one, though very fair, but the prices were unusually high."[81]

John S. Sydnor recognized the importance of slavery to his livelihood and wealth and was a full participant in assuring the South retained its slave-holding status. Sydnor and other citizens purchased arms for the defense of Galveston and the Confederacy using their own funds.[82]

John S. Sydnor died in 1869.[83] Prior to his death, with impending health concerns and the South's loss of the Civil War, John S. and his son J. B. took out an advertisement placing property owned by Sydnor for sale. It is clear his auctioneering of the enslaved brought him—and his heirs—considerable wealth. He possessed more than 23,000 acres of land outside of his properties in Galveston and Houston. The properties were in twenty counties, including the counties Harris (Houston) and Galveston.

The listed holdings were as follows:

> Sydnor's residence with 10 acres of land, about four miles from town (reference to Galveston)
> Concrete house in town (reference to Galveston)
> The equivalence of seven city lots with location noted as 1-2 int. S.E. corner of 10 acres, out-lot No. 115 (Galveston property)
> Lots located in Section 1, Galveston Island: 57 acres, 189, 202, 205; .84 acres,

1-2 int. lots 532, 533, 534, and 535

10 acres, 1-3 int. lots 234, 235, and 243 in Galveston

700 acres (Galveston being 52 lots)

"The above will be divided in 24 acre lots – each tract will front a street."

Lots 1, 2, 3 and 4, block 14 and lots 1, 2, 3 & 4 in block 18, Harby addition to city of Houston

Blocks 3, 10, 15, 16, 23, and 24, containing 12 lots on Sydnor addition, city of Houston

202 1/2 acres, one-half interest in 405 acres, about two miles from Lynchburg in Harris County

Lots 3, 4, 5, 6, 7, 8, 9, 10, 11, 12, 13, 14, 15, 16, 17, 19, 20, 21, 22, 23, 24, each lot containing 50 acres in Harris County

457 acres known as Sydnor's Farms, about five miles from Houston on Bray's Bayou

200 acres enclosed with buildings; 150 acres of woodland in Harris County

84 acres near Harrisburg on the Galveston, Houston, Henderson Railroad in Harris County

6642 acres in Brazoria County, between Flores and Austin Bayous

369 acres in Austin County and Brazoria County

220 1/2 acres between Bastrop and Chocolate Bayou

2214 acres south, half Andrea Morales league, Big Sandy, Polk County

480 acres land and improvement three miles from Sumpter

2600 acres out of the H. Webb League in Jasper County

100 city lots in Beaumont in Jefferson County

640 acres in Menard County (two separate tracts of 320 acres each)

320 acres in Mason County

640 acres in McCollough County (two separate tracts of 320 acres each)

640 acres in Bexar County

1280 acres in Medina County

640 acres in Medina County

1280 acres in Medina County

320 acres in Medina County

640 acres in Medina County

320 acres in Gillespie County

160 acres in Concha County

387 acres in Harris County

297 acres in Liberty County on Trinity River (the advertisement held out Sydnor was offered $30,000 before the Civil War)

1476 acres in Dewitt County

CHAPTER 6

555 acres on Clear Creek in Harris County
[490] acres in Bosque County
533 acres in Houston County
950 acres in Grimes County[84]

It should not be surprising that Sydnor owned land in multiple counties dispersed throughout Texas, what with his connection to the government, the military, and his slave auction houses.

John S. Sydnor had seven children. Prior to his son John B.'s joining his father's business, he worked with other partners. Four months after placing his properties for sale, John S. and John B. announced that Seabrook W. Sydnor, another son of John S., would be joining them as an additional partner on May 1, 1867.[85] John S. Sydnor died in 1869. His son, John B., died in 1875.[86] Seabrook Sydnor was the executor of his father's estate.[87]

Seabrook W. Sydnor purchased land in Harris County in 1893. In March 1903, Seabrook W. Sydnor filed a revised layout for a proposed Seabrook Townsite.[88] The city of Seabrook, Texas, is named after Seabrook W. Sydnor. Today, the city of Galveston continues its slave heritage by honoring John S. Sydnor in a multitude of ways: a street (Sydnor Lane), a body of water (Sydnor Bay), and an entire subdivision (Sydnor subdivision).[89] The subdivision was platted by John S. Sydnor in 1846.[90] In Houston, a street and subdivision bear his name. The subdivision is located east of downtown Houston.[91] Another author has previously identified the address of Sydnor's auction house in Houston.[92]

This type of tracing of a person's business interests, heirs, and wealth—as related to slave trading—goes back to one of the original points: those men, women, and children who stood in enclosed structures, on docksides, in small rooms, were valuable commodities in the development of this country's economy. These human souls also contributed to the wealth of the slaveholders, auctioneers, commission agents, real estate brokers, attorneys, insurance companies, plantation owners, small farmers, pressmen, bankers—permitting these men to bequeath and devise considerable outsized wealth and influence. This wealth benefited cities, states, the country, Wall Street, banks, religious institutions, etc. Their brains and bodies were used to construct infrastructure, clean gutters, build cities, maintain homes, plant, pick, harvest crops, care for animals and children, and to satisfy others' sexual deviances/desires.

The elected officeholder, John Henry Brown, knew his resolution to the Texas Legislature prior to the Civil War was a lie; he, like others, refused to admit the nature of the distasteful institution of slavery. State Representative Brown did, however, admit to the institution's importance. His were words crafted over centuries to justify the enslavement of a people.

CHAPTER 7

WHY IS THE TRUTH IMPORTANT?

On November 25, 1857, a joint resolution on the importation of African slaves was introduced into the Texas House of Representatives. The resolution was submitted by Galveston's state representative, John Henry Brown. The resolution was referred to the House Committee on Slaves and Slavery. Brown had been the mayor of Galveston in 1856. He later served as the mayor of Dallas in the years 1885–1887, where he moved after the Civil War.[1]

Joint resolution in relation to the importation of African Slaves
WHEREAS, In the All-wise laws of nature, there has existed from the days of extreme antiquity, different races of men on earth, varying in intellectual endowments, from the superior capacity of the white man in the descending scale to the black man; and whereas, from the earliest dawn of social organization, government and civilization, of which we have any authentic knowledge to the present time, the black man, or negro, has shown himself to be a distinctively inferior intellectual being, incapable of self-elevation or moral improvement, as evidenced by the absence of a single fact to the contrary, on the continent of

Africa, though in greater or less contact with civilized nations for thousands of years: And Whereas, we find recorded in the Holy Bible, immediately after the deluge, a distinct classification of man in these words: "Cursed be Canaan (*i.e.* Ham, the black son of Noah,) a servant of servants shall he be unto his brethren. And he (Moses) said: blessed be the Lord God of Shem, and Canaan shall be his servant. And God shall enlarge Japhet, and he shall dwell in the tents of Shem, and Canaan (the negro) shall be his servant. And

Whereas, It is further provided, in the Holy Bible, in the Book of Leviticus (ch. xxv, vers. 39, 46,) that – "Both thy bondmen and thy bondmaids, (meaning, according to learned divinee, *slaves* in the modern sense,) which thou shalt have, shalt be of the heathen (negro) that are round about you; of them shall ye buy bondmen and bondmaids, *** and they shall be your possession. And ye shall take them as an inheritance for your children after you to inherit them for a possession; they shall be your bondmen forever. And

Whereas, In addition to many other and abundant commands, both in the Old Testament and the New, instituting, ordaining, or regulating the enslavement of this inferior or negro race of men, we find Paul enunciating the Divine Law to Timothy, (1 Tim. VI 1–8) in this unequivocal language – Let as many servants as are *under the yoke* count their own masters worthy of all honor, that the name of God and his doctrine be not blasphemed. And they that have believing masters, let them not despise them because they are brethren, but rather do them service because they are faithful and beloved, partakers of the benefit. These things teach and exhort. *If any man teach otherwise, and consent not to wholesome words, even the words of our Lord Jesus Christ, and to the doctrine which is according to godliness, he is proud knowing nothing, but doting about question and strife of words, whereof cometh envy, strife, railing, evil surmising, perverse disputings* [sic] *men of corrupt minds, and destitute of the truth, supposing that gain is godliness, from such withdraw yourself.* And

Whereas, From the first introduction of negroes as slaves into the American colonies, to the present proud development of our country, all experience hath demonstrated their removal from a state of degradation, slavery and barbarian wretchedness in their native African wilds, to their present continent, to have been, and still to be, for their greatest known good as a people; and of incalculable benefit to all civilized nations, through the instrumentality of slave labor, the modern productions of which have done more, directly and indirectly, than all other causes combined through ages of centuries, to spread commerce, civilization, religion, "peace and good will" among mankind; and the destruction of which, would spread darkness, gloom and desolation over the earth; burst asunder the now growing bonds of universal peace, progress and liberty; and by one fell swoop, uproot the foundations of civilized society, disintegrate modern fellowship among men, and re-inaugurate the "weeping, wailing, and gnashing of teeth" of the dark ages, under a system of remorseless, petty despotisms, now and then, as of old, eclipsed by the dazzling elevation of a more stupendous villainy in the achievements of a Nero. And

Whereas, Experience hath further demonstrated that the amalgamation of the white with the black race, inevitably leads to disease, decline, and death, and also that the efforts in our own country and of the European governments in the West India Islands and elsewhere, to emancipate the negro with a view to his freedom and self-government, however sincerely made, have been founded in ignorance of the law of races, of the negro character and inferior organization, and in defiance of the mandates of an All-wise Creator, and in every instance have lead to results disastrous to the black man, sending him back with painful rapidity into the gloom of hopeless barbarism and self-abasement, as abundantly shown in the West Indian Islands, Mexico, the refuge slaves in Canada, and portions of our northern States, and indeed wherever negro slaves have been emancipated and thrown upon their own resources in communities. And,

Whereas, after long and fair trials, the governments of Great Britain and France, through the experiment of emancipation, have destroyed the foundations of society and rendered barren and desolate several of the most fertile and highly cultivated islands of the world, as in San Domingo and Jamaica, where the freed slaves and their descendants now exhibit the most deplorable state of barbarian degradation and idolatry, the lamentable truth of which, standing forth in all the deformity of a prostrate, ruined, and beastialised [*sic*] people, has at length arrested the attention of the wise in the parent governments and lead to the adoption of incipient measures to retrace the unfortunate steps which caused such dire results, and to restore the institution of slavery in those islands of social, moral, and political woe—presenting to the mind of the patriot and philanthropist, the germ of hope for the future, saddened only by the fact that the ultimate good is sought to be accomplished through a temporary resort to an apprentice system, full of inhumanity, and embracing within its grasp the people of another and greatly superior race, neither adapted nor designed by the Great Creator for a state of slavery. And,

Whereas, The experience of nations, aside from the unparalleled prosperity of our own country, demonstrates the value and conservative effect of African slavery on government—as its perpetuation in Brazil has given strength, liberal views and stability to that government, wherein anarchy and revolution are comparatively unknown, and religion and law prevail—while its abolition in all the other Spanish American States, has been succeeded for a period of near forty years by continuous revolution, anarchy, internecine war, and the disruption of all those ties, without which no nation or people can prosper or long retain even the semblance of civilization; and the history of this country has already in a large sense, and is now, demonstrating the same great truth in the science of government, viz: that the institution of African slavery, as existing in a portion of these States, stands in bold antagonism alike to aristocracy and agrarianism, to despotism and anarchy; to tyranny and faction—and sustains just laws, good government, the stability of Republican Institutions and the rights of man to self-government, as proclaimed by our forefathers of 1776. And

Whereas, in view of all these facts, and others of equal magnitude, and of the check given to the progress and development of the slaveholding States by the legislation of the general government in the year 1503, inhibiting the further importation of African slaves, by which they were denied a supply of labor suited to their climate and production, and the door was closed against the further amelioration of the condition of the debased and dependent black man of that continent, whose degraded state then and now appeals to the philanthropy of the Christian world for protection, control and instruction, suited to his capacity to understand. And

Whereas, the State of Texas, in her vast unsettled territory, demands only labor to place her in the front rank of civilized States – being capable of receiving, reclaiming and controlling a large number of those hapless beings, with advantage to them, benefit to herself and blessings to all classes, but especially to the laboring masses of the northern States, Europe and every other land open to trade and commerce. *Now, therefore,*

Be it Resolved by the Legislature of the State of Texas, That our Senators in Congress has instructed and our Representatives to urge upon the Congress of the United States the repeal of all laws and the abrogation of all treaties prohibiting the importation of African slaves into the slaveholding States and territories of the Union: And the passage of such laws as shall effectually guard against every species of cruelty in such future purchase and importation of African slaves; and requiring that they shall be imported in such numbers, on board of such vessels and under such safe guards as shall be necessary to their health, comfort and general protection in life and person.

Resolved further, That the Governor is requested to transmit copies of these resolutions to our members of Congress and the Government of all the States of the Union.[2]

Galveston's representative proclaimed the superior capacity of the White man in the descending scale to the Negro, who has shown himself to be a distinctively inferior intellectual being, incapable of self-elevation or moral improvement; reaffirmed the Negro was cursed by Canaan ... and the Negro was a servant of servants shall he be unto his brethren; the Negro character and inferior organization, and in defiance of the mandates of an All-wise Creator, and in every instance contrary to the All-wise Creator has led to results disastrous to the Negro. He said what he wanted to say in the resolution: the State of Texas needed the slaves to further the prosperity and development of the state for the White race, and for the benefit of those supposed hapless beings. At the time of his submission of the resolution, State Representative Brown reported to the United States census he owned twenty-three enslaved persons—the youngest, 2 years of age, the oldest, 50.[3]

After the South lost the war in June 1865, Representative Brown moved to Mexico, where he remained until 1871. When he returned, Brown moved to Dallas, Texas. He remained politically active and was elected again in 1872 as a state representative for the Dallas area and as mayor of the city of Dallas from 1885 to 1887. There remains a street in Dallas's Oak Lawn neighborhood named in Brown's honor. In 1912, an elementary school in South Dallas was named in his honor: John Henry Brown Elementary.[4]

The acts of honoring John Henry Brown are no different than the previous cited occasions for others. This author believes the same permits the fatal lies to remain in place.[5] In a historical context, Brown's resolution submitted to the Texas Legislature was consistent with the United States Supreme Court's proclamation in *Dred Scott*, issued the same year.

On June 19, 1865, General Gordon Granger read General Order No. 3.[6] Granger's order created an inherent contradiction, announcing freedom (ordering "all slaves are free"), but ordering the previously enslaved to remain in place:

> The people of Texas are informed that in accordance with a Proclamation from the Executive of the United States, all slaves are free. This involves an absolute equality of personal rights and rights of property between former masters and slaves, and the connection heretofore existing between them becomes that between employer and hired labor.
>
> The freedmen are advised to remain quietly at their present homes and work for wages. They are informed that they will not be allowed to collect at military posts and that they will not be supported in idleness either there or elsewhere.[7]

"On June 18, hours before Granger's arrival, Galveston's mayor C. H. Leonard called on Rankin G. Laughlin, Union provost marshal general for the State of Texas. Leonard was concerned with the immediate freeing of the slaves in that he was worried about harvesting the crops in the interior. Laughlin appeased many

CHAPTER 7

of Leonard's concerns."[8] The order reinforced the priority of keeping the formerly enslaved populations at work on their respective plantations. The changed order stated the importance of keeping the freed slave population working on their respective plantations as paid employees both to ensure a cotton crop and, in his opinion, to provide for the best possible outcome for the Black population.[9]

Granger's conflicting order, or clarifying order—now celebrated on Juneteenth—was the country's first declaration of all deliberate speed. Galveston's outsized influence should not be shocking, in that the city remained the most influential city in the state, home of citizens who controlled Texas's commerce and political discourse.[10] Even after the South's capitulation, the city's influence remained in place.

The phrase "all deliberate speed" comes from the United States Supreme Court's decision of *Brown v. Board of Education of Topeka*, issued in 1954.[11] The Supreme Court's decision struck down the "separate but equal" doctrine in the field of education, ultimately leading to the integration of public schools. The Court required the states to integrate with "all deliberate speed." The states and governmental entities took the Supreme Court at its word and deliberately delayed enforcement of *Brown v. Board*'s jurisprudential sea change. Again, it is this author's position that the freeing of the slaves was the first such declaration. General Granger's orders did not and do not represent absolute equality.

> Why do we tolerate the myth that General Granger supposedly read his General Order in three different places in Galveston (Ashton Villa, Osterman Building and Reedy Chapel AME Church)—mere blocks from each other? For years there have been celebrations at Ashton Villa, while telling the public Granger's Orders were read from Ashton Villa. Then she whispered, really? ... The application for the National Register of Historical Places, Inventory-Nomination Form submitted for historical designation for Ashton Villa was submitted by the Texas State Historical Survey Committee. The submissions: "The Brown House [Ashton Villa] was the headquarters for the Confederate Army and later the Union Army after the battle of Galveston Bay"—there was no mention of Granger's reading at Ashton Villa. Wouldn't this fact be historically significant, if true? In the autobiography of General Granger, the author, Robert C. Conner, references this myth, by describing the supposed reading in a non-historical manner—"possibly from the balcony."[12]

A bit of personal history is in order. Momma explained that Albert Wright was freed at the age of thirteen. His birth was in 1865, which means he was not freed until 1880, much after the emancipation of slaves. How is that possible? Let me

84

explain this way—I never bought the wise tale that George Washington never told a lie.[13] I will always believe that Georgia seldom lied.

Trust me, this unspoken historical relic is possible, particularly when the words of the general orders are read and when one appreciates the conditions that existed in Texas at the time. Texans possessed no resolve Negroes should be free and equal. They needed their cotton picked, cane harvested, cattle herded, children breast fed, cities built. In addition, the federal government did not have enough troops in place to protect the newly freed persons of color, nor the commitment.[14] At the conclusion of the Civil War, the United States census revealed Texas had more Negroes than any Western state and territory. In 1870 there were 253,475 Negroes in Texas, with a White population of 564,700. In the ten-year period before, the Negro population was 182,921, the White population 420,891. The Department of Commerce, Bureau of the Census in a report titled "Negro Population 1790–1915" provided a warning on any data related to the early decennial census reports:

> At the earlier censuses, returns relating to the slave and to the free colored population were generally restricted to a few simple inquiries. At the census of 1790, for example, the number of slaves was ascertained without distinction of either sex or age, and at the five succeeding censuses, 1800–1840, age was recorded for Negroes, free and slave, in less detail than for whites. At the censuses, of 1850 and 1860, also, the returns for the slave population, which were made upon special schedules (referred to as slave schedules), were less detailed than those secured for the free colored and white population. In 1870, however, since all Negroes were free, the returns for the total Negro population were made upon the schedule provided for all free habitants, and at this census, as at each succeeding census, they were made in the same detail for Negroes as for whites.[15]

Quintard Taylor, in his book *In Search of the Racial Frontier: African Americans in the West, 1528–1990*, explained that the next two most populated states at the time were California—with 560,247 in total population, but only 4,272 Negroes—and Kansas—with a total population of 364,399, but only 17,108 Negroes. Even though Texas was included with other Western states by the Census Bureau, Dr. Taylor explained, "Post–Civil War Texas, however, remained closer to the old South than the new West. . . . Other such actions were taken in concert as dozens of planters in the county sought to punish the blacks for their freedom. In the fall of 1865 white citizens in Freestone County, for example, resolved to hire no blacks and to whip any freedman who tried to sign a labor contract with a white employer. Whites who violated the resolution were to be warned on the first offense and whipped or hanged on the second. Other owners were so disturbed by emancipation that they poisoned water wells or shot slaves who persisted in proclaiming their freedom."[16] Freestone is the county of my maternal great-grandparents.

Lawrence D. Rice explained, "Although there was some migration of the freedmen in the summer and fall, in fact enough to create social and agricultural problems, evidence points to a greater stability than contemporary observers are willing to concede. The overwhelming majority of the ex-slaves remained in their accustomed homes and eventually entered into contracts with their former masters, either as tenants or laborers. If they did wander, it was not far and most soon returned to their former abode."[17]

"Your great-grandfather's slave name was Longbottom. When finally freed he refused to carry the Longbottom name and changed his name to Wright. They—Albert and Lillie—had nine children, Mary Etta, Sanford, Lovely, Ardena, Gena, Precious, Nola, and Alma and Louis," Momma said.

Daddy Louis (Louis Wright) lived to just days short of 100. Three of Daddy Louis's sisters lived into their nineties. Louis married Chesterana Demus (Muh Chest). They had four children, Clinton, Mildred, Ezekiel, and Georgia. The newspaper recorded Albert Wright's age at death at 99.[18] Lillie Wright was born in 1868, her age at death 104.[19] Lillie too incurred a delayed freedom, not until 1881/1882.

When the couple celebrated their 75th wedding anniversary, none of their history as slaves was recorded. At the time of the anniversary party, I was seven and met, for the first time, other branches of the family tree. Momma had said something about them, not in a complaining manner but in passing. I didn't understand what she meant. Perhaps I was too young to fully comprehend. In hindsight, I know the segregated world in which we lived; 1961 Texas remained a proud apartheid state, tightly controlled, segregated.

The newspaper article on my great-grandparents' anniversary did not mention their having come from the state of Virginia, nor the slaveowners' name. If they were slaves in Texas, what was the name of the plantation? Who sold them? Who bought them? How many times? Who held them in place? Where? Is the oral history of Albert and Lillian traveling from Virginia part of the fatal lie to conceal the additional years of delayed freedom after the previously acknowledged historical delay of June 19th?

Albert's mother had seven first names, or was that Lillie's mom? The absence of information is part of this historical void the institution of slavery has tainted and continued to taint. The inhuman deprivation and silence slavery bequeathed plays out in real time. They—the news reporters—did not ask any questions related to slavery. Strangely, I do not think anyone else did either.

When I met those other branches? They looked *so, so different than we*: hair, eyes, skin tones, voices. They looked *so, so much like us*—twitches and mannerisms, bodies and facial contours and angles, different but alike—hands, backs, faces, arms. Same-same—but different—we were.

The cicadas did not care, their unique sound reverberated in the trees, the grasses—over—over—over—again, screaming, much like the voices I heard near the waters. I told Muh Chest and Daddy Louis as much, running as fast as I could to tell. Neither said a word. They did smile.

Muh Chest remained in place—rocking—rocking—rocking—holding those hands, which Bill Withers sung about years later,[20] in rhythm with the cicadas' screech—looking, listening, from afar. I moved closer and held onto Momma's leg.[21] Muh Chest kept her distance; the wind was not moving, she too was silent. The sun's intense stare watched over us; she provided a clear picture of the different hues moving about on the land, making, some renewing, acquaintances, others meeting for the first time. The birds too remained in place. I continued my grip, not understanding. Momma's arm rested across my body, the palm of her hand rested in the middle of my back, holding me close.

CHAPTER 8

WE MUST SAY THEIR NAMES AND MORE

Galveston County citizens elected Latonia Wilson, an African American female, to the countywide District Clerk Office in 2006. The District Clerk Office is a constitutional office, meaning the duties of the clerk can only be taken away by constitutional amendment. Wilson previously served out the term of Evelyn Wells Robison, who retired because of illness in 2004. Robison's term expired in 2006; Wilson was elected for a full term in 2006.[1] She left office in 2010, losing her bid for reelection.

During her time as district clerk, Wilson listed as one of her greatest accomplishments beginning the process of preserving old district court records. These records were in a state of deterioration. Wilson approached the Texas Supreme Court and obtained an order placing a moratorium (unanimous vote) to protect these historical documents. She was also able to obtain training for designated employees. Wilson explained, "Among the documents restored were slave records, which were in different forms. They were not files labelled 'slave records,' however; in your search and review of records one would discover these records could be easily misplaced or lost."

Wilson continued:

One must remember: Galveston County records are important and unique in several respects: Galveston was one of the port cities and received a considerable number of immigrants; New York and New Orleans were the other cities. Galveston was the home of the first government of Texas and courts. All lawsuits—no matter where the facts originated—were brought in Galveston. My office maintained the Supreme Court of Texas and the Court of Appeals' records. When Texas was established, my office housed unique records related to Texas's history. Slaves were not necessarily recorded in the immigration documents; most were simply registered with the animals—pigs, horses, cattle, dogs. Some had names, others didn't.

Prior to leaving office I had entered discussions with George Mitchell[2] surrounding initial funding to house the records in a special facility. Although Mr. Mitchell was open to the project and providing funding, the election results interfered; I lost the election.[3]

Records curated by Ancestry.com contain images of original slave manifests dated primarily between 1840 and 1860.[4] Ancestry.com provides additional evidence of Galveston's port being an active slave hub, particularly between the ports of New Orleans and Galveston. There are 10,959 manifests recording slaves transported to Galveston from New Orleans between 1840 and 1860.[5] During the same period, 86,530 slave manifests documented slave ships transporting slaves from Galveston to New Orleans.[6]

Slave manifests contain space for multiple people on one document.[7] Slave manifests provide a ship's name, port, date of departure, date of arrival, name, estimated birth, height, gender, color for the enslaved (you know the ritual by now—documenting the tone/variation/shade of the color brown), the captain's name, and date of certification by the collector of customs.[8] The bulk of the shipments between Galveston and New Orleans occurred between 1846 and 1860.

Remember, Galveston was not incorporated as a city until 1839. Texas did not join the Union until December 29, 1845; Louisiana was admitted to the Union years earlier on April 30, 1812.[9] In context of the numbers, notably, this compilation of records is incomplete; an entire decade's worth of records of inward manifests (shipments of slaves arriving at New Orleans from other ports) is missing from 1808 to 1818.[10] Outward manifests (or records of shipments of slaves departing from New Orleans for other ports) are not available for 1813–1817, 1837, and 1859.[11] Ancestry.com provides an additional preface to the records: "Though an 1807 law banned the trans-Atlantic slave trade to the United States as of 1 January 1808, slaves could still be bought and sold (and transported) within the country."[12]

To help decipher the meaning of the numbers of ships to and from, a review of Solomon Northup's accounting seems appropriate. After being kidnapped, Northup spent several days in a holding facility until additional slaves were collected for shipment. "In the course of several days the outer door was thrown open, allowing me the liberty of the yard. There I found three slaves—one of them a lad of ten years, the others young men about twenty and twenty-five."[13] Northup remained in the slave pen for about two weeks. "The night previous to my departure a woman was brought in, weeping bitterly, and leading by the hand a little child.... Emily, the child, was seven or eight years old, of light complexion, and with the face of admirable beauty."[14] By the time they were shipped out the port of Richmond to the port of Orleans, Northup's writing appears to indicate there were fifteen enslaved on the brig to New Orleans.[15]

The Ancestry.com records mean Galveston and the historians have long hidden the extent of slave trade in and out of the port of Galveston. Modern technology helps to readily dispose of Galveston's incidental myth. "There were none." "There was one location." Ours was minimal involvement.

In 1840, in one particular transaction, John Sydnor identified his residence as Richmond, Virginia.[16] The manifest involved two slaves, a thirty-year old female (Clary) and a child who was fourteen years of age. Sydnor was shipping the slaves from the port of New Orleans to the port of Galveston. Sydnor's activities were consistent with those of other Galveston families: migration from an established slave state, bringing with them well-established practices, methods and means of buying and selling, and the establishment of slave auction houses.

Slavery was the dispute that remained constant between the North and South, particularly after Congress banned the transatlantic slave trade in 1807. The South and its allies in the North were in a constant flux: seeking workarounds, turning a blind eye to the continuation of illegal trafficking, using alternative arrangements such as kidnapping free people of color, the establishment of slave colonies in Cuba, South America, the Caribbean.

Southerners were in a constant state of protecting their vested interest, preaching the gospel of slavery, working the halls of Congress and state governments to change the ban, even proceeding to war to protect their possession of their things of value. The lost records, the transaction logs, the known and unknown numbers identified by Ancestry.com, represent why Latonia Wilson worked frantically to protect Galveston's historical records.

What is the point?

Galveston's port moved millions of souls through its waters during a relatively short period. Galveston served as a hub for Texas's economic growth and development of wealth while serving other parts of the country with goods, services, and slaves. The number of shipments from Galveston to New Orleans provided is a conservative one. One cannot ignore Galveston was also the hub for the distribution of slaves to the plantations located inland. The footprints left in the sands of time are telling.

CHAPTER 9

FOR HISTORY'S SAKE

And yet, in the midst of all this ruin and suffering they were harassed by thugs and thieves and ghouls in human shape, who looted property, assaulted citizens who resisted them, and despoiled and disfigured the dead in shockingly savage manner to secure rings and other jewels. Devoid of any feeling or sympathy or pity, they seized upon this awful disaster as an opportunity to enrich themselves. As soon, however, as the authorities could recover from the first shock of the disaster the city was placed under martial law, and the troops patrolling the island did not hesitate to kill every one of the vandals caught in the commission of his infamous work. Public opinion sustained this prompt style of punishment. It was a species of Southern lynching to which no objection was ever raised.[1]

Galveston is a small but historic city in context of politics, history, architecture, and the economic development of the greater southwest portion of this country. Save for the historic plaques located in the front of some of the African American houses of worship, recognition of the contribution of the African American community to Galveston proper is deficient.[2] Abject curiosity and anxieties forced the additional research; unable to sleep, waking in the middle of night, and extended periods of anguish provided no other option. Childhood nightmares returned, different voices—whispering in the recesses of my brain. Night sweats, images of the well-worn path of tormented souls, unexpected outbursts and tears. Forever—over, above, circling. When existing in the other world—as a lawyer—I subconsciously/consciously understood when the challenges to my existence were getting to me—a subject I have refused to talk about. However, I believe time has passed sufficiently to violate this self-imposed social grace. From the bed to the floor, thinking too much, consumed, wondering what next?

Wandering from room to room, not because I had misplaced anything or I needed to be in one room or another, but because my mind compelled me to walk, walk, walk. Sometimes I went back to bed, attributing the anxiety to sleepwalking; most times, I stopped at the stereo. Reaching and putting headphones in place, placing the music on the turntable or in a slot, listening with head bowed, partially dressed/undressed. In this condition, the song was always the same, Gil Scott-Heron's "95 Down South: All of the Places We've Been." The tears flowed freely while I spoke inaudibly, unintelligibly—mutterings, purported song.

Then—always—seeing the faces of my elders who made the privilege of our struggle possible. No, no, this was not an everyday occurrence—only when the challenges seemed overwhelming, insulting, persistent. I am sure no one could—with sanity intact—navigate their world if this was a daily occurrence. This only occurred when race stained my existence, when the challenge seemed insurmountable. Sometimes this activity was compelled by fear, most times not—uncertainty is a better adjective.

Confusion, worry, wonderment, all contributed to this combustible mix. I just needed reminding of the others who had preceded me down these roads. Down, down south, "all the places we've been." Gil Scott sang, "I've been in places where you could not eat / Or take a drink of water wherever you pleased / And now that I meet you in the middle of a mountain." . . . I lowered my head. . . . I always lowered my head . . . to futilely wipe. . . . "And all I can think of are chapters and scenes of / All of the places we've been / I'm not such an old man so don't get me wrong / I'm the latest survivor of the constantly strong." The reminder permitted me to lift my head and know I was going to be fine. "Cause all I can think of are chapters and scenes of / All of the places we've been."[3]

If my great-grandparents remained enslaved in rural Texas for an additional thirteen to fifteen years, what happened to those who looked like me in Galveston and the surrounding cities and counties? What did they do? Where did they live? What struggles did they face? With the auction houses located, what next? What can be done—as a collective society—to remember all of these places we've been?

From a historical perspective, we have failed in several respects: not retaining buildings/structures in order to recognize how slaves and their heirs contributed to the development and wealth of the city, state, and country. This means something other than cursory, and sometimes false, recounting of history by public entities and private concerns.

Our sin is not an original one. Other cities have also hidden and obscured the locations of these hallowed places. I am also sure our acts of placing vague, misleading plaques and writing false, incomplete stories without citations is not original.

These obstacles have hindered growth and caused the bulk of the African American population to remain mired on the lower rungs of the socioeconomic

Figure 10: Construction of seawall. (Fair use/public domain.)

ladder. Like for the rest of the country, this failure has intruded into other areas: birth and death rates, housing, development, jobs, sickness, and death. Documenting history will also correct the persistent and unmistakable out-migration from the island and other areas of the country. How is this done?

In *The Alleys and Back Buildings of Galveston: An Architectural and Social History*, author Ellen Beasley provided the common historical refrain for Galveston's colored population.[4] Her view represents the persistent and continued diminishment of a people.

> Fat and Tin Can Alleys were located in Ward Five, which was bordered by 25th Street, 29th Street, Avenue J, and Galveston Bay. The blocks northward from Avenue E composed "the district," the less respectable side of Galveston's port economy, with its concentration of saloons, boardinghouses, gambling halls, and brothels. Galvestonians preferred to talk instead about the city's importance as a cotton port, second only to New Orleans, as a port of entry for thousands of immigrants every year.[5]

Beasley does what historians have normally done to the African American community—no matter how well-intended. Let me try to be clearer: in the seminal work *The Galveston That Was*, Peter Brink, the former executive director of the

Galveston Historical Foundation, provided a concise history of Galveston and its architectural wonders.[6] However, Brink never mentioned the contribution of those former slaves or later freed colored citizens to the development of the city.[7]

> In the 1950s and early 1960s there remained in Galveston one of the finest collections of nineteenth century architecture in the United States. Some 300 blocks of the island city were packed cheek-by-jowl with hundreds upon hundreds of Victorian structures.
>
> In the residential areas, high above their compact yards, sat raised cottages, intricate frame houses and imposing mansions. They presented a dazzling array of porches, double galleries, crazy-quilt rooflines cut by multiple dormers, grand entryways with massive ten-foot-high doors, beveled and stained glass, and rusticated stucco on piers and chimneys. Those built of wood were accented—even frosted—with elaborate patterns of millwork, giving rise to the popular "Carpenter Gothic" to describe this vernacular exuberance.
>
> ...
>
> These structures represented the dreams of European immigrants, who saw in the promised land of Galveston and Texas the opportunity to build for themselves the castles, chateaux and ornate stone masterpieces so familiar, yet so unobtainable, in their homelands. Never mind the lack of stone and stonemasons in this new city on its island of sand; with characteristic tenacity they built in brick, then covered the brick with stucco and finally rusticated it all to look like stone—or, more frequently, they simply recreated the glories of carved stone out of wood, paint, and carpentry genius.[8]

Brink's assessment of Galveston's deterioration was correct, in a sense. The Galveston Historical Foundation and the city have done a wonderful job of saving others' landmarks but have done considerably less in saving properties and history related to the African American population. There has been a pattern of simply ignoring these communities of interest, never mentioning them when recounting history, and/or failing to provide the full context of the city's history.

The city's neighborhood plans compound this bias, relegating neighborhoods to little or no value, planning for improvement by the destruction and the removal of the heirs of the previously enslaved. So instead of improvements and keeping the population in place, this disparate population is ignored or their numbers used for funding purposes for others' projects. The city of Galveston's description of the Old Central/Carver Park neighborhood is a prime example of this bias.

The recovery period following the Civil War saw the area from 26th Street through 29th Street, and Postoffice and Market, develop into a vice district replete with bawdy houses, saloons and "[V]ariety Shows." This colorful history was to dominate certain areas of the neighborhood until the 1950s. On a more constructive note, from its earliest days as the port of entry for the Republic of Texas, this neighborhood area has provided the labor pool for the port facility.[9]

The Texas Historical Commission visited this area in the 1950s and conducted a pictorial survey. The results of the survey? The bulk of the structures in the area have since been demolished. Between 25th and 27th Street, Winnie to Market, entire blocks of housing were demolished and replaced with a CenterPoint plant/facility (electrical) and a parking lot for the federal courthouse/post office. This represents four city blocks.[10]

Thus, the use of governmental powers to acquire properties under the rubric of urban development and then writing/recounting/retelling history in a different light; time and memories fade, which permits historians and governmental officials to paint a different and far less inclusive picture.

Contrary to the assertions of John Henry Brown, we are not an inferior people. We are not cursed, less intelligent, nor a people that has not contributed one iota to the civilized world. John Henry Brown's views, at one time, were the views of policymakers in this country and the populace. The historian Arnold Toynbee was much more succinct in expressing this view: "It will be seen that when we classify mankind by color, the only one of the primary races, given by this classification, which has not made a creative contribution to any one of our twenty-one civilizations is the Black Race."[11] If we as a community remain captured by these views of the African American community and history—even slightly—we will continue to make the same mistakes. Learning how to hold one's tongue and silence are no different. We were indeed enslaved for four hundred years. The effect of slavery and its mindset lives on in various iterations.

When the residential and commercial structures were built, of which the historians so proudly write, who are they ignoring? When John Henry Brown pleaded with his fellow legislators about the need for the enslaved to build the cities and cultivate the land, why do we now refuse to acknowledge the profound contributions and wealth that was derived from the illicit and immoral trade? Does it follow that some of the craftsmen/laborers were the enslaved/colored/Negroes?[12] We continue to lacquer over this history, or papier-mâché, perhaps, is a better description. Putting in place inaccurate plaques and supposed tributes—knowing but not knowing, acknowledging but not—absolving our city and city leaders

Figure 11: Wedding portrait of Charles Aaron and Willa A. Bruce. (California African American Museum, https://www.npr.org/2021/10/10/1043821492/black-americans-land-history; public domain.)

while continuing to condemn at the same time. We should know by now: all of these attempts are imperfect masking materials.

A freed people, regulations, the power of eminent domain: The *Los Angeles Times* was the first to report the county of Los Angeles was considering giving back property taken from a Black family in 1924 by the process of eminent domain. Willa and Charles Bruce bought the property in 1912. The land is located on the California coast. "In this affluent town of 35,000—known for its manicured homes, the community fair, the Strand by the sea—few know of this racist past. Others would prefer to gloss over the uncomfortable details in a community where Black residents make up less than 1% of the population."[13] The condemnation was based upon a claim by the city that the city needed a public park. After a trial, the city paid a total of $14,500 for the land.

In 1912, Willa Bruce purchased for $1,225 the first of two lots along the Strand (in Los Angeles County) between 26th and 27th Streets. While her husband, Charles, worked as a dining-car chef on the train running between Salt Lake City and Los Angeles, Willa ran a popular lodge, cafe, and dance hall—providing Black families a way to enjoy a weekend on the coast. By setting up a beachside community, Charles and Willa Bruce "did what every other Californian was doing during that time," a historian says.[14] Many referred to this area as Bruce's Beach. A few more Black families bought and built their own cottages by the sea.

Izola Collins, in her book *Island of Color: Where Juneteenth Started*, tells a similar story:

> Property ownership in Galveston was very elusive in those early days of the 20th century, and so African Americans placed more importance on it than many do now. Ownership is more important to those who have difficulty accomplishing it. From one book about the back-alley houses and businesses of Galveston, by Ellen Beasley, one might get the mistaken notion that most African Americans lived in Galveston's alleys. Not so.[15]

Collins explained that the two-block area between 27th and 28th Streets (Seawall Boulevard) was owned primarily by Robert McGuire for a generation. "The bathhouse area, where he had his businesses and homes, was known by people who did not live in Galveston as 'The Beachfront.' In the days of segregation, many African Americans, both residents and visitors, thought it was the only place they were allowed to use the Gulf of Mexico, other than at the end of the seawall at 61st Street, where one could drive down a ramp onto the sand."[16]

McGuire acquired the property in 1904; in 1910, he and two others applied to the City of Galveston for a park license. "Articles of copartnership were filed with the County Clerk's Office, 'to organize the McGuire Park Co. . . . the purpose . . . to erect a pavilion for entertainment . . . to be located on lots 1, 2, and 8 in the northeast block of lot 140. This property is on Twenty-Eight Street and Avenue R.'"[17] The county of Galveston granted McGuire a liquor license in April 1911.[18]

The McGuires' property was ultimately taken from them by the city through eminent domain.[19] In reference to the plural, Alberta (Mabson) was Robert McGuire's spouse. The 1913 city directory lists Robert McGuire as colored with the following location/address: "Mgr. Bob Hack Stand, 2219 Postoffice, ph. 157, also prest and mgr McGuire Park Co., 2725 R, r. 2724 R. 5. Ph. 2461."[20] In 1914, the listing for McGuire reflected "McGuire Park and Bath House,[21] R. E. McGuire, prop. 2725 Avenue R." There is an additional reference to McGuire, "McGuire Park and Bath House, also hack line 2219 Avenue E,[22] r 2724 Avenue R."[23]

CHAPTER 9

"Let Me"
Let me take you to the beach
Eat a peach
By Sérgio Mendes, performed by Jill Scott and Will.i.am

Figure 12: *Let Me Take You to the Beach*. Photographer unknown, date unknown. (Part of collection date 05.24.2002; contributed by Melba Pope. Anthony P. Griffin Collection.)

McGuire's land was targeted by Galveston Commercial Association, a group of White businessmen. GAC was not part of the city government. The organization wielded power in conjunction with city officials, making the decision to attack McGuire's business interest—their business interest—becoming the will of the city.[24]

In 1916, the year after the eminent domain proceeding, McGuire went back to being a "cabman," with a residence at 2818 Avenue R.[25] The remaining neighbors in the two-block area were colored, and they too were affected, no different than the Bruces and their neighbors.[26] Do you see the pattern?[27]

In Manhattan Beach, "[i]n time, a small community of Black landowners bloomed around the resort . . . [t]hese included George Priolean, a formerly enslaved retired army major whose family developed a duplex along the shore; Mary Sanders, a caterer from Canada who was known as a skilled entrepreneur; and John and Bessie McCaskill, who hosted elaborate beachside breakfasts."[28] The *City Times* (Galveston)—a Black newspaper at the time—takes away the mystery of the race of the other property owners, informing the public that these folks were indeed colored.[29] The cause and effect of the city's action was that the colored population started to migrate to the mainland.

Bruce Beach prospered, even with harassment by White neighbors and city officials. Izola Collins confirmed the same for the land surrounding McGuire's property: the area prospered.[30] Remember, Manhattan Beach took the Bruces' property in 1924; Galveston took the McGuire's property in 1915.[31]

The supposed need for a park in the Bruces' case? The park was not put in place until three decades later.[32] The City of Galveston's exercise of eminent domain powers permitted it to take possession of private property and rename the park Menard Park. The newly christened Menard Park opened on July 4, 1915.[33]

A recreation center was not built on the land until 1941.[34] With respect to Robert McGuire, the city took an area dedicated for the specific purpose of the entertainment of colored people—a park, pavilion, bath house—one of few places people of color could go—and created a publicly segregated beach park, replacing the coloreds with Whites only.

The park was renamed after one of the city's founding fathers, Michel B. Menard, a slave holder and slave trader; Menard appeared in the 1850 U.S. federal census of slave schedules and was reported owning nine enslaved persons.[35] Menard died at his home in Galveston on September 2, 1856. He is buried at the Catholic Cemetery in Galveston. He is the namesake of Menard County, Texas.[36]

The city's message in the exercise of eminent domain was just as clear as Menard's participation in the sale with J. L. Darragh of fifty-six human beings on March 1, 1854.[37] As previously set out, Michel B. Menard traded under the firm of Doswell, Hill and Co.[38] The sale took place in the offices of Doswell, Hill and

CHAPTER 9

Company. The firm's name is listed in the 1859 city directory; R. B. Doswell's address in 1859 was on 23rd Street. In Heller's *Galveston Directory*, after the Civil War—1886–1877—the name of the firm had changed to Arnold, Menard & Co. with an address of 120 E. Strand, 2nd Floor.[39]

The year 1915 was only a mere fifty years—two generations—out from emancipation. After the ouster of the McGuires' businesses and the colored families, the city paid Mr. McGuire and the others in the two-block area a pittance. In 1999, the city erected a commemorative plaque and named the center sitting on the land after McGuire's daughter.[40] We, as a city, mention Robert McGuire nowhere. Naming the facility after his daughter is misplaced and designed to avoid discussing how race was the dominant factor in the city's taking the land.

There are other tributes that sit on the southern portion of Menard Park, facing the Seawall—one is a tribute to World War II troops ("honored for their service"), explicitly distinguishing between the White and colored troops. This plaque was put in place by the George Washington Chapter of the National Society of the Daughters of the American Revolution (NSDAR).[41] The Daughters of the American Revolution (DAR) is "an organization whose members can prove they are related [direct descent] to someone who aided the rebels in 1776."[42] The second statue was put in place on April 21, 1937, also by the DAR, in tribute to the Texas navy. The state chair at the time of installment was Mrs. E. C. (Mary Moody) Northen.[43] The city has taken a similar position by placing a Korean War statue in the place where City Hall was located (along with John Sydnor's slave auction house).[44] Perhaps camouflaging is a more apt descriptor.

The city's stated intent for appropriating the property for a park was specious since Mr. McGuire had already developed the property as a park. McGuire entered into a partnership with two other individuals—a registered articles of co-partnership in which the others partners were to construct a two-story building, complete with a third-story cupola, for a price that had been estimated at $6,000.00 (the co-partnership agreement stated $3,500.00)[45]—or the equivalent of an approximate range of $93,000.00 to $160,000.00 in today's dollars[46]—assuming the cost of construction of the building was as initially contemplated by the articles of partnership. The city purchased the building from McGuire for cost and paid $5,500.00 for the land, for his additional land, and the home in which he resided. The city also targeted fourteen additional property owners, all of whom were African American. After the taking, the property became a segregated city park—for Whites only—with the city creating and designating Wright Cuney Park as a segregated park for Negroes.[47] The City of Galveston effectively ousted the population of African Americans adjacent to Seawall Boulevard, purchasing

> "Maria, Maria"
> *When the wind blows, I can feel you*
> *Through the weather*
> *And even when we are apart*
> *Still feels like we're together*
>
> By Wyclef Jean, Jerry "Wonda" Duplessis, Carlos Santana, Karl Perazzo, and Raul Rekow. Performed by Santana, featuring The Product G&B

Figure 13: *Thank You for Being My Friend.* Photographer unknown, date unknown. (Part of collection date 05.24.2002; contributed by Melba Pope. Anthony P. Griffin Collection.)

5.75 acres of land, including two blocks of frontage on Seawall Boulevard, for $18,500 (equivalent to $558,740.41 in December 2024), $11,500 going to Mr. McGuire and the remainder to the other landowners.[48] The site is now worth tens of millions of dollars. Sadly, there are currently no African American business property owners on the Galveston seawall. The seawall is ten miles in length.[49] This exclusion has not been by happenstance.

The Bruces' land currently houses a lifeguard training facility owned by the County of Los Angeles. Los Angeles County officials admitted the land is worth millions and the heirs have been shorted on their inheritance. The State of California ultimately agreed to reverse the taking and agreed to give the property back to the family.[50] Galveston is not yet there and may never get there. Our city remains in the stagnant position, not yet willing to admit the basic fabric of the city's history—the most active slave port west of New Orleans. The Wall Street of the southwest, indeed, indeed. By painting an incomplete picture, we have become complicit in silencing history's voice.

The wind moved the car from one lane to another, causing the dashboard to flash in response to the abrupt movement; the rain lashed out, striking at an angle, giving an appearance she was in full agreement with her companion. We were traveling the 289 miles from Galveston to Dallas, and each of them remained with us the entire trip. Their breath was cold, causing the dashboard to display snowflakes, a warning I assume in that no snow was visible to the naked eye. I was driving my brother Gregory's car. He sat in the rear talking to Ellyn, who sat in the front seat marveling at the technology; she controlled the sound system, deciding what music to cue, and repeatedly provided a running commentary about the seat warmers and the massage she was being administered as we moved closer and closer to Dallas. Gregory—a preacher and radio talk show host—was practicing/prepping/pontificating for future shows. Ellyn—a lawyer—was in and out of conversations, doing the lawyer thing—addressing the anticipated and threatened eminent domain suit for an entire block by the electricity provider in Galveston. She obsessed over the pandemic, the law. I had yet to discover how and in what manner the McGuires' property was taken. I was a mere fifty pages into this work. The stacks of papers, books, and research papers I left at the office comprised considerably more pages than my progress. The trip was welcome.

The electronic wizardry continued to dance, dance, and dance in front of me. I veered out of the lane slightly again—only slightly, I swear—the thing beeped. When cars passed on either side, the thing flashed yellow lights. I nodded slightly—the thing kindly warned me and displayed a cup of coffee with steam. I would have lightly stopped and walked if it had been a sponsorship for a particular brand. Farther down the road, it—the thing—demanded I pull over. Sorry, Shakespeare, the man didn't protest much ["The lady doth protest too much, methinks"][51]—I pulled over two exits down and took a break.

When we resumed our travel, I opened my eyes and straightened my posture to lessen the nice bullying I was enduring.

The day was February 19, 2020. The public emergency began on January 31, 2020. We were less than one month into the pandemic and travelling to make an appointment with the congresswoman on a timely basis. Years before, I had represented Congresswoman Eddie Bernice Johnson in two redistricting trials against the State of Texas.[52] Each trial was separated by the census conducted by the United States Census Bureau (every ten years). The first trial was so paper intense I still bear a scar on my left eye, caused by eye strain and the lack of sleep over an extended period. Both trials spanned weeks.

I worried too much as a child. One of my most profound fears as a child was travelling in Texas—traveling on old Highway 75, knowing certain stops were fraught places for colored/Negroes/Blacks. We were never welcomed. Momma knew this history and gave the same speech every time. "We are not stopping. If we stop it will be for 'gas, and gas only.' If you have to go to the restroom, go in groups. Do you hear me?!" As Momma drove, a palpable worry radiated and filled the air until we arrived at the stoop of her parents' home (located between

Teague and Mexia), her sister's home (Aunt Mildred and Uncle Warren, in Fort Worth), or our paternal grandparents' home (also in Fort Worth). On the day of our travel, we pulled into one of the places that seemed inconsistent with rural Texas—a smiling bucktoothed beaver perched high above. Seventy-five to a hundred and twenty gas pumps, 60,000–75,000 square feet, taking on the appearance of a carnival when exiting the car. Go figure, leaving the city to go to a monstrous city complex in rural Texas.

We—the congresswoman and I—no longer talked to each other every other day. Our visits were now limited to once a year; however, she remained someone I trusted. I wanted to talk to her about the eminent domain threat and sought her advice. I decided to bring along a lawyer (Ellyn) and a preacher (Gregory)—who also wanted to meet the congresswoman, having heard so much about her.

Technology did what technology does: it efficiently moved us over the continuum of time and distance allowing us to arrive approximately thirty minutes early, in a much more efficient manner than I would care to admit—directing movements, directions, calculating time, beeping, talking, scolding. Thousands of thousands of synchronized inanimate/animate movements working together, befuddling the driver, broadcasting the temperature in real time, isolating us from the elements. The wind's howl was a gentle blow on our side of the window. Ellyn continued to swoon over her pampered treatment. Yes indeed, the thing delivered on the Ford Motor Company's latest slogan, "What a Luxury Car Should Be." Not he, not she—the thing—I say, did deliver. Indeed, we were as comfortable as bugs, like those who compelled me to think too much and who were probably burrowed deep near the same pavement in which they rudely introduced themselves to me. Gregory's car told me we too had accomplished silent, coordinated movement, although not as silent as the *Solenopsis*.

"Your destination is on the left."

We entered a large conference room and awaited the congresswoman and her assistant. Our visit was before masking had been suggested by the Centers for Disease Control and Prevention. However, even in the early stages of the pandemic, this strange new unknown was not as predictable and comforting as our travel.

"The congresswoman will be with you in a minute."

We talked for a couple of hours about why I was there. The first part of the meeting was catching up, telling stories—some we had shared long before, others new. As we neared the end of the meeting, the congresswoman told me her family was from Galveston. "At slavery's end, the White portion of the family received one portion of the land, my family received another portion." The land owned by the formerly enslaved was taken by the State of Texas, again pursuant to its eminent domain power. "The land is where the University of Texas's Medical Branch Hospital is located."[53] As the congresswoman talked, sadness invaded my body and mind.[54]

Figure 14: *Old Hospitals, University of Texas Medical Branch, Galveston.* (Fair use/public domain).

Mindy Thompson Fullilove, MD, argues the Fifth Amendment's takings clause was derived from the commonality about which Peter Brink wrote—of immigrants building their American dreams:

> In fact, many of the revolutionaries who founded the United States had lived through or knew about the excesses of English law that permitted the enclosures in England. They were aware that land was taken for the purposes of economic development that profited the well-to-do. They were also aware that the loss of shared common lands—woods, fields, and marshes that provide grazing for livestock, firewood, and wild foods—had a devasting effect on the survival of the poor. Perhaps to protect against the excess of English law, the framers wrote in the Fifth Amendment to the United States Constitution "... that private property [shall not] be taken for public use, without just compensation."[55]

Dr. Fullilove's study found that during a 24-year period, 2,532 projects were carried out in 922 cities that displaced 1,000,000 people, two-thirds of them African American. The study dealt with the period of 1949–1973.[56] The deterioration and displacement of businesses and persons of the colored citizens—again—has not been by happenstance.

CHAPTER 10

MAYBE THE NEGROES WENT TOO FAST

Laying Myths to Waste

In 1866, George T. Ruby moved from New Orleans to Galveston to continue his work as a teacher. He established a newspaper, the *Galveston Standard*, in 1871. The newspaper was issued semi-weekly through 1873.[1] "In 1869 [four years after the reading of General Granger's order], Ruby was appointed deputy collector of customs at Galveston. He was active in the Republican party, serving in 1868 as a delegate to the national Republican convention and to the state Constitutional Convention." Ruby was elected as a state senator during Reconstruction, representing the Twelfth District—which included Galveston, Brazoria, and Matagorda Counties. Ruby served in the 12th and 13th Texas Legislatures from 1870 to 1871 [five to six years after the reading] and in 1873 [eight years after] respectively. As state senator Ruby served on the judiciary, militia, education, and state affairs committees. Bills he introduced successfully incorporated the Galveston, El Paso, Harrisburg, San Antonio, Houston, and Tyler railroads, as well as the Harbor Trust Company and several insurance companies. "He did not seek reelection in 1873 and moved back to Louisiana."[2] At the time of Ruby's election to the senate, two other colored men were also elected: John F. DeBruhl, justice of the peace, and Jo[h]nson Reed, district clerk.[3]

CHAPTER 10

Norris Wright Cuney ran against C. J. Allen for an alderman position in 1885, a mere twenty years after Granger's reading and eighteen years after John Henry Brown prepared the Joint Resolution for the Texas Legislature, telling the world of Ruby's, Cuney's, and others' inferiority. Chief Justice Roger Taney wrote his opinion in *Dred Scott* the same year John Brown submitted his resolution, proclaiming a Black man had no rights a White man was bound to respect in 1856, nine years before emancipation.[4] The Texas Historical Commission reports that Norris Wright Cuney initially ran for mayor in 1875 but lost to Robert L. Fulton.[5]

In 1885—twenty years after Granger's reading—Cuney was elected as an alderman over C. J. Allen. Initially, Cuney was declared the loser. He challenged the election and sued because of the irregularities in the ballots. Norris Wright Cuney's daughter, Maud Cuney Hare, explained:

> In the eleventh ward, the vote stood 309 for Allen and 21 for Cuney, against 162 in the tenth ward and 221 in the twelfth ward—contiguous wards. The total vote was 2389 for Cuney and 2492 for Allen. In the eleventh ward which was credited for 21 votes for father, 97 citizens made affidavits of having voted for him. In the meantime, other affidavits were taken. More than 300 identified ballots as having been changed. Many ballots were destroyed, and others substituted Allen's name on them.... One of the prominent citizens who took the stand and swore he had voted for N. W. Cuney and that ballot had been changed was Chief Justice A. H. Willie of the Supreme Court of Texas.[6]

In 1886, Cuney opposed a charter amendment which "moved to make six wards in the city, one alderman to be elected from each ward, and in addition thereto, six aldermen to be elected from the city at law." Cuney argued that electing the entire body by the vote of the entire city worked to disenfranchise minorities' vote. The amendment to the charter passed.[7]

Cuney had local, state, and national influence. He complained to the federal government of colored citizens being run out of adjoining counties under threat of violence, requiring these elected officials to resign their offices. Norris Wright Cuney was able to get the United States government to indict sixty-two citizens of Fort Bend County, including the sheriff and county attorney, for forcing colored men to leave their homes. There was also an indictment by the same jury of twenty-six citizens of Richmond charged with the murder growing out of the Richmond riot.[8] One of the victims was C. M. Ferguson, who had travelled to Galveston to the Cuneys' home. "It was thought best to take precautions for his personal safety, and that night he was taken to the home of my father's brother, Joseph." Mr. Ferguson brought a civil suit in Galveston County.[9]

One researcher, Lovette, cites a local historian (Clarence R. Wharton) in describing antebellum Fort Bend County, "Slavery was the cornerstone of plantation life." Lovette explained the historical background of these coastal counties and why, ultimately, emancipation proved problematic for a previously master-servant society: "As part of the first area of Texas to be settled, Fort Bend was also part of the initial expansion of slavery into the state, which moved the coast inward along the Colorado and Brazos rivers. By 1840 the area—including the coastal counties of Brazoria and Matagorda and the inland counties of Fort Bend, Colorado, Austin, and Washington—contained one-third of Texas's slave population. Increased movement into east Texas in the 1840's only slightly reduced the coastal a region's slaveholding majority to one-fourth of the state's slave population by 1845."[10]

Norris Wright Cuney's daughter, Maud Cuney Hare, described her father as follows:

> Negro, Indian and Swiss descent. The Negro and Indian blood came through his mother, Adeline Stuart, for whom free papers were executed by Col. Cuney, and who was born in the State of Virginia. Her mother, Hester Neale Stuart, was of Potomac Indian, Caucasian, and Negro blood, and belonged as a slave to a family named Neale of Centreville and Alexandria, Virginia. Our grandmother was a woman of medium height and slender; of olive complexion and regular features, with straight black hair and dark eyes.[11]

As related to C. M. Ferguson's taking refuge on the island when violence erupted in Richmond, Maud Cuney described a gathering of laborers in the streets of Galveston to deter others who may have travelled to the island looking for Ferguson.

> [H]is loyalty to the best interests of his race, the utter fearlessness which marked his conduct in this bitter contest was not unappreciated by the equally fearless men who followed him. In order to be prepared to meet any officers of the law who might come upon them and try to disperse them, the men had brought with them their guitars and other stringed instruments, that they might claim a "serenade" as an excuse for their loitering in such ambers before our home.

The duplicity is seen in various ways:

> Another incident amusing in some of its aspects, occurred about the same time.... My uncle Joseph had gone to the depot with mother to see her off to Houston, where she was to join father, who was there attending a matter of business. The

Figure 15: *Impudent and Insolent*, dock workers. Photographer unknown, date unknown. (Part of collection date 01.01.1985. Anthony P. Griffin Collection.)

conductor of the first-class coach saw them coming and, knowing them to be colored, he quickly locked the door of the coach as he knew from experience that no argument or force could compel mother to enter a second class car. After locking the door he disappeared. It was then nearly train time and the coach was nearly filled with passengers. For a second, disconcerted, mother looked around then innocently turning to Uncle Joseph, said: "Well, Joe, there are people in the coach and I see but one means of entrance and that is the window, so give me your hand as a mount." And, then, as if mounting a horse, she got in the window and took her seat demurely.[12]

Norris Wright Cuney's father, Col. Philip Cuney, migrated from Virginia and Louisiana. He settled in Waller County near Hempstead. He maintained a large plantation and held slaves; he had eight children with Adeline Stuart, a slave.[13] He was one of the largest slave owners in the state, owning 105 slaves.[14] Norris Wright Cuney was the middle child, fourth out of eight children.[15] He was born on the Sunnyside Plantation on the Brazos River and at the age of thirteen was sent to Pittsburgh for schooling; two older brothers were already there.[16]

In 1883, Norris Wright Cuney formed a stevedoring company, employing "500-colored men to load and unload vessels passing through the port of Galveston." Prior to his enterprise, only White longshoremen worked on the wharves.[17] "He had secured laborers not only in Galveston, but from New Orleans."[18] After working some time on the Morgan wharves, Cuney attempted to secure contracts on the New York docks.

J. B. Stubbs of Galveston wrote an open letter, which was published in the *Galveston News*, complaining of Norris Wright Cuney's denunciation of the race riots that were occurring in the state:

> It is just such inflammatory speeches as that delivered by Mr. Cuney last night that incites Negroes when in the majority to domineer over their white neighbors until the latter rise to either precipitate bloodshed or force them to leave.... I am surprised at Mr. Cuney. He is a man of intelligence and has been the recipient of many honors at the hands of the people of this city; yet one would think from his speech that Negroes were not safe in Texas.[19]

J. B. Stubbs was the child of Theodore Bonaparte Stubbs and Ellen Kirkpatrick Stubbs of Montgomery, Alabama.[20] T. B. Stubbs is the same person who, in February of 1861, was a partner with J. S. Sydnor next door to the slave auction business. Other evidence reveals T. B. was a slave trader. J. B. served as the city attorney and as a senator. J. B. was a graduate of Washington & Lee University in 1872 and returned to the island to practice at the Ballinger, Jack, and Mott law firm.

On July 20, 1889, Norris Wright Cuney was nominated as the collector of customs. The *Galveston News* supported the nomination: "The President did Texas proud today by naming three of her citizens for important places. They were N. W. Cuney for Collector of Customs at Galveston; James J. Dickerson of Fort Bend County for Marshal of eastern district; and Joseph W. Burke of Austin for Collector of Internal Revenue for the third Texas district."[21] The *Houston Post* view was starkly different: "Down at 'Cuney Island' last night, the elaborate reception prepared for Mr. Cuney, the dark-skinned white man, who was recently given the most important Federal position in Texas by Benjamin Harrison, took place."[22] With his appointment, Cuney had the highest-ranking appointed position of any Negro in the late nineteenth-century South. Please do not work too hard trying to suppose "Cuney Island" was not intended to insult, either Norris Wright Cuney or others.

Norris Wright Cuney was a high-ranking official in the Republican Party. He was active in the founding of an orphan's home for colored children in Mexia. As a younger man, he served as sergeant of arms of the 12th Texas Legislature. Cuney supported the legislature's establishing a school for the deaf, dumb, and blind colored youth. He was a candidate for the legislature in the 66th District in 1882. The district comprised Galveston, Brazoria, Matagorda, and Wharton Counties. One of his campaign positions was the elimination of the convict labor laws adopted by the State of Texas.[23] Galvestonian Harris Kempner signed an agreement with the State of Texas in 1883, using the convict leasing system for his land. Ike Kempner executed a similar contract twenty years later for Imperial Sugar. "Texas furnished the prisoners, tools, and guards, plus their horses and tracking dogs. The Kempners provided food and housing for the laborers, guards, and animals and paid the state a nominal amount per day per convict."[24] Howard University awarded Norris Wright Cuney an honorary degree, Master of Laws, in 1896.[25]

When the State of Texas decided to recognize Juneteenth as a state holiday, it did so in context of a political compromise. The day was required to be shared with Confederate Heroes Day. There exist no plaques, streets, or public acknowledgment of George T. Ruby. The one plaque in existence honoring Norris Wright Cuney is located at the Galveston County Courthouse located at 722 Moody (21st Street), among several others in the square, surrounding a statue (a soldier) supporting the Confederacy. The display in and of itself is insulting. It is proper to chant: history does repeat itself.[26] The establishment of Wright Cuney Park as a segregated park by the City of Galveston in 1937 is an additional insult. Remember the creation of the Norris Wright Cuney Park took place after the taking of Robert McGuire's land. Currently the city of Galveston still has more statues honoring Confederate war heroes than it does honoring African Americans,[27] and there are none denoting those hallowed places in which humans were traded and sold the same as cattle.[28]

The 1880 Galveston city directory lists Norris Cuney as follows: "Cuney, N. W., custom house, res. L, between 8th and 9th."[29]

In 1884, after graduating from Meharry Medical College in Nashville, Tennessee, John Henry Wilkins, MD (1853–1917) was the first African American to open a medical practice in Galveston.[30] His office was located at the Pix Building, 420 22nd Street, with a residence located at 905 Avenue K. After the 1900 storm, he moved to Victoria, Texas. His brother, Lewis Melton Wilkins, MD (1859–1928), who had graduated from Meharry in 1887, remained in Galveston.[31] Lewis Melton's office was located at 24th and Market (2420 1/2). His residence was at 1111 Postoffice. An advertisement in June 1922, in the *City Times*, reflected Dr. Wilkins' office moved from 315 1/2 Twenty-sixth Street to 3501 Avenue L.[32]

The Lone Star Medical Association was established in Galveston in 1886. The initial meeting was in the office of John J. Wilkins. The organization was created because of the Texas Medical Association's Whites-only policy.[33] The founders were all classmates at Meharry. The officers elected in the initial meeting were "Greene J. Starnes, MD, of San Antonio, as president; Reed Townsend, MD, Victoria; Ernest M. Blakney, MD, Columbus; N. Hill Middleton, MD, Oakland; William H. Scott, MD, Helinora; Edwin B. Ramsey, MD, Houston and Monroe Majors, MD, Brenham."[34] Four years later, an announcement was placed in the *Galveston Daily News* on June 3, 1890, wherein the meeting of the organization was announced:

> The Lone Star Medical Association, an organization of the colored physicians of the state, will meet in annual session here today, commencing at 10 a.m. The meetings are to be held at Excelsior Hall on Postoffice street, between Twenty-third and Twenty-fourth. Mayor Fulton will deliver an address of welcome at the opening session in the morning.[35]

In 1898 an operating charter was issued for the Lone Star Cotton Jammers of Texas, a Black union. Cotton Jammers—or screwmen—were longshoremen who loaded cotton into the ships. The Briscoe Center for American History provides the following history for the Screwmen's Association:

> Black longshoremen began to organize their own association starting in 1879, the Cotton Jammers' Association. Norris Wright Cuney, a powerful and prominent black Galveston businessman and politician, was one of the primary movers of this organization, which he pushed into competition with the Screwmen's Benevolent Association. In 1883, Cuney brought black longshoremen in from New Orleans and obtained a contract with the Morgan Lines, which broke the White longshoremen's monopoly.[36]

Cuney's group was named the Colored Screwmen's Benevolent Association (CSBA).[37]

In 1913, the charter was issued for International Longshoremen's Union Local 851. Local 851 ultimately absorbed the Cotton Jammers; its president was Doc Hamilton. Doc Hamilton was the first Black man to be elected to the district executive board of the South Atlantic and Gulf Coast District ILA. He also served that board as vice president and was elected to the vice president position on the International Longshoremen's Association Executive Board.[38] In the 1909–1910 Galveston city directory the following listing is found for Doc Hamilton: "Hamilton, Dock (sic), (c), screwman, r. 2818 Postoffice."[39]

On December 26, 1908, John Arthur (Jack) Johnson knocked out Tommy Burns in Sydney, Australia, becoming the boxing world's first Black heavyweight champion. Johnson's victory sparked race riots. These riots too were cemented in racist mythology: "At the beginning of the twentieth century most Americans believed that Whites were physically superior to Blacks and the heavyweight champion of the boxing world was considered the epitome of physical strength." The hate generated by Johnson's victory and his history of taunting his White opponents led to a search for the next Great White Hope, or stated differently, a search for any White man who could defeat Johnson. Years later, Muhammad Ali played on this history—talking, bragging, taking unpopular positions—becoming

Figure 16: Ads for Pope's Bath House (27th & Beach) and rooms for rent (Mrs. A. Roberts, Proprietress, 3528 Winnie Street). (Public domain.)

a public figure and inviting comparison, hatred, and mystique, for anyone who could beat him. The movie and play *The Great White Hope* were loosely based on Jack Johnson's life.[40]

Johnson was born on March 31, 1878, to Henry and Tiny Johnson; both parents were former slaves.[41] Johnson died on June 10, 1946. In his youth, Johnson worked the Galveston docks. He participated in a spectacle referenced as "battle royale," wherein four to twelve Blacks were placed in a ring for the entertainment of a White patron. The lone standing fighter was declared the victor. In 1910, Jack Johnson still called Galveston home and maintained his residence at 2310 Avenue H.[42]

Johnson was criticized for his relationships with White women. This latter behavior existed in a milieu in which Black men were prosecuted and even lynched for flirting with White women. Johnson openly dated and married White women. Johnson was prosecuted; he was indicted for taking Lucille Cameron, his second wife, across state lines. Cameron's mother was the complainant. There was little dispute their relationship was consensual. Johnson and Cameron later married.[43] The government's criminal case failed because Cameron refused to provide evidence against her husband. The government filed a new charge based upon a past relationship with Belle Schreiber.[44] In 1913, Jack Johnson was convicted for violating the Mann Act, "the transportation of a White woman across state lines for immoral purposes." Johnson was sentenced to a year in federal prison.[45]

On June 13, 1908, an advertisement was taken out in the *Galveston New Idea* that reflected Thos. Pope's establishment (a bathhouse) was in the same location as Robert McGuire's bathhouse.[46] In 1906, the *Galveston Daily News* reported Thos. Pope and others proposed the city pass an ordinance allowing the opening of a bathhouse on 37th Street.[47]

On May 1, 1909, the *City Times* published an article titled, "Various Businesses, Professions, etc., of the Race in Galveston and Total Value," which provided the following information as the location of Black businesses in the city of Galveston:[48]

> W. D. Lewis, Lone Star Motel; Mr. M. W. Webb, Banner Hotel; Mr. W. T. Matthews, Sea-wall Hotel; Ida Bennett, Alamo Café; The Green Front Café (without reference to the owner); John Williams's Restaurant [406 25th Street]; The Scott Restaurant located at 29th & Postoffice; Mr. Homer Hollier, caterer at Harmony Club, 2111 Postoffice; Mr. A. M. Sutton and wife, The Causeway Hotel and Café; Mr. Benj. Lockett Hotel, 2627 Church; Mr. Jesse Atkinson, 407 25th Street (restaurant and barber shop); Mr. A. Harris, restaurant next to the S. E. corner 29th and H; Mr. R. Sims, 27th [& Mechanic Street]; Messrs. Oliver, Young & Porter [saloon keepers and café] at 2712 Market Street; Mr. W. H. Brown Café, 2512 Market Street; Mrs. Jennie Thomas, 1729 Strand (restaurant); Mr. Ben Thomas at 1712 Strand; Mr. Smith's restaurant;[49] Mr. C. Laster (shoemaker); Messrs Jim Pope, T. P. Pope, J. L. Tankersley and other (house raising contractors and builders).

The article also identified wood dealers:

> Mr. Moses Evans, 1410 A; Jas S. Stewart, 2519 Avenue H; Mr. Sam Edwards, 3007 M; Mr. J. W. Griffin, 1613 Avenue A; Mr. Eugene Crutcher, L between 27th and 29th Street.

The tailors were located in the central business district of the city, with a few of these businesses extending into the current boundary line for Old Central Carver Park:

> Mr. A. Gilmore, 418 25th Street (Rosenberg); Mr. J. M. Gray, 2724 Market Street; Messrs. Zollah & Green, No. 415 25th Street (Market); Messr. Richard Jones and John Bell, 2307 Postoffice; Mr. J. B. Spiller, 25th and Winnie Street; Mr. E. T. Chissell, 318 26th Street.

Grocers, W. D. Lewis and Geo. W. Williams, were located at 2607 Mechanic St. There were three grocers at the time. The city possessed a colored furniture dealer, colored drugstores (e.g., Mr. E. T. Thurston was located at 30 . . . L); barbershops (e.g., "Mr. A. Pinder, 317 25th for 35 years in business in this city, the oldest of the race, employs 3 besides himself"); blacksmiths, a longshoremen's office, physicians, attorneys, and vegetable stands. Joseph Cuney took out a small advertisement notifying the public of his new office location, 2125 Mechanic Street, second floor. Joseph Cuney was Norris Wright Cuney's older brother.[50]

The city directory reflects Dr. L. M. Wilkins's, physician and surgeon, address at the Lone Star Screwman Hall, 2712A Market Street,[51] with additional offices at 3505 Avenue I. Dr. T. Adolph Jones, General Practice, was located at 901 30th Street. Mrs. E. Silas was listed as a trained nurse and midwife.[52]

In 1920 the Galveston dockworkers went on strike. The strike involved Local 807's approximately 250 members,[53] the White dockworkers of Local 385, and Black screwmen, Local 329.[54] "On March 3, 1920, after months of futile negotiations with coastwise shipping companies, sixteen hundred coastwise longshoremen in Galveston struck the Morgan and Mallory steamship lines."[55] The strike was part of a nationwide walkout. Labor's demand was an hourly wage hike. Another underlying issue in the dispute was the hiring of nonunion labor on the wharves. Prior to and during, the strike exploited racial animosities. Mallory Shipping Company had employed Black longshoremen; Morgan Line had hired only Whites. Shortly after the strike began Mallory brought in White workers to replace the striking Black longshoremen, and Morgan hired Blacks to work the company's docks in place of White unionmen.[56] There were roughly eleven White and eleven Black ILA locals in Galveston when roughly 1,600 of the island's coastwise dockworkers and screwmen joined the strike against Mallory and Morgan companies. The strike was led by Black Local 807 and Local 329 along with the White Local 385.[57] The cooperation of the Black and White locals led to local, state, and national business interests working to defeat the strike, including the governor's declaring martial law in Galveston.

In a speech to Galveston's Black workers, J. S. Lewis, a Black organizer, activist, and longshoreman, urged such solidarity across racial lines: "No wage earner is doing his full duty if he fails to identify his own interests with those of his fellow workmen."[58] Other Blacks who were notable during this period of unrest and entrenchment include: Laura A. Piney, union organizer and leader of the Woman's Progressive (Texas Association of Colored Women's Clubs); Anna Bradley, a charter member of the Galveston NAACP, who owned and operated a restaurant with her husband; and Edward Henderson and Luther Graves, who were officials with Local 807.

Governor William P. Hobby sided with the business community (Galveston Commercial Association). Governor Hobby sent "troops to control alleged violence on the docks." Racial eruptions "only occurred when both shippers began to employ Mexican braceros as strikebreakers, at which time both White and Black dock workers began to harass the newcomers."[59] Martial law remained in place from June 7 to October 1920, with militia on the streets of Galveston. Galveston's mayor and commissioners were suspended and restrained "from performing their duties appertaining to their respective offices with respect to the enforcement of the penal laws of the State and City of Galveston." The order also suspended all members of the Galveston police department.[60]

FBI agent J. V. Bell, investigating the 1920 longshoremen strike, wrote in his case file: "The negroes in Galveston, through their long association on an equality basis with white Union Labor, have about arrived at the time where they think they should be accepted on a par or equal with the white race." He warned that the "insolent manner" of local African Americans "toward the white race will, in time, lead to serious disorders between the races." More accurately, he indignantly reported, "I have never been in any city where the negroes are so impudent and insolent as they are in Galveston."[61]

Labor's history is important because of the leadership by the colored labor leaders and workers during this period of Galveston's history. The International Longshoremen's Association was formed in Chicago in 1877. In 1898 the colored cotton jammers and screwmen were represented by Wilford H. Smith. The laborers had struck the Mallory Wharf.[62]

Galveston's initial labor charter was issued in 1900 for Local 310. Local 329 and Local 851 (Black locals) were chartered in 1911 and 1913 respectively.[63] "Galveston's Dock and Marine Council tried to follow the example set by New Orleans longshoremen."[64] "Organized on August 25, 1909, and chartered by the ILA on July 1, 1910, the Galveston Dock and Marine Council worked to moderate racial tension and advance the common interests of waterfront workers." Galveston Dock and Marine Council work was obviously successful in that the 1920/1921 strike was by both the Black and White workers.[65] This history was remarkable in light of the fact that these events were fifty-five years after General Granger's order and occurred in a deeply segregated South. The State of Texas's reaction to the labor organization's actions was even more remarkable.

In the 1915 city elections, A. P. Norman, who had served as police commissioner since 1901, broke ranks with the City Club and endorsed a different candidate for mayor. "With exception of the years between 1917 and 1919, Norman held elected office until 1923, thanks mainly to Black and White longshoremen's votes and support of small businessmen who opposed control of city government by Kempner-Sealy forces."[66] The City Party was an example of labor cooperation.[67] "At an organizational meeting of a new political club on March 25, 1919, attorney

Henry O'Dell, acting as temporary chairman, appointed a committee composed of three Black leaders—Willis Woods, [68] D. H. 'Doc' Hamilton, and Thomas Jamison[69]—and three White leaders. Black and White waterfront workers had a majority influence on the committee."[70] The City Party was successful in the 1919 city election: H. O. Sappington, a former commissioner, defeated Isaac Kempner in the mayor's race.

Professor Andrews's research revealed a split between the Black newspapers on how labor's activism was covered. The *City Times*, "a black Republican newspaper in Galveston, offered no public support to the longshoremen, remaining virtually silent during the strike with very little coverage of it or the underlying issues. Nor did the newspaper's editor, William H. Noble Jr., support the City Party that longshoremen had elected in office. In contrast, editor David T. Shelton's *New Idea* had been harassed by the federal government during the war but reemerged in 1920, printed speeches by black labor organizers."[71] Professor Andrews explained, "There were efforts to suppress the Galveston *New Idea*, a Black newspaper regarded by the intelligence community as a tool of German capital to stir disloyalty. Military intelligence and Bureau of Investigation agents urged application of the Espionage Act against the newspaper because of its attacks on lynching and other forms of racism."[72]

We cannot ignore the history of retrenchment that occurred in Texas after emancipation. Perhaps Negroes were going too fast.[73]

In Matagorda County:

> In the summer of 1887 racial friction reached a boiling point in the county when two white men refused to work on the county road with Negroes and under the supervision of a Negro commissioner. In the ensuing controversy a Negro constable was slain when he attempted to bring one of the white men before a justice of the peace. Suddenly the county became an armed camp as Negroes secured weapons to defend themselves and armed whites from Matagorda, Brazoria, Fort Bend and Wharton appeared on the scene. Violence erupted and ended only after the death of five Negroes and the wounding of seven others. Governor L. S. Ross promptly dispatched the militia to prevent further lawlessness.[74]

In Fort Bend County, on September 5, 1888, the Jaybirds called a meeting at the courthouse in Richmond. A decision was reached to rid the county of the Negro leaders. The resolution read:

> Resolved, that in view of the crimes lately committed in our midst, we consider it necessary to the public good that the following persons be notified to leave

this county when ten hours from notification, to-wit: C. M. Ferguson, H. G. Lucas, Peter Warren, J. D. Davis, Tom Taylor, and O. M. Williams. That the above named be forever warned from returning to this county.[75]

After emancipation, the colored men of Fort Bend and other counties exercised their right to vote. Whether they were going too fast or too slow depends on one's prism.

> In Fort Bend black men at one time or another functioned in the roles of sheriff, county commissioner, tax assessor, voter registrar, treasurer, cattle and hide inspector, board of appeals ... district clerk, justice of the peace, and constable.... Between 1869 and 1889 at least forty-four black men served Fort Bend County as elected officials ... most notably Henry Ferguson and his brother Charles Ferguson.[76]

Charles M. Ferguson was also one of the men who brought the lawsuit to federal court in Galveston at Norris Wright Cuney's insistence. Dr. Lawrence Rice identified Henry Ferguson as the older and more prominent of the two brothers. "Henry succeeded Walter Burton as sheriff in 1874 and was destined to be the leader of the Negroes in the county for many years. He had been a slave of a planter named Ferguson in Jasper County, granted his freedom when he was thirty years of age."[77]

Neighboring counties—Brazoria, Matagorda, Colorado, Marion, Grimes, Jefferson, and Jackson—duplicated Fort Bend's activities and instituted violence and exclusionary tactics to remove the Negro officeholders (White primaries) and exclude the Negro voter. This pattern effectively eviscerated the Black vote.[78] These activities were precipitated, particularly in the agricultural counties, when the newly freed Negro men outnumbered White men and were able to nominate and elect their own to fill the county seats.[79]

In the years 1917–1921, violence erupted in Longview, Texas;[80] Washington, DC;[81] Chicago, Illinois;[82] Houston, Texas;[83] Knoxville, Tennessee; Omaha, Nebraska;[84] Elaine, Arkansas;[85] Tulsa, Oklahoma.[86] The 1920 labor strike in Galveston was preceded by the strike of October 1917 and 1898 of Black dockworkers.[87] Texas's violence was post passage of the state's constitutional adoption of the poll tax in 1902 and the establishment of White primaries in 1903.[88] In context of the collective action by White and Black workers, the strike caused a second invocation of martial law, the first being after the 1900 storm. Seemingly, Texas

CHAPTER 10

Figure 17: Klan Parade, Waco, Texas, July 4, 1924. (Public domain.)

considered the collective action of working-class men to be on par with a natural disaster. "From 1901 to 1910, 846 persons were lynched in the United States. Of this number, 92 were White and 734 were Black. Ninety percent of the lynchings took place in the South."[89]

The Texas legislature in 1866 put into effect its version of Black Codes, policies that were being enacted throughout the South directed at the newly freed formerly enslaved to limit their autonomy.[90] These laws constituted the cornerstone of the postwar social order orchestrated by the ex-Confederates. Examples are in order:

> SECTION 1. Be it enacted by the Legislature of the State of Texas, That all persons desirous of engaging as laborers for a period of one year or less, may do so under the following regulations:
>
> **All contracts for labor for a longer period than one month shall be made in writing, and in the presence of a Justice of the peace, County Judge, County Clerk**, Notary Public, or two disinterested witnesses, in **whose presence the contract shall be read to the laborers**, and, when assented to, shall be signed in triplicate by both parties, and shall then be considered binding, for the time therein prescribed.
>
> SEC. 2. **Every laborer shall have full and perfect liberty to choose his or her employer, but when once chosen, they shall not be allowed to leave their place of employment, until the fulfillment of their contract**, unless by consent of their employer, or on account of harsh treatment or breach of contract on the part of the employer, and if they do so leave without cause or

permission, **they shall forfeit all wages earned to the time of abandonment.**[91] [Emphasis added.]

These newly freed persons were told to stay in place, that freedom didn't really mean freedom, and any agreement was not valid unless and until it was signed in front of the county officer and two disinterested witnesses—if these conditions were not met, again, the contract was not valid and all wages were forfeited. The ultimate effect of any such laws was to remind the formerly enslaved where control was still vested. This author can only imagine the lawyers sitting around laughing—no, bellowing seems a more apt word—as they constructed a legal house of restrictive riddles. State Representative Brown's siren song indeed.

> SEC. 5. **All labor contracts shall be made with the heads of families**; they shall embrace the labor of **all the members of the family named therein, able to work, and shall be binding on all minors of said families.**
> SEC. 6. **Wages due, under labor contracts, shall be a lien upon one-half of the crops**, second only to liens for rent, and **not more than one-half of the crops shall be removed from the plantation, until such wages are fully paid.**
> SEC. 7. **All employers, willfully fully failing to comply with their contract, shall, upon conviction, be fined in amount double that due the laborer**, recoverable before any court of competent jurisdiction, to be paid to the laborer, and any inhumanity, cruelty, or neglect of duty, on the part of the employer, shall be summarily punished by fines, within the discretion of the court, to be aid to the inured [*sic*] party; provided, that this shall not be so construed as a remission of any penalty, now inflicted by law, for like offences.[92] [Emphasis added.]

Mayor Leonard's and other Galvestonians' plea to General Granger was just that—to have the previously enslaved stay in place. General Granger's order complied, Texas law engrafted the condition, everyone was expected to comply, and even if the laborers were not paid, their remedies were explicitly limited.

One other example:

> SEC. 9. **The labor of the employee shall be governed by the terms stipulated in the contract; he shall obey all proper orders of his employer or his agent, take proper [c]are of his work-mules, horses, oxen, stock of all character and kind; also, all agricultural implements; and employers shall have the right to make a reasonable deduction from laborers' wages for injuries done to animals or agricultural implements committed to their**

care, or for bad or negligent work. Failing to obey reasonable orders, neglect of duty, leaving home without permission, impudence, swearing or indecent language to, or in the presence of the employer, his family or agent, or quarrelling and fighting with one another, shall be deemed disobedience. **For any disobedience, a fine of one dollar shall be imposed on, and paid by the offender. For all lost time from work hours, without permission from the employer or his agent, unless in case of sickness, the laborer shall be fined twenty-five cents per hour**. For all absence from home without permission, the laborer will be fined at the rate of two dollars per day; fines to be denounced at the time of the delinquency. Laborers will not be required to labor on the Sabbath, except to take necessary care of stock, and other property on the plantation or to do necessary cooking or household duties, unless by special contract for work of necessity. For all thefts of the laborer from the employer, of agricultural products, hogs, sheep, poultry, or any other property of the employer, or willful destruction of property, or injury the laborer shall pay the employer double the amount of the value of the property stolen, destroyed or injured, one-half to be paid to the employer, and the other half to be placed in the general fund, provided for in this section, No livestock shall be allowed to laborers without the permission of the employer. Laborers shall not receive visitors during work hours. All difficulties arising between the employer and laborers under this section, shall be settled, and all fines imposed by the former; if not satisfactory to the laborer, and appeal may be had to the nearest Justice of the Peace, and two free holders, citizens, one of said citizens to be selected by employer, and the other by the laborer; and all fines imposed.[93] [Emphasis added.]

Even with only a portion of the codes set out, the intent is clear. Keep them in place, fine them, never pay them, make sure they will never be given full freedom! Keep them enslaved and, if necessary, kill them. The lawyers and state legislators were howling about the time they reached this point of the document. The contract labor code bound entire families to their employers, who could impose fines on any worker guilty of disobedience or unapproved absence. In fact, laborers who missed three days of work forfeited an entire year's wages.

Texas, like other ex-Confederate states, promulgated a vagrancy law to pressure Blacks into accepting the convict leasing system. Those serving time in city or county jails for petty crimes could be hired out to railroads, iron foundries, ore mines, and public utilities. It could be said Sugar Land, Texas, and the sugar industry (Imperial Sugar) prospered under these laws and the free labor designed to benefit Texas's development. When a Northern newspaper correspondent asked a White Texan if using prison labor to build a railroad through Rusk County was a safe practice, he was assured, "Of course, [the prisoners] haven't done anything bad." The reassurances provided were accurate. By way of example, one Black male convict served three years for stealing a twenty-five-cent can of sardines.[94]

The treatment of the *New Idea* newspaper was not power exercised in a void; it was part of a social milieu and a byproduct of the freeing of the enslaved. The authorities simply needed the newspaper to march in lock step, and if not, it would be forced to cease business. The criticism directed against Norris Wright Cuney by Stubbs, whose ancestor was a slave trader, was much the same. Again, Cuney Island was never intended to be a compliment. Representative Brown was honest in one respect—Texas needed the bodies and, unwittingly, the brains of these formally enslaved men and women (and of course, this also applied to their heirs). With the abolition of slavery, mythmaking alone wasn't enough to permit the continued control by the dominant society, thus laws (Black Codes), threats, and violence became an adjunct to previously institutionalized system of slavery.

On October 30, 1865, an article titled "Coolie Negroes" ran in the *Galveston Tri-Weekly News*. The article had run for 134 days starting June 19, 1865:

> Clearly, our agricultural labor system is now the chief concern and while it must be that time will have to contribute much to the settlement of the questions arising out of emancipation, it is also true that attention cannot be too earnestly directed at every scheme which seems to promise the deliverance of our planters out of a state of dependence, and the rescue of our lands from the encroaching jungle.[95]

The concern expressed by State Representative Brown in 1860, by Mayor C. H. Leonard, just prior to General Granger's order, remained the same—how was the work going to be done?

> Our readers are aware that the platform of the Radicals is to force the black man upon the South which the Northern States would not tolerate for themselves. The attempt to do this is unfair, and it cannot succeed without trouble. We do not wish to face the extermination of the negro on one hand, nor his equality on the other.[96]

In context of the labor strike that occurred in Galveston, Professor Andrews explained how effective retribution was:

> The political activism of black longshoremen raises important questions about the swift collapse of the Galveston NAACP chapter after the strike. After all, three of the four charter officers in the local branch worked on the waterfront. In 1919–1920, while most fledging chapters of the NAACP were being decimated

or wiped out completely in Texas, the Galveston branch was the only one that increased its membership. Whereas membership in the Dallas and San Antonio chapters, for example, plunged, respectively from 1,152 to 317 and from 1,746 to 607 between 1919 and 1920, the Galveston Branch grew from 173 to 259. By 1921, however, in the demoralized aftermath of the strike and establishment of the open shop, only 15 members remained in the Galveston branch.[97]

Even with the period of cooperation between White and Black labor, leading to the 1920 strike, during and after the period of retrenchment, the International Longshoremen's Association remained a segregated entity until the 1970s. The union integrated because the United States brought a suit against the ILA and ordered the unions to integrate.[98] The ILA stipulated at trial that "the I.L.A. chartered the locals on the basis of race, and there is no question that it has maintained these locals on the basis of race, has at all times been aware of their segregated nature and has done nothing to seek their merger, or to charter integrated locals since the passage of the Civil Rights Act."[99]

In 1893, Joseph Cuney opened a law office in Galveston after serving as chief clerk for the United States Customs Service.[100] By 1895, several other Black lawyers established practices in Galveston.[101] Wilford Horace Smith arrived around 1895. Smith was a native of Mississippi. In 1901, his office was located at 420 20th Street according to an advertisement in the *City Times*, May 18, 1901, 4. On the same date an advertisement can be found for Dr. L. M. Wilkins.

Smith had practiced law in Greenville, Mississippi, for eight years after graduating from Boston University's law school in 1883. "In 1901, Wilford Horace Smith became Booker T. Washington's personal attorney, and with Washington's encouragement and support, he was designated by Washington as the legal strategist to challenge the laws of Alabama which excluded blacks from voting."[102]

Smith was the first Black lawyer to appear before the United States Supreme Court.[103] He prevailed.[104] Smith was also counsel to Marcus Garvey—the head of the Universal Negro Improvement Association (UNIA) based in New York—and Booker T. Washington, who was in Tuskegee, Alabama.[105]

In other words, Smith did what good lawyers do. He represented a diverse clientele, oftentimes with different views on important societal issues. Marcus Garvey and Booker T. Washington were on opposite polar ends of the political spectrum. It can readily be assumed Wilford Smith understood the importance of protecting others' rights.[106]

J. Clay Smith recounts Wilford Smith left Galveston in 1905 and moved to New York. "With the departure of Wilford H. Smith from Galveston in 1905, Cornelius J. Williams, Allen G. Perkins, and Joseph Cuney assumed the burden

Figure 18: Central High faculty. Photographer unknown, date unknown. (Part of collection date 05.24.2002; contributed by Robert Hoskins Esquire, 1980. Anthony P. Griffin Collection.)

of civil rights litigation in the area. They fought a local ordinance excluding blacks from riding White streetcars."[107]

"Between 1895 and 1920, the following Black lawyers practiced in Galveston, Texas: Cornelius J. Williams, Joseph Cuney, Allen G. Perkins, J. Vance Lewis, Alex Green, Henry H. Swanson, Allen D. Bridge, Webster Wilson, M. G. Lewis, M. H. Broyles, John H. Barbour and Thomas H. Dent."[108] Considerable evidence exists that lends credence that Smith remained active in both New York and Texas after 1905.[109]

In 1920, African Americans made up about 21 percent (11,123) of Galveston County's total population of 53,150.[110] The bulk of the population was in Galveston (44,300); the remainder of the county was sparsely populated.

Central High School was established in 1885. It was the first African American high school in the state of Texas. It was established for the purpose of "providing higher educational opportunities for the colored in a free public school in the city of Galveston, Texas. In 1904, an annex to Central High was built."[111] Central High School and grades 6, 7, and 8 occupied a structure on 15th Street and Avenue N from 1889 to 1893. After 1893, a new two-story building was erected on the corner of 26th Street and Avenue M.[112] In 1905, the Colored Branch of Rosenberg Library was placed on the site, opening on January 11, 1905.[113] This location is the current location of the Old Central

Cultural Center.

In 1913, the sorority Delta Sigma Theta was founded. Izola Collins observed, "The National American Woman Suffrage Association (NAWSA) was trying to get the Susan B. Anthony amendment passed, sponsored a march on the evening before Woodrow Wilson was inaugurated as president. An internal dispute arose surrounding participation in the march with the sorority, Alpha Kappa Alpha (AKA). The dispute caused a split and the formation of Delta Sigma Sorority. Jessie McGuire Dent of Galveston was one of twenty-two founding members of the organization."[114] Jessie McGuire was the daughter of Robert McGuire and Mabson McGuire.[115] McGuire was a graduate of Central High, graduating in 1908. She thereafter attended Howard University in Washington, DC. After graduation, she returned to Galveston to teach English and Latin in Central High in 1913. In 1924, Jessie McGuire married attorney Thomas Dent.

In 1943, Jessie McGuire Dent brought a lawsuit against Galveston Independent School District because the district's standard practice was to pay Negro teachers a salary that was twenty percent less than that of White teachers because of their race. She prevailed in the case. Thomas Dent Jr. was born of the union of Thomas Dent and Jessie McGuire Dent. He died in 1940 at the age of eleven. Jessie McGuire Dent passed on March 12, 1948. Thomas Dent Sr. passed in 1998.[116]

A March 28, 1914, advertisement informed the Galveston public Maud Cuney Hare was scheduled to perform in Galveston on March 31, 1914, at the Lincoln Theatre [Ave D Lincoln Theatre, 413–15 25th].[117] She was accompanied by W. H. Richardson, a baritone. Tickets were available at the Oleander Drug Store located at 417 25th Street. Walter A. Davis was the pharmacy's general manager.[118] At the time of Maud Cuney's initial tour, she had already penned a book about her father, *Norris Wright Cuney: A Tribune of the Black People*. The book was on sale at Purdy's Bookstore, at 2217 Market, Galveston, Texas.[119] Purdy was located a block down from Pullman's Café for Colored People, located at 507 25th Street: "This Café will have things first class for the colored people."[120] The book's publication was noted in the *City Times* in July 1915.[121]

On February 22, 1922, Maud Cuney Hare returned to Galveston. She performed at Wesley Tabernacle Methodist Church. She was again accompanied by W. H. Richardson, who also lived in Boston.[122] Their other engagements included performances in both Carolinas, Georgia, Florida, Louisiana, in addition to concerts in Washington, DC, and New York City. Maud Cuney Hare was the daughter of Norris Wright Cuney[123] and Adelina Cuney. She was born on February 16, 1874, in Galveston, Texas.[124] She was a graduate of Central High in 1890. After Central, she attended the New England Conservatory of Music in Boston. She studied piano and music theory.[125] After completing her studies at the New

England Conservatory, Cuney attended Harvard, where she studied music privately and took courses in English literature. At Harvard, she met W. E. B. Du Bois. The two were engaged for a period of time. After their engagement ended, Maud Cuney returned to Texas.[126]

Maud Cuney went to work as the director of music at the Texas Deaf, Dumb, and Blind Institute for Colored Youths in Austin, Texas, from 1887 to 1898. In 1897, she was scheduled to appear at the Austin Opera House. She cancelled the appearance because the Opera House administrators refused to integrate the house. She rebooked at the institute.[127]

Tuberculosis claimed her mother on October 1, 1895, and her father on March 3, 1898. Tuberculosis also left her brother, Lloyd, incapacitated.[128] Maud Cuney was married briefly to Dr. J. Frank McKinley. They lived in Chicago and had one child during the marriage. Maud Cuney moved back to Texas and worked as a music instructor at Prairie View A&M before moving back to Boston. In Boston, she met William P. Hare; they married on August 10, 1904.[129] In 1908, her daughter died at the age of eight. Maud Cuney Hare died in 1936 at her home in Boston.[130]

Maud Cuney Hare's contributions included: editor of a column for *The Crisis* (the NAACP magazine also edited by her former fiancé W. E. B. Du Bois); published articles for the periodicals *Musical America*, *The Christian Science Monitor*, *Musical Quarterly*, and *Musical Observer*;[131] publication of a collection of *Six Creole Folk-songs* with commentary in 1921; writing and producing a play in 1929; and founding the Allied Arts Center in Boston (W. E. B. Du Bois was one of her sponsors; she served the center as its director).[132] Her book, *Negro Musicians and Their Music* (1936), represented a lifelong dedication to music and her race.[133]

> The African tom-tom, the drum, although not always used as a musical instrument, is of unusual importance. It is claimed that in a hot climate, the older the drum gets, the tauter the string becomes. The method of tuning is by placing the instrument over a fire to contract the skin or in water to expand it.
>
> . . .
>
> The African tom-tom has had parallels abroad. Daniel Alomia Robles, a Peruvian musician and archaeologist, has a flute which was found in one of the old tombs in Peru. Among the old Inca instruments, some of which are over 3,000 years old, is a 5-string harp. Of the 4-note instruments, the scale was found to be Re, Fa, Sol, La, though later enlarged by the interval of a third, which is a complete Inca pentatonic scale. Mr. Robles claims this is in advance of the Greeks. As we know, this Inca music, later absorbed by the Spanish, was again

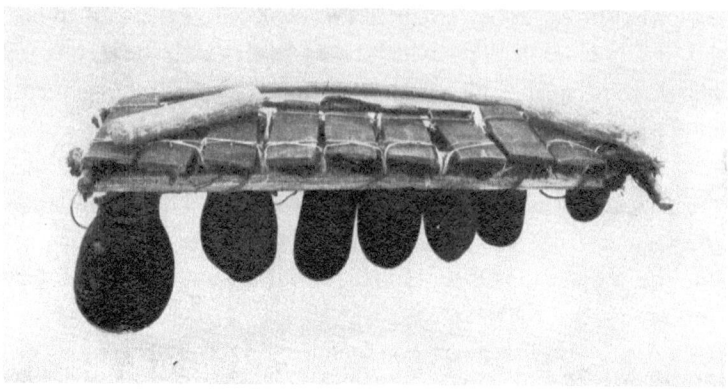

Figure 19: Marimba. (Public domain.)

modified by African influences. In this the "marimba," or xylophone—a native African piano—was an important factor.[134]

If Maud Cuney Hare is considered a starting point for the arts, she also provides a guidepost in discussing others' work. Those listed below should absolutely not be considered exhaustive but representative of a sampling of colored/Negro/Black/African American artists and musicians originating from Galveston whose work helped to prove the ultimate point of the initial search, the focus of chapters 9–11, and the proposals set out therein.

Camille Howard: Her birth name was Deasy Browning; she was born on March 29, 1914, in Galveston, Texas. She was the daughter of Cecilia Hines and Samuel Browning.[135] Howard was also known as Camille Agnes Browning and Camille Browning Howard. She died on March 10, 1993, in Los Angeles, California. Browning was a rhythm and blues singer and pianist "who first came to prominence in Roy Milton's Solid Senders in the 1940s."[136] During her teens, she was a member of a local group called the Cotton Tavern Trio.

By 1935, she was performing as a club musician in Galveston. She moved to Los Angeles in the early 1940s. Her first hit, under her own name, was in 1948 called "X-Temporaneous Boogie," which reached number 7 on the R&B chart and sold close to a quarter of a million copies. She toured "with Roy Brown, Little Willie John, The 5 Royales, and Joe Tex."[137]

Dr. Frederick Tillis: Frederick C. Tillis was born on January 5, 1930. Dr. Tillis died on May 3, 2020.[138] Dr. Frederick C. Tillis graduated from Wiley College; he received his BA at the age of 19. He later received an MA and PhD in Music Composition from the University of Iowa. His catalog includes more than 125 compositions and commissions, spanning both jazz and classical European traditions in various media—orchestral, jazz, instrumental, choral, chamber music,

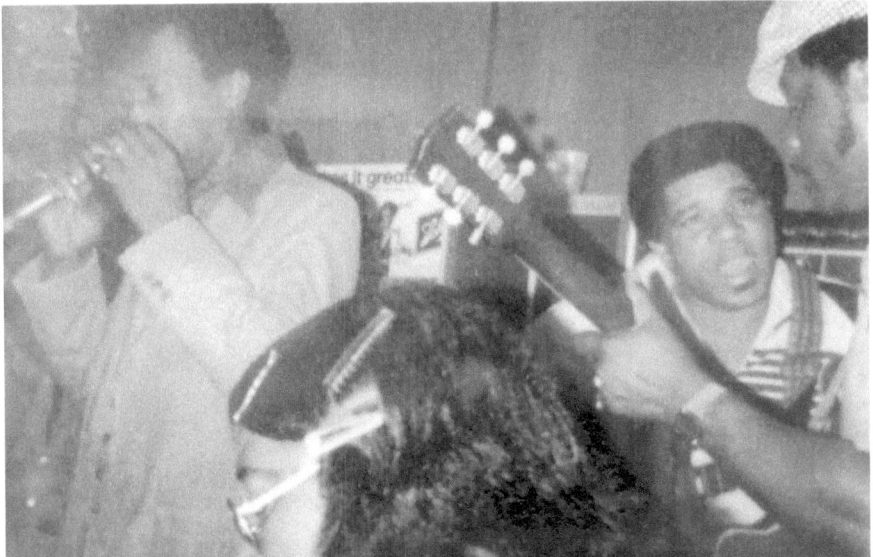

Figure 20: *The Day That I'll Always Remember*. Photographer unknown, date unknown. (Part of collection date 01.15.2005; contributed by Matlene Finch. Anthony P. Griffin Collection.)

and vocal works. Melodic and harmonic textures reflect elements of various music of the world, including Asian and Western cultures, as well as natural outgrowths of his ethnic and cultural background.[139]

He was the recipient of numerous honors and awards, including the 1997 Commonwealth Award from the Massachusetts Cultural Council and an award for outstanding service from the International Association of Jazz Educators. As a professor of music at the University of Massachusetts, he taught music composition and a survey course in the history of Afro-American music & musicians.

Beginning his professional performing career at the age of 12 as a jazz saxophonist, he traveled with the Tillis-Holmes Jazz Duo and the Tradewinds Jazz Ensemble to Australia, Austria, Belgium, China, England, Fiji, France, Germany, Greece, Italy, Japan, Luxembourg, Mexico, Netherlands, New Zealand, Poland, the former Soviet Union, Switzerland, and Turkey.[140]

The *Galveston Daily News* noted of Dr. Tillis:

> Dr. Tillis was a proud son of Galveston, born January 5, 1930. His mother was Zelma Bernice Gardner and his stepfather, General Gardner.[141] He was a graduate of the public Galveston schools including Central High School. . . . His musical talents were recognized at a very early age by his mother and by his music teacher and mentor Mr. Fleming Smizer Huff. Mr. Huff played the trumpet and that inspired Dr. Tillis to learn the instrument.[142]

Figure 21: *Florence & Izola, 1944*. Photographer unknown. (Part of collection date 05.24.2002; contributed by Izola Collins. Anthony P. Griffin Collection.)

Figure 22: Izola and Roy Lester Collins Sr., 1951. Photographer unknown. (Part of collection date 05.24.2002; contributed by Izola Collins. Anthony P. Griffin Collection.)

After his retirement from UMass, Dr. Tillis traveled back to Galveston in 2000 to perform at Reedy Chapel, AME. The program was dedicated to his mother.[143]

Izola Collins: *The Houston Chronicle* characterized Izola Collins as both a musician and an educator.[144] *The Chronicle* was right—she was a third-generation educator and musician. "Born in Galveston on Oct. 26, 1929, to a family of educators, Collins graduated from the segregated Central High School at 14 and from Prairie View A&M University at 18. She was awarded a master's degree in music from Northwestern University in Illinois. Izola was a gifted musician and played trumpet with an all-girl jazz band that toured the East Coast while attending Prairie View."[145] Izola was born on October 26, 1929, to Viola C. and Brister Fedford. She died at the age of 82.[146]

"As a lifelong member, pianist, and organist of Galveston's Reedy Chapel, A.M.E. Church, Collins is passionate about musical storytelling and theological import of Christian hymns."[147] During her career as a teacher, she taught in Bay City, Hitchcock, and the Galveston Independent School District. She served as band and choir directors in each district. She taught in Galveston for 20 years with a specialty in music.[148] In 2002, Collins and other female students were honored by

Prairie View A&M for their serving in the all-girls band in the 1940s. "They were known throughout the country and were compared to the Darlings of Rhythm and other famous groups of their time."[149] They performed at dance halls, military bases, and the Apollo Theater. On September 4, 2016, Izola Collins directed the Galveston Symphony in the performance of the symphonic composition *Galveston Survives* at the 1894 Grand Opera House.[150] She was the founding director of the Galveston Heritage Choral Choir.[151]

Esther Mae Jones: On Esther Mae Jones's death the *New York Times* wrote: "The blues singer Esther Phillips, who got her start with Johnny Otis and was acknowledged by the Beatles as a major innovator of rock, died today in U.C.L.A.-Harbor Medical Center in Torrance, Calif. She was 48 years old and had been ill for some time."[152] Esther Phillips was born Esther Mae Jones and performed under the name of Little Esther Phillips, later as Esther Phillips. She was the child of Lucille Green and Arthur Washington.[153] The website Discography describes her as a soul and blues singer. She started singing when she was fourteen.[154] Her parents divorced when she was a child; she spent time in Houston with her father and with her mother is Los Angeles.[155] Esther Phillips died on August 7, 1984.[156]

Louis Prince Jones Jr.: Louis Prince "Blues Boy" was a blues singer, musician, and songwriter. He was born in Galveston, Texas on April 28, 1931. His parents were Rebecca Prince Jackson and Louis Jones Sr.[157] Jones was drafted during the Korean War under the name of Louis Prince. He served as a medic. In his early life in Galveston, he worked as a longshoreman. In his mid-twenties, he changed his name, adopting his biological father's surname Jones.[158] Jones was the lead singer of two bands. The second band was called Louis Jones with Bobby Scott Orchestra. They toured with noted artists Jerry Butler and Otis Redding in the 1960s. The City of Galveston approved a section of 37th Street to have an additional name: Louis Blues Boy Jones Street. On August 12, 2015, the mayor signed a proclamation declaring April 28th of each year to be "Louis Blues Boy Jones Day."[159]

Barry White: "Barry Eugene Carter, commonly known as Barry White, was a three-time Grammy award winning singer, songwriter, producer, and arranger. His music focused primarily on funk, rhythm and blues, soul, and disco. Over the course of his career, he generated 106 gold and forty-one platinum albums, twenty gold and ten platinum records, and accrued sales in excess of 100 million records."[160] He was born in Galveston on September 12, 1944, to Melvin White and Sadie Carter. He was raised by his mother. At the age of three, she moved him and his brother to South Central Los Angeles where he was raised.[161]

Why mention this artist if he left Galveston so early in his life? The answer is simple: a child sees the world through possibilities, emulating the success and determination of others who look like him or her. Tapping into their individual

Figure 23: *The Idle Wyle's—The Annual Picnic, with Their Wives and Sweethearts*, July 3, 1938. Palmer Studios. (Part of collection 05.24.2002; contributed by Patricia Ann Tate. Anthony P. Griffin Collection.)

talents, whether the talent is math, English, or music. It is not a question of the talents leading to wealth and fame; the point is the broadening of the disenfranchised and disadvantaged's view of the world and of themselves. Barry Eugene Carter's (and others') success and triumphs in turn enhance the given community of the child's birth, thus the power of history.

White also enjoyed success as an actor, providing voice-over performances for animated films and television shows, including *The Simpsons*. His voice was in demand for commercial work, and he did spots for cars, restaurants, and other products. He was featured in person on the television show *Ally McBeal*, which also featured his music prominently.[162]

Celestine Beyoncé Knowles-Lawson: Célestine Ann Beyincé was born in Galveston on January 4, 1954.[163] Her parents were Agnéz Deréon and Lumis Albert Beyincé. This artist/entrepreneur's contributions: a fashion designer known for establishing the brands House of Deréon and Miss Tina by Tina Knowles. She helped launch the careers of her children, Solange and Beyoncé Knowles.[164]

CHAPTER 10

In an interview with the artist, *USA Today* shared a story told by the entrepreneur:

> Knowles-Lawson does not spell her last name the same way her other relatives do. According to the businesswoman, only she and her brother, Skip, spell their last name B-E-Y-O-N-C-E, while, for others in her family, it is spelled B-E-Y-I-N-C-E.
>
> When Knowles-Lawson asked her mother about the discrepancy, her reply was simple: "That's what they put on your birth certificate."
>
> "So, I said, 'Well, why didn't you argue and make them correct it?'" Knowles-Lawson said[,] "And she said, 'I did one time, the first time, and I was told, 'Be happy that you're getting a birth certificate,' because at one time Black people didn't get birth certificates."[165]

On July 3, 1938, the Idle Wyle's 7th Annual Picnic with their wives and sweethearts took place at City Paty Park, Galveston, Texas.[166]

What was the name of the park? City Paty or City Party? Where was the park located? Who were the Idle Wyles?

In 1932 there was a debate over where to place a proposed colored park in the city of Galveston. An article appeared in the *Galveston Daily News* that provided a bird's-eye view of the colored populations in the city at the time, identifying the areas in which the population was at least 70 percent Negroes.[167] The article is instructive:

> [T]he proposed site for a negro playground selected by the city commissioners, and which is the basis of the special election January 27 gives an idea of the sections of the city which are predominantly occupied by Negroes.[168]
>
> The present predominantly colored areas, which are practically seventy percent (70%) or more inhabited, are the following areas: Avenue A to C, 12th to 17th streets; Avenue I to F, 26th to 46th street; Avenue K to M 1/2, 10th to 14th streets; Avenue L to N 1/2 (varying), 26th to 35th street; Avenue K to M 1/2, 51st street to 57th streets.
>
> Beach front area now used by colored: Boulevard to R, 28th to 29th street (bath house); Boulevard and 10th street; Boulevard and 10th (bathing only), no construction.
>
> One can find colored living practically in every neighborhood in Galveston, with one exception. This exception is an area predominantly white which lies west of 39th street and south of Broadway (Avenue J) (exclusive of the colored area K to M 1/2, 51st to 57th streets). This predominantly white area was established by Galvestonians, realizing the necessity and need of such an area, having restricted the major portions of this area for exclusive white use.

Figure 24: *The Working Girls' Social Club*, April 2, 1942. Palmer Studios. (Part of collection date 01.01.1995. Anthony P. Griffin Collection.)

The proposed west end park was from land sold by Dr. R. T. Stanton, who sold the city one-half of his land. The other half of the site the city proposed to take by eminent domain.[169]

On April 21, 1942, the Working Girls Social Club had its Fourth Anniversary Spring Banquet. The president of the club was Julia Allen, a sister of Augustus "Gus" Allen.[170]

The Working Girls' Social Club's event occurred at the Virginia Pavilian [*sic*]. When did the Working Girls' Social Club come into existence? Does the organization still exist? If it doesn't exist, when did it cease operation?

The photographer of the above and previous images was John E. Palmer, whose pictures documented Black Galvestonians' daily activities and celebrations during the time he lived in the city.[171] Palmer moved to Galveston in 1916. He lived in the city for forty-eight years. His business's name was Palmer Studios.

The *City Times* reported on October 17, 1917, John Palmer attended a meeting of Galveston Colored Men's Business League. The meeting was in the office of Dr. L. D. Davis 2513 1/2 Market Street. "New members received Prof. Thos. H. Love and Mr. Wm. Woods."[172] Other businesspersons noted in the report: C. J.

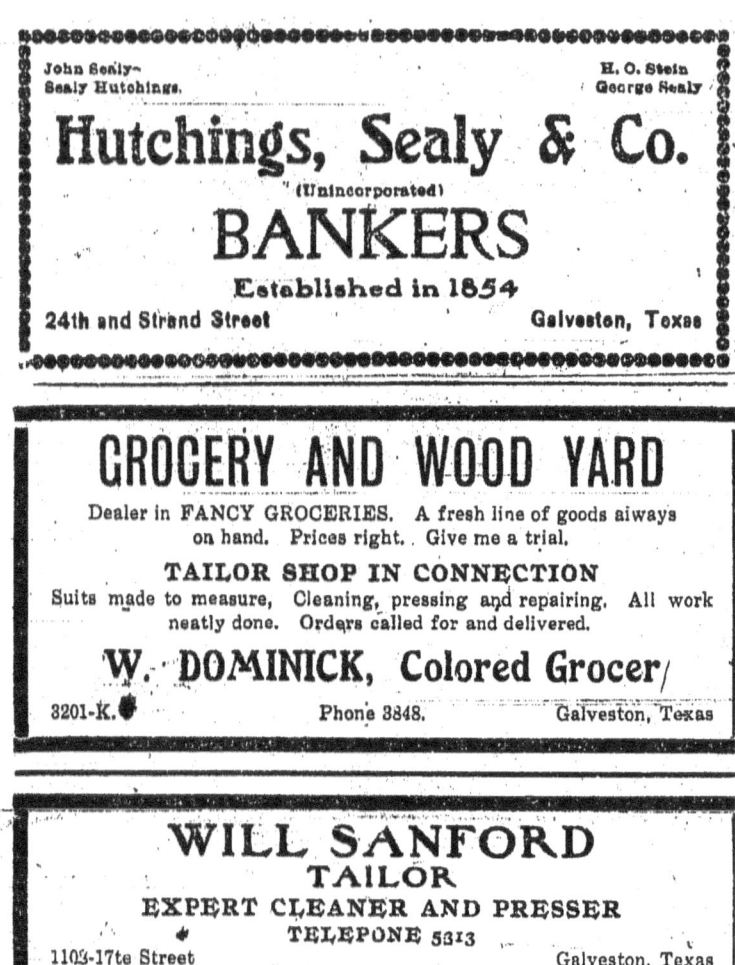

Figure 25: Hutchings, Sealy, etc. ads. *City Times* (Galveston), December 8, 1917.

Reedy, Thos. E. Hall, Will Sanford, Dr. L. D. Davis, John L. Lewis, J. E. Palmer, W. Dominick, F. E. Stewart, H. McKenna, R. A. Mills, W. C. Hollinsworth, J. S. Lewis, W. T. Price, W. H. Noble Jr. A Women's Auxiliary meeting was scheduled to meet at the same location the next day, with the men's next meeting on Monday night, November 5, at the Thos. E. Hall office at 2601 Mechanic Street.[173] Did the Colored Men's Business League and the Women's Auxiliary cease operation with the demise of Black businesses on the island and/or the population moving elsewhere? How long did the Colored Men and Women's Business League stay in operation?

John Palmer was born in 1891 in Many, Louisiana. He died on March 7, 1964.[174]

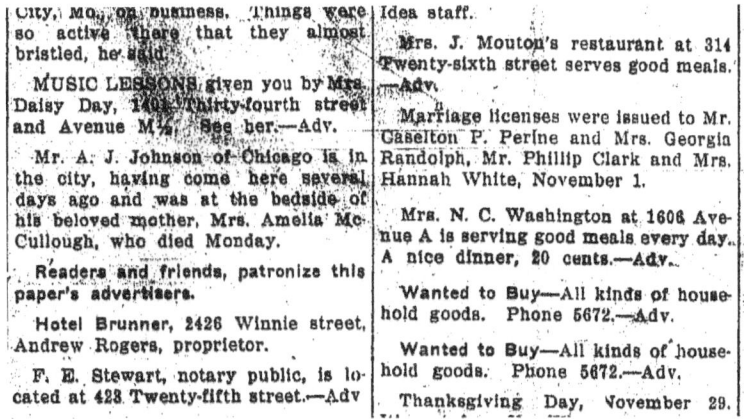

Figure 26: F. E. Stewart, Mrs. J. Mouton's restaurant & Mrs. N. C. Washington ads, *City Times* (Galveston), November 10, 1917, 1.

At one time, there existed numerous African American businesses in the corridors between 25th and 28th Street. Why are these corridors of commerce not recognized and cherished the same as others? I am willing to bet there were craftsmen in their ranks. Fortunately, the Black press at the time left indelible imprints in the sand to track the businesses' existence. More is needed, however. A community's history can be tracked through oral histories, pictures, and deed records. Shon Arthur, the current owner of Busy Bee Cab Company, identifies the company as the oldest Black business in Texas. Is this true? What additional information is needed to reestablish this history so as to document the struggles and successes of minority businesses on the island? Judge Pope's records yielded a picture of a social club wherein her mother was a member. What is the history of social clubs on the island? After the retrenchment and hostility that exploded around the country from 1915 to 1921, how did this retrenchment affect the island and other communities throughout Texas?

Even in context of being able to retrieve the information from various archives, the reality remains we have failed as a community in assuring African American businesses share in the wealth this island has created for others. Our community should not continue to feel comfortable with the assumption that Blacks are/were not productive, contributed nothing to the island, existed in a small area on the island, or that the island would be better served with a smaller Black population.

After the retrenchment (the post-Reconstruction period), segregation became the law of the land. No attempt will be made to identify state by state how this separation played out. One could readily argue segregation was an exclusive Southern malfeasance. Other evidence, however, forever gets in the way: membership exclusion, national loan policies, housing policies, and redlining belies the attempt to

CHAPTER 10

Figure 27: Galveston chapter of the Circle-lets. Sitting, L–R: Doris Thompson, Vicki Taylor, Lynne Nita Pope, Natalie Douglas. Standing, L–R: Georgia Cashin, Thelma D. Armstrong, Lillian Ross, Janice Stanton, Marie Mosely, Jeanette Ward. (By permission of Penny Pope.)[176]

blame only the South for this disease. This is much like the previously discussed mythology that only the Southern states benefited from human slavery.

During segregation, Blacks were prohibited—to a greater extent—from travelling and if they did travel, their families were forever endangered by a hostile America. *The Negro Motorist Green Book* (*Green Book*) was a byproduct of these societal conditions.[177] *The Green Book*, 1947, provided some evidence of these conditions.

The following Galveston properties were listed in 1947 as providing a respite for the Negro traveler: "Hotels: Oleander—421 1/2 25th Street; Restaurants: Mitchell's—417 25th Street; Tourist Homes: G. H. Freeman—1414 29th Street; Mrs. J. Pope—2824 Avenue M; Cotton's—2907 Avenue L; Taverns: Gulf View—28th and Blvd."[178]

Mrs. J. Pope would be Rachel Pope. Rachel Pope who was married to J. Pope, a Galveston police officer. J. Pope's first name was Joe. He and his brother, Thomas, both appeared in the newspaper in 1908 advertising their businesses.[179]

Figure 28: Rachel Pope. (By permission of Penny Pope.)

Reginald Pope is Rachel Pope's son. He married Lynne Nita Pope. They had three children: Penny Lynne Pope, Reginald Pope Jr., and Reggie Nelle Pope. Both Reginald and Lynne Nita Pope were teachers in the Galveston Independent School District. Daddy was the physical education teacher at Central back in the fifties, then he taught at Goliad Junior High, which was located between Thirty and Thirty First Street, the south side of Broadway.[180] The property was purchased by the Galveston Housing Authority, which put in place low-to-moderate income housing. Mother was a math teacher and Assistant Principal at Goliad. Goliad was the one Black junior high school. There were three White junior highs: Weiss, Lovenberg, and Stephen F. Austin.[181]

Galveston's schools integrated in 1967–1968; at that time, Penny L. Pope was in the tenth grade and transferred to Ball High School. Her father, Reginald Pope, moved from his school to Ball as the assistant principal. Penny L. Pope recounted, "George Washington Carver and Booker T. Washington were the Black elementary schools between 1930 and 1950. I do not remember their locations. One was located on the block next to the football stadium and when they tore the school down years ago, nothing has ever been built back to replace the building."[182] The land is still owned by the school district.

• • •

Conversation with Judge Pope

Q. What changes have you most noticed about Galveston since your childhood?
A. [Penny Pope] [laughter] . . . I don't know. Wait, I can tell you a couple of stories. The carnival came to Galveston once a year for two weeks. They set up on the seawall, at the bunkers, where the San Luis Hotel is located. Daddy used to bring us to the carnival and park on the seawall across the street. We would sit in the car and just look. I would always ask, "Why are you bringing us here and we can't go across the street and ride the rides?" Daddy never said anything.
Q. Did you, your brother [Reginald] and sister [Reggie Nelle] ever get to ride the rides?
A. Yeah, the last day. The last day was the only day when black kids could ride. The last day the carnival was in town. The other thirteen days, only the Whites could go. [Laughter.] So, one change is, we can go to the carnival now.

• • •

Anita Barksdale was my mother's mother. She was also an educator. The home for travelers was located between 28th and 29th Street on Avenue M 1/2. My great-grandfather, J. Pope, died before I was born. My great-grandmother died when I was 5. Coming from a family of educators I attended Texas Southern University and obtained degrees in government and secondary education (1976). I also went to Atlanta University to obtain a master's in political science (1983). I attended South Texas College of Law in Houston and obtained a law degree (1988). I graduated in 1988.[183]

Figure 29: Marie Harderman's second-grade science classroom, Booker T. Washington Elementary School, September 1957. Sheila Roque is located on the second row, second child from the left. The teacher, standing, is Marie Harderman. (By permission of Sheila Roque.)

• • •

In *The Green Book*, 1954, the following Galveston properties were listed: Hotels: Oleander—421 1/2 25th Street; Gus Allen—2710 Avenue F; Tourist Homes: Mrs. J. Pope—2823 Avenue M; Taverns: Gulf View—28th & Blvd.; Night Clubs: Manhattan—2802 Avenue R 1/2; Barber Shops: Imperial—1814 Avenue O 1/2; Garages: Sunset, 2928 Avenue H.[184]

The Green Book, 1963–64, listed the following properties: Gus Allen Hotel—2710 Avenue F; Little Shamrock Motel—1207 31st Street; Oleander Hotel: 421 1/2 25th Street; Tourist Home: Mrs. J. Pope, 2824 M 1/2 Avenue.[185]

Gus Allen Café was located on the northern half of block 387 on the corner of Church and 27th Streets (2702–2704 Church Street). Gus Allen Hotel was across the street.[186] Were the takings by the city and other governmental entities contributing factors in the demise of landownership and the appreciable decline in the Black population?

If one were to conduct a survey of Galvestonians, few would know this history, particularly as related to persons and businesses of color. Even if requested to take an educated guess, most of us would not know the businesses' locations/addresses in the city. The deterioration of the African American business community and population is not tied solely to integration, particularly when integration did

CHAPTER 10

Figure 30: Restrooms sign. (Anthony P. Griffin Collection.)

not take place until three generations later. Out-migration because of diminishing opportunity, violence, the misuse of eminent domain, the failed promises of Reconstruction governments, and local and statewide Jim Crow laws have contributed to these conditions. Galveston was not exempt from these societal maladies. These are some of the reasons the search for the locations of auction houses was imperative.

And what about our institutions of faith?

There is scant historical recognition of our existence on the island as evinced on the plaques placed in front of the houses of worship. As previously written, the practice is to mislead or mask over history. This section briefly discusses religious institutions and the insidiousness of the institution of slavery. The churches were willing participants and benefited financially. So that it is clear, this section is not designed to diminish the importance of these institutions of faith—this last statement is this author's way of not being slapped silly by his grandparents, on both sides, looking over him as he writes, ready to strike him at any moment for his transgressions. However, the dichotomy between considering human beings as things of value and praying for the enslaved's salvation is the vortex in which religious institutions participated, particularly in the slave trade and molding laws to protect their investment.[187]

In the book *Five Hundred Thousand Strokes of Freedom*, Wilson Armistead estimated the "number of people of colour in the New World" was 12,370,000. "Of those, seven million and a-half are in slavery in United States, Brazil, and Dutch colonies; one quarter of a million in [the] process of emancipation in South American republics; and the remainder, four million six hundred and twenty thousand, are free."[188] In addition, Armistead sets out the religious denomination, number of ministers, members, and "the total number of slaves held by Ministers of the Gospel and Members of different Protestant Churches."[189]

Slaves Held by Ministers of the Gospel and Members of Protestant Churches

Denominations	Ministers	Members	No. of Slaves
Methodists	5,080	1,178,637	291,563
Presbyterians	3,264	333,458	77,000
Baptists	6,598	812,921	125,000
Campbellites	----	----	101,000
Episcopalians	1,404	67,550	88,000
Other Denominations	----	----	50,000
Total			660,563 [*sic*]

"The denominations above cited under their control 80 colleges, with 5,495 students, and 26 theological seminaries, with about 700 students. Some of these colleges and seminaries have been built and endowed partly by the sale of slaves, and all are looking for slaveholding patronage."[190]

Armistead's documentation was designed to persuade the slave holding countries slavery was untenable, at a time the institution was full-fledged.[191] No attempt is made to document every instance where institutions of faith have grappled with the duality created by its support of slavery. The purpose of this brief section is to point out that, without documentation and recognition, we will remain captive to this history until and unless we recognize how faith has been indeed duplicitous. This is something as simple as the songs we sing, the prayers we pray, the images we display, and as complicated as the active participation in the slave trade (owning, buying, selling, mortgaging) setting up the conditions, including theology, to continue the debasement of the enslaved.

Avenue L Baptist Church on 2612 Avenue L, Texas's oldest Baptist church, "organized initially in 1840, it was comprised of five members, all who were slaves. The church was known as the African Baptist Church. The land was donated by First Baptist Church trustees, John S. Sydnor, Gail Borden, Jr. and Reverend James Huckins in 1855."[192] The Rev. I. S. Campbell became the pastor in 1867 and organized the church as the First Regular Missionary Baptist Church. In 1891, a new building was erected; the 1900 storm destroyed this structure. The current name of Avenue L was adopted between the years of 1903 and 1904.[193]

The mood of Baptists toward slavery began to shift to a more regional perspective by 1831. In the mid-1820s, Richard Furman, a prominent pastor from South Carolina, forwarded a document to the governor defending slavery as biblically sound and beneficial to Blacks. This became one of the first shots fired by Southerners in defending the institution. What had been a "necessary evil" now became protected as a positive good. In the North, William Lloyd Garrison, who had a strict Baptist upbringing, began his uncompromising attacks on the institution in 1831—in Virginia, Nat Turner, a slave and self-styled Baptist exhorter, was about to sow terror into the hearts of Southerners with his bloody rebellion later that same year. The polarization of Baptist opinion paralleled that of the nation. The formation of the American Baptist Anti-Slavery Convention in 1840, followed by the American Baptist Free Mission Society the same year, began the schism that resulted in the creation of the Southern Baptist Convention in 1845. Although slavery was not the only reason for the split, it was the primary reason and became a harbinger of Southern secession from the United States fifteen years later.[194]

Absolutely, there was a north-White divide with respect to slavery; by way of example, this divide led to the establishment of the Southern Baptist Convention and ultimately influenced the development of faith institution on both sides of the Mason–Dixon Line, Black and White institutions alike. One 1857 committee urged Whites to attend Black gatherings "in order to aid and give character to such meetings and to prevent any disorder that might otherwise occur."[195]

The Texas State Historical Association website fails to tell us fully about the donors who helped form Avenue L. "In Galveston, pastor James Huckins was accused of violence toward his slaves. A letter from member George Fellows to 'Brother Sawyer' stated that he (Fellows) [c]ould not listen to preaching, with profit where the remembrance of sound of the sighs and groans of the slave of Mr. Huckins will wring [sic] in my ears . . . from the hands of her master, a minister of the gospel. . . . Huckins' slave ownership may have been partly responsible for creation of the Southern Baptist Convention as Baptists in the North refused to condone such a practice by missionaries."[196] Huckins was also involved in the establishment of Baylor University.[197] Baylor University in 2020–2021 started the process of addressing this hidden and/or previously unspoken history.[198]

At the inception of Avenue L:

> Business was usually conducted under the watchful eye of whites, but the business was that of the blacks. First Church, Galveston, allowed the most freedom for black members. Slaves joined that congregation only eleven days after its

inception, and in 1852 African Americans constituted the majority. By then, they had already reorganized themselves into the African Baptist Church under the direction of a white leader, David B. Morrill. Although they were granted a semi-autonomous status, they remained under the guidance of the original congregation. In July 1851 black members elected their own deacons: James (Hall), Isaac (Boswell), and Luke (Hall). A year later, Matthew (Crozier) was chosen to replace Isaac. Both James and Luke Hall were freemen, perhaps indicative of the extent of license allowed to black congregants. This liberty was further enhanced by the acquisition of a lot in 1855, deeded by a white member, Judge J. P. Cole. Although the white pastor and others remained in attendance, the minutes stated in 1856 that the "Coloured members of the Baptist Church met at their house of worship," and the business they conducted, particularly of a disciplinary nature, was brought by their own deacons. The minutes noted that in 1859, the African Americans chose the Reverend James Langley (a white man) as their pastor.[199]

John Sydnor's history has previously been recounted, no need to repeat the same in this section. "Gail Borden was a wealthy businessman and inventor who was instrumental in beginning one of the first newspapers in the state. . . . [Borden] served as alderman and secretary of the Galveston City Company. He was also collector of customs for the Republic at the Port of Galveston."[200] Gail Borden's papers tell of his involvement with and ownership of slaves.[201] The United States census of slave schedules reveals Borden in 1850 as having six enslaved, in 1860 none.[202]

Another example would be the foundation of Wesley Tabernacle United Methodist on the island. Wesley Tabernacle United Methodist Church is located at 902 28th Street.

> The Reverend Peter Cavanaugh organized the church in 1869 as an independent congregation. Church members met in a one-room house between 38th and 39th on Broadway. . . . After losses of church buildings to fire and 1900 Storm, a one-story building was erected. In 1924 the church was remodeled by raising the building and constructing a new first floor. The new construction gave the building a unique combination of architectural styles.[203]

At its founding in 1785, the Methodist denomination was explicit in calling for emancipation. But thereafter the church grew quickly. So quickly that it was the largest denomination in the United States by 1840. As they evangelized in slaveholding areas, Methodists compromised—in 1800, the church shifted to calling for "gradual emancipation, in 1808 local churches were allowed to make their own rules 'regarding buying and selling slaves, and in 1824, slaveholders were gently encouraged to allow slaves to attend church.'"[204]

By 1844, the problem could no longer be avoided. The leadership took a vote, condemning the slave-holding bishop.

> James Osgood Andrew . . . asserted that his slave Kitty refused freedom because she loved her owners so dearly. Northerners argued that a slaveholding bishop was the last straw, the most offensive of a long series of slaveholding demands. Andrew responded that he held a slave "legally but not with my own consent." This argument conveniently ignored that Andrew had a long history of slave ownership and just that year had married a woman who brought at least 14 additional enslaved people to his household. Nonetheless, Andrew was offended that his private affairs were a matter of discussion, objecting to "impertinent interference [by antislavery Northerners] with my domestic arrangements."[205]

Andrew had been elected bishop by the General Conference of 1832 and "many northern delegates were concerned that holding slaves would undermine the moral authority of a bishop functioning outside of slave territory."[206] The Methodist Episcopal Church was the forerunner to today's United Methodist Church. The separate denominations that resulted—the M. E. Church and the M. E. Church, South—were separated by a border that stretched some 1,200 miles, a good portion of which passed through the state of Virginia. Years later, after the split in northern and southern divisions of the church, the United States Supreme Court, in the case of *Smith v. Swormstedt*, permitted the southern division of the church to share disputed funds.[207]

Holy Rosary Parish, 1422 31st Street:

> Holy Rosary was the first African American parish in the South, with Texas's first Black Catholic School. Holy Rosary was established in 1886 in a small cottage at the corner of 12th and Avenue K. In 1927, a high school curriculum was added to the school program. This was the first accredited Catholic high school for African Americans in the state of Texas. Holy Rosary School closed its doors on May 28, 1979.[208]

The Jesuits recently vowed to raise $100 million to atone for their role in slavery. "This is an opportunity for Jesuits to begin a very serious process of truth and reconciliation," said the Rev. Timothy P. Kesicki, president of the Jesuit Conference of Canada and the United States. "Our shameful history of Jesuit slaveholding in the United States has been taken off the dusty shelf, and it can never be put back."[209]

The intensive involvement of religious institutions is seen in the infrastructure put in place to process the enslaved:

> Cape Coast Castle was built in the 1650s and passed through Swedish, Danish, and Dutch possession until becoming a headquarter for British colonial administration in the 1660s. Africans were taken from their homes and held in dungeons at the castle, with squalid, overcrowded conditions and little ventilation. It was one of 50 castles on Africa's west coast, 39 of them in Ghana, that served as points of embarkation for slave ships. An estimated 12 million to 25 million Africans passed through Ghana's ports to be sold across the Atlantic as slaves.[210] These castles served as places in which church was held while "enslaved people were beneath crying out in agony, starving, [Anglicans] were having a church service."[211]

What do we make of religious institutions being also part and parcel of the skeleton of the institution of slavery, institutions that admittedly were formed to pacify the slave? These conclusions are not this author's but are supported by religious institutions' internal documents and history's tales and are repeatedly demonstrated as the enslaved were placed in both North and South America and the Caribbean. Grandiose plans by Galvestonians to place slave colonies in Mexico, Nicaragua, and Cuba weren't particularly new or unique ideals but an idea implemented repeatedly throughout the New World, sometimes successful, other times not—guns in one hand, faith in another—to subjugate those enslaved. Our duality—our faith has worked for us and against us in telling these histories. Some of the schools and faiths whose development and wealth were established off Black bodies are beginning to open their records, admitting to the financial benefit these centuries of subjugation have brought them. Whether these admissions are also being done in the name of the Gods is not within the province of this author.

> Out of the worst of systems, or the most deplorable of events, Providence may often bring results full of promise. But let not the planter who holds the slave, or the minister of religion who supports him in it, imagine that the wrong he does is any the less wrong because good may sometimes arise out of it. Let him not flatter himself that even if God did pronounce a curse on Canaan and so make slavery the inevitable lot of the negro (a question we do not care to argue), he will look with a gracious eye on those who make themselves the ministers of his will that they may promote their own selfish interests.[212]

- Baltimore, Maryland: Baltimore Episcopal Church, which was founded by slaveholders in the 1860s, says it will spend $500,000 over the next five years to establish a fund intended as reparations for slavery. Members of Memorial Episcopal Church in Bolton Hill voted to set aside $100,000 to donate to community organizations doing "justice-centered work."[213]

- Washington, DC: Georgetown University, run by the Jesuits, sold 272 slaves to save the university.[214] Georgetown announced it would raise $400,000 yearly for a goal of $1 billion for reparations for the descendants of the 272 slaves. Of course, the difficulties lie in identifying accurately the heirs.[215]

- New York, New York: The Episcopal Diocese of New York. "The New York Diocesan Reparations Committee was created by the 330th Diocesan Convention in response to three 2006 General Convention resolutions calling on dioceses to respond to the transatlantic slave trade and its aftermath of segregation and discrimination. The role of the Reparations Committee is to collect and document information on the complicity of the Diocese of New York in the institution of slavery and its subsequent history of segregation and discrimination. The committee will consider the benefits the Episcopal Church derived from the institution of slavery and collect, through documentation and storytelling, information on historical and present-day privilege and under-privilege in order to discern a process toward restorative justice. The Committee's findings will help to determine whether the diocese is called to conduct a truth and reconciliation process regarding the legacies of racial discrimination and oppression."[216]

- Hampton, Virginia: "No Episcopal parish has been a witness to a longer span of American history than St. John's Episcopal Church in the heart of this coastal city's downtown. . . . Also in 1619, the settlers here were witness to the first arrival of enslaved Africans in British North America. The story told by Jamestown colonist John Rolfe describes '20 and odd Negroes' who were taken ashore at nearby Point Comfort and sold for supplies. That transaction only hinted at how slavery soon would dominate the economy and the social life of Virginia and slaveholding communities like Hampton. Black chattel slavery was codified in Virginia law in the second half of the 17th century and began to surge, replacing White indentured servants as the preferred labor source for tobacco cultivation. In Hampton, Black residents, most of them slaves, made up nearly half or more than half of the population throughout the antebellum period."[217]

CHAPTER 11

HISTORY'S VOICES CONTINUE TO CIRCLE

Stopping the Deterioration and Loss

The information and stories preceding are merely a small part of history's tales: there are names omitted, persons not interviewed, locations obscured, family albums and records lost to floods, natural disasters, neglect. Displacement, out-migration, memories that have faded—always, always, always fading—with time, age, illness, and death. Sometimes the lost is based on destruction, neglect, and political and wrongheaded policy decisions that have affected the community in a disparate manner. Sadly, other times history has been lost because of ignorance and/or not understanding the importance of same.

This history should be part and parcel of the stories told to visitors and islanders alike. It is also this author's position that these past and present histories should be told and funded with the same vigor as we do for others' tales. We as a community should take bolder, more substantial steps—leaps perhaps—to tell the truth about Galveston's substantial involvement in the slave trade and the location of the auction houses. This would be in homage to those who stood still, in rooms large and small, by the water, in pens on streets bustling with commerce—indeed in strange places. If we do not talk about all of the places we've been, we will forever tell only part of the story, creating pure and utter fiction—as needed—to patch holes in the well-worn and historical narrative. Bill Moyers' notion of the fatal lie is apropos—telling an incorrect story. It seems abject silence is the same as creative lying.

Galveston is a unique community, but it is no different from other Southern port cities (the importation of slaves and serving as a center of commerce for the distribution of those human souls to other parts of the country). Galveston is also not unique in its failure to recount this history fully.[1] This author contends Galveston lags in efforts to correct and address this historical malady. It seems appropriate to comment on other communities' efforts to address this history.

- Cambridge, Massachusetts: Harvard University, a private institution, recently released a report finding slavery was "inseparable from the University's rise to global prominence, and included enslaved individuals on campus, funding from donors engaged in the slave trade, and intellectual leadership that obstructed efforts to achieve racial equality."[2] The president and corporation dedicated $100 million to implement recommendations of the university's findings.[3]

- Stone Mountain, Georgia: Stone Mountain, the mountain park near Atlanta with a giant carving of Confederate leaders, is proposing changes. "The park 15 miles (25 kilometers) northeast of downtown Atlanta is a popular hiking and tourist destination but is replete with Confederate imagery, including a colossal sculpture of Gen. Robert E. Lee, Confederate President Jefferson Davis and Gen. Thomas J. 'Stonewall' Jackson on the mountain's northern face. It is the largest Confederate monument ever crafted." The park's CEO, Bill Stephens, explained, "'The proposal was not going to satisfy everyone,' but he called them a 'common sense middle ground.' The park has lost corporate sponsors and revenues are down, he said."[4]

- Charleston, South Carolina: Much like Galveston, Charleston was a port of entry for the enslaved, importing and enslaving millions of souls for work in the sugar cane and rice plantations that surrounded the city and the port. Charleston is home of the oldest free museum (Charleston Museum)[5] in the United States, and it possesses an extensive collection of historical documents unveiling the contributions of slaves to the wealth of the city and its people. The community has raised more than $100 million to construct the International African American Museum.[6] "[Gifts Officer Ginny] Deerin said IAAM also is netting $3.4 million from New Markets Tax Credits, a federal initiative meant to attract private investment and stimulate community development and economic growth in distressed communities. That total takes into account a $14.4 million allocation from TD Bank that was just announced this month." The debate that took place in the low country is *our* debate and the purpose of this book. Recognition of the past, while also never forgetting the present.[7] Charleston's International African American Museum opened on June 23, 2023.

- Memphis, Tennessee: There was a $10 million restoration of "Cobblestone Landing, the largest stone-paved riverfront wharf in the country. Completed after the Civil War, it was used for loading cotton and timber, but in earlier days, enslaved people were made to assemble there. A nearby throughfare was called Auction Avenue before it was renamed A. W. Willis Avenue, after the civil rights lawyer, in 2008. Parks that glorified the Confederate leaders Jefferson Davis and Nathan Bedford Forrest have also been renamed, with statues of the two removed in 2017."[8]

- Los Angeles, California: Getty Conservation Institute and the Office of Historic Resources within Los Angeles's Department of City Planning announced the launch of African American Historic Places Project, a three-year initiative to identify and preserve landmarks that represent Black heritage across L.A. "The goal of the project is to more accurately reflect the history of the city."[9] The *Los Angeles Times* reported the cooperation between Getty and the city began as early as 2005. "In 2018, after the deaths of Breonna Taylor and George Floyd, the Office of Historic Resources developed a model to guide preservation work in Black communities, using themes including civil rights, visual arts, and religion and spirituality."[10] Getty and the city intend to soon launch a search for a project leader and will convene an advisory group from the Black communities. According to a Getty spokesperson, the organization is contributing about $500,000 toward the project.[11]

- New Orleans, Louisiana: New Orleans has a $10 billion annual tourist economy. "Visitors to New Orleans in 2019 spent $10.05 billion, a 10.3 percent increase over 2018, according to D. K. Shifflet & Associates' (DKSA) reporting."[12] The City Council in 2017 voted to remove the Confederate statues, declaring the statues as a "public nuisance."[13] New Orleans is also home of Tremé, a historic, predominantly African American community just north of the French Quarter.[14] Tremé is recognized as a historic district by the National Register of Historic Places.[15]

- San Antonio, Texas: San Antonio Community Archive and Museum plans to move out of its current location and set up shop downtown (in the Kress-Grant building). This is an anticipated $40 million investment. The complex will contain a cultural center, a 500-seat auditorium, and a working lunch counter. The anticipated move is in 2026.[16]

- Fort Worth, Texas: The National Juneteenth Museum intends to open in 2025. The museum is a "key part of an effort to revitalize Fort Worth's Historic Southside neighborhood."[17] The City of Fort Worth has pledged $15 million of the total fundraising goal of $70 million.[18]

- State of Maryland: "For the past decade, the Maryland General Assembly has authorized $1 million annually for the African American Heritage Preservation Grant Fund, which provides grants for projects that restore and preserve African American history in the state. But last year the state quintupled its contribution, upping funding to $5 million to be spent on buildings, communities and sites that are integral to Maryland's African American experience."[19]

National Register of Historic District/African American Neighborhoods:

- Mound Bayou Historic District, Mississippi: "Mound Bayou differs from communities in the surrounding area because of its history as a municipality founded by, developed and governed by African Americans. Although the range of building types, whether commercial, institutional, or residential, would be similar in neighboring communities such as Merigold or Winstonville, none of these other communities feature resources like the I. T. Montgomery House or the Taborian Hospital which link Mound Bayou with the African American experience in the Mississippi Delta during the 'segregation era.'"[20]

- Paine College Historic District: Augusta, Richmond County. Georgia Paine College Historic District in Augusta, Georgia was listed in the National Register of Historic Places on December 26, 2012. At the time of its listing, "Paine ... join[ed] the 2,072 listings from Georgia on the national register."[21]

- American Beach Historic District: Nassau County, Florida American Beach was developed as an oceanfront resort for African Americans on the south end of Amelia Island, Florida, in 1935.[22]

- Sherwood Equal Rights Historic District: Cayuga County, New York. "The district is historically significant because of its association with numerous social reform movements popular during the mid to late nineteenth century, including issues related to abolitionism, the Underground Railroad, women's rights and education."[23]

- Richmond, Virginia: Capital of the Confederacy Richmond is home of Jackson Ward, a historic African American neighborhood. Jackson Ward has been recognized and listed as a National Historic Landmark District. This occurred in 1978.[24] Richmond, too, has undertaken the long-overdue removal of the tributes to the Confederacy, removing more Confederate statues than any other community.[25]

- Emmett Till's Funeral Site: Chicago, Illinois. "The Chicago church that hosted Emmett Till's funeral. The theater in Cleveland that is the oldest African American producing theater in the country—where Langston Hughes once had an in-house apartment. The sole remaining Black owned and built historic building along Southeastern Ohio River Valley's Underground Railroad corridor. These are just a handful of the 40 historic sites across the country that will receive a portion of $3 million in grant funding for preservation today."[26]

Admittedly, the second portion of this manuscript provides little of the period between 1945 and 1963 (the period between World War II and the second civil rights movement—the first civil rights movement was after the Civil War,[27] the second in 1963).[28] In addition, there is sparse information from integration to the present. These omissions were intentional and are the subject of further storytelling and research.

Public accommodations, voting, protests, the inequitable distribution of resources, inequitable taxation, theft of land and wealth by hook or crook, vice, and scheme have always been part of the struggle and will remain part of the struggle. This has been a historical struggle indeed and documentation is needed in every community. By way of example: recently the City of Palm Springs formally apologized for its city's action in the 1960s, wherein the city wrongly evicted, demolished, and burned out residents within a one-square-mile area of downtown known as Section 14.[29] The majority of residents in Section 14 were Black. The city wanted the land for development purposes.[30] "A 1968 report prepared by California Assistant Atty. Gen. Loren Miller called the destruction, most of which took place two to three years earlier, a city-engineered holocaust." The destruction began in 1959 and continued through 1966.[31]

Did I say race is an artificial construct? I think I did. Did I say the challenge in this century, too, remains the color line? I did not. . . . W. E. B. Du Bois did—a century ago. His observation still resonates.

Years ago, an old man—whom this author knew only as Shed—approached and held his hand out to me. I held mine out to him. He deposited a handful of old coins and prayed for me to tell these stories and ultimately tell his own. I accepted the coins and requested the privilege of looking through his picture album. Death interceded. I never did see his pictures. I remain in possession of those coins. I write this to say, there remains much work to be done—through pictures, artifacts, stories, and writings. Time is not our friend in this context.

At different points in this work, the use of language and words may have been difficult to translate. Sometimes this is because of colloquialism, other times cultural. It is the author's hope one is not insulted when the common use of pronouns was deemed inadequate to express *our* commonality. By way of example, sometimes in conveying history or expressing findings, I used "them" or "they." These references mean exactly that—*them* and *they*. No, no, not in a Southern sense, but in the ordinary context. As this work developed, the pronouns varied and changed. These references were directed at a collective people, pointing inward, meaning *our*, *us*, a given community. The author also recognizes our cultural canyons may be too wide or deep and words inadequate to explain anguish and fear, which remain a persistent stain and byproduct of slavery's inhumanity. This may forever remain nonsensical, confusing, opaque. I pray it does not.

History can be dynamic, static, revealing, hurtful, sad. I write this to say, history and recounting history can be deemed emotional, attacking, and yes, again hurtful. Absolutely, I have a personal stake in the topic. I expressed this early on—I saw it coming when drafting, writing, proofing, worrying. Honestly, history tells us that we all have a personal stake in the enslavement of others. I hope the documentation provided in this book, accompanied with futile swings at objectivity, while enveloped and surrounded with words, brings home this point.

Isabel Wilkerson explains, "While all the countries in the New World created hierarchies with Europeans on top, the United States alone created a system based on racial absolutism, the idea that a single drop of African blood, or varying percentages of Asian or Native American blood, could taint the purity of someone who might otherwise be presumed to be European, a stain that would thus disqualify the person from admittance to the dominant caste."[32] The consequence of this system of racial absolutism has been devastating to our communities and societies. Jean Guerrero tells a poignant and touching story of her Puerto Rican grandmother hiding from her, for years, that her mother was African. "She was beautiful and undeniably Black, with dark chocolate skin. '*Tu mamà arà afro-puertorriqueña*,' I said.[33] Abuelita Coco's face crumpled. 'Her skin was as white and as beautiful as mine,' she replied in Spanish, lifting her shirt to expose her pale belly. When I replied that there is nothing wrong with being Black, her eyes filled with tears. Perhaps her mother was 'trigueña,' or wheat-colored, she said. But she certainly wasn't *Black*."[34]

Nothing in this manuscript is intended to engage in the debate surrounding what percentage of the population owned slaves. "My parents didn't have slaves... none of this affects me." I have listened to this exclusionary, "don't bother me," language, over the years. I forever wanted to provide a more complicated answer: Slavery, race, and the color line are far more detailed than owning slaves.

Old news? Not relevant? Why do you bother?

Telling the story of Maud Cuney Hare, Izola Collins, Rachel Pope, Julia Allen, Penny Pope, and Georgia does not threaten one's maleness or make men an endangered species. African American athletes have passed by cameras and audiences from time immemorial, saying hello to their mothers. This behavior is historically grounded: Black women are and remain the glue to our survival. The stories of women should be told equally. When Martin Luther King Jr. stood to deliver his speech at the march on Washington, we can never ignore the contributions of the women—known and unknown, who outnumbered the men—who made the march successful. This, too, should be part of our truth. Mahalia Jackson didn't necessarily (even though her comments were part and parcel of the call and recall of the church) want to be heard when she demanded of Martin, "Tell them about the dream, Martin."[35] We heard her.

Telling these stories allows others to know more of a strange breed of people—Southerners—of differing colors and hues, relatives, kin, somehow invariably connected by their language, music, genetics, stories. Told and untold tales, the tale of skin tones, hair textures, noses, eyes, mannerisms.

The oft-times silent story—of rape, a necessary story for each of us to rethink and reposition our view of women and their bodies. Remember, the dividing lines of race and color are artificial constructs. The biological difference between men and women is not artificial. The adage of "it is her body" should apply equally to a woman of color. Our historical treatment of women is and should be part of our examination.

Speaking the truth of Galveston's first Black lawyers permits others to see the fallacy of another artificial construct—this notion of the "firsts." Gil Scott-Heron said it best—or sang it best—reminding us that others before us have traveled the same road. We should henceforth never let the history of silence and ignorance continue to control the discussion. We must study, tell these stories, and recognize the term "the first" reinforces the mythology of a false history. Oh, what our forebears have bequeathed us and we simply don't know.

CHAPTER 11

We as a community should be proud of those newly freed souls, those in the medical profession who attended medical schools and colleges after the Civil War, who came to this community to provide medical care. They successfully matriculated and came to Galveston looking for opportunities. They traveled to Galveston to form their own group. These men clearly saw Galveston as the ideal place to organize. They visited the city and held their conventions here for at least the first eight years. Did you know their organization still exists to this date? Telling this story permits us to tell other stories, including those of Drs. Rufus Hezekiah Stanton, Robert Thurston Stanton, Rufus Hezekiah Stanton Jr., Herman A. Barrett, and the modern-day heroes of color—men and women—who have matriculated from the University of Texas Medical Branch at Galveston and other institutions. Today, medical students should not come to or leave the island without knowing this history.

So . . . we danced! So . . . we sang! So . . . we have been disobedient.

We are an impudent, insolent bunch who have never hesitated to disagree. Maybe it was the water: Heman Sweatt (unspoken about herein), Eldrewey Stearnes (also not mentioned), Jessie McGuire Dent (briefly covered), and Linda Arceneaux are all part of this strange breed of negroes (said with affection, even in the lower case) whom the island's sun and water nurtured. The water cries. It also nurtures.

While conducting this research, I didn't initially notice the subtle changes that were occurring with me internally: anxiety, thinking too much, flights of thought. I initially thought the changes were normal until the night I dreamt of the man who was dragged out of the slave house, stabbed repeatedly, and watched his abductors move him downstairs and to the street to hang him in downtown Galveston. When his severed head was retrieved, it was used to play soccer/football on the Strand the next day. I was awakened by my own screams and slamming my fist into the headboard. I initially wondered at the source of the noise until I saw my fist still balled. The pain assured me of what had occurred. I rolled around in the bed until morning—sleeping, not sleeping, thinking. I continued to read and found more lynching—before and after Granger's order—documented lynchings in the city and an untold/told number of Southern-style lynchings of Black people after the Great Storm of 1900.

No more than a month after slamming the headboard, I was awakened by words that moved involuntarily from the recesses of thought to lips—over, over, and over again, audible, inaudible. This new behavior forced me out of the bed. I retrieved paper from the bureau and scribbled—two, three, four pages of barely readable script. I then moved upstairs to a computer to type out a disjointed and frightful poem. This new behavior was accompanied by tears and a compelled blindness—barely able to see because I typed in the dark, not turning on any additional lights as I typed. I read the scribble the best I could to complete the compelled poem; this, too, was the byproduct of my internal struggles—seeing men, women, and children treated as chattel and auctioned to the highest bidder, feeling my great-grandparents' touch, hearing their voices, and understanding more why the water cries. Some of the stories will always create anguish and make us cry—I now understand this—man's inhumanity to man does this. Muh Chest nodding and Georgia's insistence to always think and use your brain made sense. These stories are necessary, too. They allow us to move forward while never forgetting. History repeats itself, doesn't it? We do forget, don't we?

We must retain the talented folks who flee to other communities to sing, dance, practice—seeking their fortune, or even just practicing their craft. New Orleans would be Disneyland if its colored palette were wiped clean, removing its musicians, musical history, and culture. We should establish venues and encourage the arts, permitting our children to remain in place—for our stake and survival, for history's sake. We as a community need to correct the ever-persisting deficiency of exporting talents to other communities. Bragging and explaining he/she was born in Galveston is not enough. This admonition also applies to medicine, the field of architecture and design, and to those who wish to study the universe, the sciences.

On the other hand, the unwitting musings by the FBI agent after the 1921 labor strike serves as the counterbalance—a compliment to the community (our community) and the gift to those men's heirs. Being impudent, insolent Negroes and having a government agent so concerned he was compelled to document, in his case report, the relationship of those working men meant the theoretical concepts of equality had a chance to work. And gosh—there is frankly nothing wrong when those colored workers were bold enough to convey a firm insistence they were equal to others. Think and read carefully: this paragraph is not quite the expression of the happy, happy Negroes and Negresses. The FBI agent's words were what they were, intended as an alarm, a warning.

When I read that the educational institution Howard University thought so much of Norris Wright Cuney it bestowed an honorary degree upon him, I was ashamed of our community for never bragging and telling this truth. This is a fact that should be part of the historical lore of this community. A by-rote exercise it should be ($1 + 1 = 2$; easy, isn't it?). Indeed, this, too, is something none of us tell. I blushed with embarrassment when I discovered he—Norris Wright Cuney—started a stevedoring company in Galveston, organizing and providing opportunity to Galveston colored longshoremen; also remember, Cuney travelled to both New Orleans and New York looking for business. One of the areas of law in which I practiced for years was labor law, representing unions, Locals 851 (integrated local) and 329 (Black union, cotton-headers). What we don't know is frightening; I didn't know any of this.

Figure 31: L–R: Sharon Baldridge Lewis, Ellis Bernard Baldridge (father), Dorothy Corine Baldridge (mother). (Contributed by Sharon Baldridge Lewis. Anthony P. Griffin Collection.)

When I completed reading Maud Cuney Hare's books and academic papers, I was incensed for not knowing. I can still see Izola's eyes watering. I always wondered whether she was crying for us or whether they were tears of pride.

When I read Professor Wells's *Kidnapping Club*, I saw the tears of my elders and the persistent fear of living under and in apartheid America. Unable to stop on Texas highways at most locations—being preached to by your elders when moving—to and from, to and from, to and from: "be safe." Theirs was a defined and palpable worry. This is the importance of *Green Book* sites and Debbie Allen's father (Augustus Allen) and Penny Pope's great-grandmother (Rachel Pope). This historical terror should never be permitted to be stolen and appropriated by Hollywood, by anyone. I heard joy in Debbie's voice when I called and was inquisitive over the phone. She didn't know I wanted to hug her and wanted to be hugged.

Reading about Norris Wright Cuney having to sue to achieve victory when he ran for city council, followed years later by Charles Scott Jones's alleging election irregularities when he ran for the Galveston College's board, is something I wish I knew when litigating on behalf of Willie Moore. Willie Moore ran for a Galveston County Commissioner position. Moore's name disappeared from the ballot on election day during the morning hours. The error was supposedly corrected after lunch. The mistake never seemed inconsequential or happenstance to me.[36] The same happened to Sharon Lewis when she first ran for the Galveston City Council.[37]

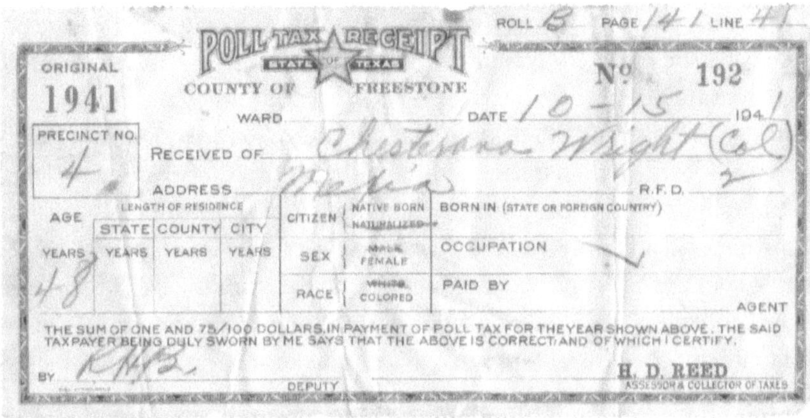

ROLL B PAGE 141 LINE 41

POLL TAX RECEIPT

STATE OF TEXAS

ORIGINAL 1941

COUNTY OF FREESTONE

No. 192

WARD DATE 10-15 1941

PRECINCT NO. 4

RECEIVED OF Chesterana Wright (Col)

ADDRESS Mexia R.F.D. 2

AGE	LENGTH OF RESIDENCE			CITIZEN	BORN IN (STATE OR FOREIGN COUNTRY)
	STATE	COUNTY	CITY	NATIVE BORN / NATURALIZED	
YEARS	YEARS	YEARS	YEARS	SEX: MALE / FEMALE	OCCUPATION
48				RACE: WHITE / COLORED	PAID BY

AGENT

THE SUM OF ONE AND 75/100 DOLLARS IN PAYMENT OF POLL TAX FOR THE YEAR SHOWN ABOVE. THE SAID TAXPAYER BEING DULY SWORN BY ME SAYS THAT THE ABOVE IS CORRECT AND OF WHICH I CERTIFY.

BY RHB DEPUTY

H. D. REED ASSESSOR & COLLECTOR OF TAXES

Figure 32: Poll tax, Chesterana Wright. (Anthony P. Griffin Collection.)

The right to vote is one thing we have never gotten right in this country, and Galveston's history is replete with the same practices occurring much too often to colored candidates. The institution of slavery was never dismantled completely: patched, mended, papier-mâchéd, maintained by fear, terror, lynching, repressive laws (Jim Crow), historians, storytellers, words, lies, half-truths, and deceit. Perpetuated by the miseducation of the public—derisively—telling of the Negro way, lack of accomplishment, or flat-out refusing to report about our community at all. The passage of restrictive laws,[38] redistricting, and violence have their modern-day extensions of an inhumane, entrenched social, cultural, political system—never disappearing.

One last point: the whole purpose of this exercise would be futile—or in vain—if it is not understood that our history is greater than the four hundred years of enslavement. Telling Albert and Lillian Wright's story was never anticipated when this journey began. Their story was compelled, by the living and dead, the seen and unseen—floating, talking, disturbing periods of rest, worrying too much, while voices and images floated overhead. Part of the worry is rather simple—how does one explain the importance of words used when such words are historically laden? When these words and terms have been used century after century, designed to dehumanize the subject of the inhumanity? The same words are used unwittingly and wittingly to limit any full discussion and research. The question when writing was how this history has been told and retold, reconstructed, and protected. It seems to me everyone is comfortable in discussing this history when the discussion is within the confines of a clearly defined and constrained box.

The previous constrained telling of Galveston's role in the slave trade is nothing more than a continuation of the Southern tradition of wiping our hands clean.

By way of example, in 1991, Gary Cartwright, a well-known Texas journalist and Galvestonian, wrote: "Slaves had never been a major factor in Galveston's economy, so the issue of slavery was more emotional than real." This statement was written in context of his citation to the news article concerning the hanging of the unnamed man (slave) and the kicking of his head down the Strand. It is my hope—by now—this myth will no longer withstand the disinfecting qualities of light.[39]

Absolutely, it is more comforting telling this story by ignoring history's persistent whispers and to pretend the images floating above are imaginary. History has shown our previous practices were not a particularly healthy exercise. Believing what we believe, even without foundation, is something this author cannot control and frankly, at the point of terminus, this represents an impossible entrenched and stained position, allowing one to appreciate brother Benjamin Franklin's observation.[40] However, this author does not possess the guile of Benjamin Frankin and positions this is why so much time was spent in this work addressing why we as a society must act.

One more example of how invasive the institution of slavery has been to our lives: I was raised in the Baptist church. One of the most ingrained memories I possess was the music—solemn hymns, sung in a low, graceful manner—shared anguish enhanced by low baritones, moans flowing downward, upward, outward in unison, filling the chapel.

Words flowing, pew to pew, high, low, high. Some hands clasped, others wayward, shaking vigorously, pointing upward—each set of hands sincerely captured by the sound, the moment. Oh, how I loved the shared hymns—a cultural treat, when done right, grabs even the sinners like me. So, we sang a song born out of the stained institution, written by a former slave trader.[41] Oh, how duplicitous this all is—our skin tone, colors; how we are categorized by others and ourselves; how we live, where we live; our life expectancies, and life stations that remain influenced by these crimes against humanity. It is a constant predictor of life's successes and failures, defining the outline and contours of the history we share, even defining the songs we sing. We still sing.

> Amazing grace how sweet the sound
> That saved a wretch like me
> I once was lost, but now I'm found
> Was blind but now I see.

It is my hope we do better in expressing, appreciating, and documenting this shared history and realize we will remain captive if we do not do so. I hope I have not failed.

CHAPTER 12

ABOVE AND CIRCLING, ALWAYS PRESENT

A Proposal for a Dedicated Historic District

I obtained the boundaries for Old Central/Carver Park from a neighborhood plan prepared by the City of Galveston Transportation and Planning Department years ago. The boundaries were designated as follows:

The Old Central area is in the North Central section of the City of Galveston. Its boundaries are Ave. M to the South, 35th Street to the West, Mechanic and Church Streets to the North, and 26th Street to the East. This neighborhood is adjacent to the central business district and the Port of Galveston.

The Carver Park area is located in the northwest portion of Galveston. Its boundaries are Ave. L and M on the South; Post Office and Church Streets to the North; 53rd and 54th Streets to the West and 35th Street on the East.[1]

A proposed designated historic district contemplates a district being carved out of Old Central/Carver Park neighborhood lines but does not include the entirety of Old Central/Carver Park as set out above. The proposed district contemplates encompassing both the north and south sides of Broadway.

The importance of district boundaries is based upon the importance of

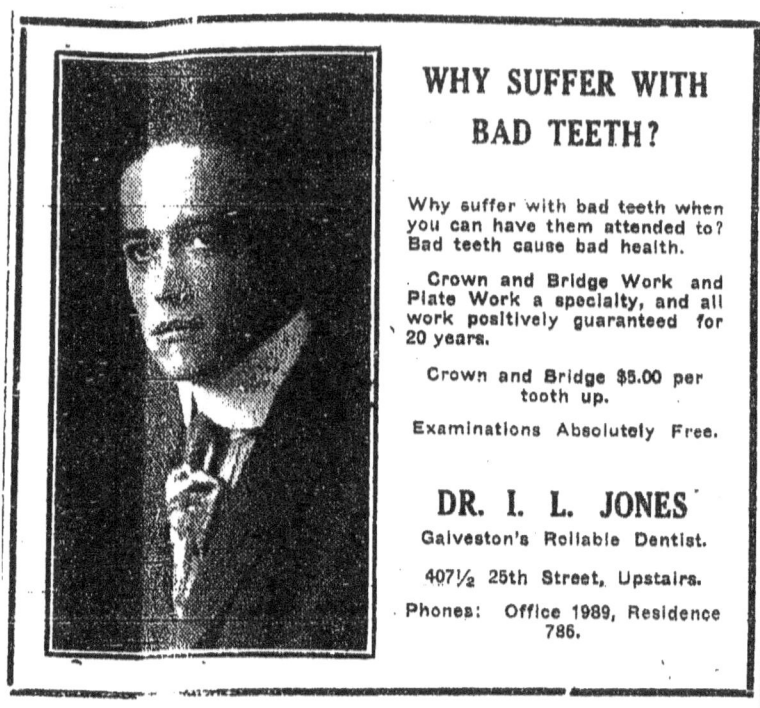

Figure 33: Dr. I. L. Jones ad. *City Times* (Galveston), January 14, 1922. (Public domain.)

addressing history in different forms: Attorney Joseph Cuney, with a listed address at 1519 Mechanic, was outside of the district. When he moved to 421 24th Street, he was just a few blocks away. Dr. William Willis, a dentist, at 426 25th Street and Postoffice—inside the district. Dr. L. M. Wilkins's physician and surgeon's office would be inside the proposed district. The Lone Star Screwman Hall at 2710 Market Street would be inside the district. Dr. Wilkins had an additional office at 3505 Avenue L, just outside the district. The Sons of Ham Brass Band (D. M. J. Sanders, manager) located at 314 26th Street was outside the district, while the developer—F. E. Stewart, 2722 Market Street (advertisement for the sale of land in La Marque, Texas, "controlled by colored men"), is an address inside the district; he also at one time took out an advertisement for notary public services at 423 25th Street. [2]

Lewis Melton's office, located at 24th and Market (2420 1/2), is just outside the district. Dr. I. L. Jones was located at 407 25th Street, inside the district. Maud Cuney's book was on sale at Purdy's Bookstore—2217 Market, Galveston, Texas—which falls outside the district. Purdy was located a block down from Pullman's Café for Colored People, which was located at 507 25th Street.[3] Purdy should be located in the proposed district.

Figure 34: Ad, *City Times* (Galveston). Idle Wyle's Club, Galveston, Texas. Grandparents of Patricia Ann Tate, Charles and Hilda Ayred (back rear, center). Date unknown. (Anthony P. Griffin Collection.)

The Gus Allen Hotel and Gus Allen Café were located in the district. The Henry Beissner House is included in the district, in that it is located on Ball between 28th and 29th Streets. Gus Allen Dog Park would be included, although this author does not understand why a dog park would be named after Gus Allen. The author's confusion is on par with not understanding why an originally segregated city park would be named after Norris Wright Cuney when the city, over the years (since the 1930s), has neglected and underfunded this park in comparison to other city parks. Gus Allen openly complained about the use of eminent domain to take from him his property north of Broadway—and his only tribute a dog park. It is this author's hope that, by now, the reader sees the pattern and the historical insult.

When referencing the *Green Book*, all the businesses listed from 1947 to 1964 fall inside the proposed district. This district picks up Kermit Courville Stadium, Old Central High School, and the Colored Branch of the Rosenberg Library (where the park is dedicated to Jack Johnson at the rear of the property), and Jessie McGuire/Menard Park/Robert McGuire's Bath House.

CHAPTER 12

Figure 35: *Behold I Send You Out as Sheep in the Midst of Wolves*. Photographer unknown, date unknown. (Collection date 05.24.2002; contributed by Sharon Baldridge Lewis. Anthony P. Griffin Collection.)

In the context of the historical houses of worship, the proposed historical district takes in the following: Wesley Tabernacle (902 28th Street), Jerusalem Baptist Church (2717 Avenue H), Compton Memorial Church OGIC (2628 Avenue H), St. John's Baptist Church (2917 Sealy Street), Live Oak Baptist Church (1020 32nd), West Point (3003 Avenue M), Avenue L Baptist Church (2612 Avenue L), Macedonia Missionary Baptist Church (2920 Avenue M 1/2), Shiloh A.M.E. (1310 Martin Luther King Blvd.), and Holy Rosary (1420 31st Street).

Remember, *City Times* provided detailed reporting of the colored businesses on the island in 1909. The *Galveston Daily News* reported the political dispute surrounding the placement of a Black park in a White area of town.[4] For purposes

Figure 36: *Reedy Chapel, We Rejoice.* Photographer unknown, date unknown. (Part of collection date 05.24.2022, contributed by Izola Collins. Anthony P. Griffin Collection.)

of this chapter, a map is not drawn; this would be the province of a cartographer, the same process used in redistricting litigation, identifying blocks and streets, carving out certain sections, excluding others.

Reedy Chapel A.M.E. (2013 Broadway) would fall outside of the district but should be in it—the same mapping technique (roadway only) recommended to encompass Menard Park should be used for Reedy's inclusion. The district lines can be drawn to avoid becoming too encompassing and to avoid threatening areas now part and parcel of other historic district(s). The district should be structured to avoid areas now fully gentrified.

Galveston Colored Men's Business League initially had its meetings in the office of Dr. L. D. Davis at 2513 1/2 Market Street (inside the district).[5] A Women's Auxiliary Meeting was scheduled to meet at the same location the next day.[6] Thos. E. Hall's office was located at 2601 Mechanic Street and the grocery store and woodyard of W. Dominick all lay inside the district.[7]

The bulk of the history recounted in this document was unknown by the author when this quest for auction houses began. Even with this effort, the project is incomplete.

As this project moves forward, treasures and histories will unfold, additional secrets and stories revealed. However, do not consider the last statement as an admission that there is not enough information, history, structures, or areas of commonality to create and carve out such a district. The creation of the Old Central/Carver Park Historic District (OCCPHD) is compelled. This is the first step.

The author has not met with representatives in the City of Galveston (planning officials and elected officials), the historical community, Galveston Historical Foundation, Rosenberg Library, or local historians and does not believe this is the type of work that can be accomplished by one person alone. What has been shared of this work with others—prior to publication—was addressed the Galveston way: rewrite around the matter or water down any such suggestions to assure little chance of success. Other communities have historically done the same thing—however, the water continued to cry. I have faith our community/state/country will continue to grow and understand that collective and cooperative work is necessary.

There is little or no mention of Thomas Green (businessman), John Henry Clouser (teacher), T. D. Armstrong (businessman and city council member), Leroy Hoskins, or other labor leaders in this work. There is no mention of Ms. Helen, who cursed too much and lived in a small cottage between 27th and 28th Street on Winnie with seventy to a hundred cats. By the time the author met her, alcohol had become her god. She was no longer a nurse, and the deplorable conditions in which she lived were seemingly tolerated while we as Galvestonians went about our business.

We can no longer pretend our island's existence and mentality absolve us from the changes taking place in other communities for a reason. We, too, should join this debate and do better than others, past and present. On the last two statements, for those not living in Galveston, these same lessons apply to communities around the country and in other countries. Our is a universal societal condition; none of our communities are exempt from the history of exclusion. A registered historic district would permit documentation and the contouring of future development.

An Old Central/Carver Park Historic District would help slow the continued destruction and rapid erosion of a community and thus give direction to a seemingly planned and in-place gentrification process. This may mean duplicating Charleston and admitting its wealth and basis for the wealth. This of course includes honestly talking about enslavement, slave auction houses, and their locations. The water still cries.

The creation of a historic district may/should mean we follow the lead of Richmond and New Orleans in removing the tributes to the Confederacy—remember John Henry Brown's words. These tributes were never about bravery.

They are nothing more than a fight to preserve the institution of slavery, subservience, and the view that the Negro was an inferior being, put on God's green earth for service and the betterment of the White race. Admittedly, the author relied upon long quotes much too many times; this was on purpose—their words, not mine. John Henry Brown's resolution was in fact a manifesto, justifying for the like-minded.

We are compelled to recognize those hallowed places in each of our communities. No amount of paint, concrete, writings, pretending, misdirection, or silence can cover the burnt grounds, the smell, the screams, and deaths. An Old Central/Carver Park Historic District would permit the communities of interest, policymakers, and politicians to redirect and reshape priorities: telling history's truths and equalizing taxes and funding (roads, flooding, correcting disparate public funding). Addressing the displacement of people of color will permit private-public partnerships to flourish and would mean also Old Central/Carver Park Historic District should receive adequate/the same funding as the East End Historic District (hotel/motel tax funds) and other organizations (Galveston Historic Foundation). The city should modify that inter-local agreement in place to the extent that OCCPHD is designated as the organization granted the first right on tax foreclosure properties in the district. This also means that other organizations with properties within the district should be required to transfer these properties to OCCPHD. The creation of building and heritage standards for the district empowers the OCCPHD and community. This last point can be seen as providing a guiding hand to enhance the district, steering development and assuring the survival of the district, and establish an adequate endowment, like Charleston, like Memphis, and step back and permit the African American leadership and community to identify those to be assigned to run any such institution. This means we act like San Antonio and Fort Worth and that government funds are directed by policymakers and elected officials to make this work (sufficient financing and endowment). Policy decisions and funding fights must be addressed on the front end to avoid the continual reliance on the volunteer efforts of the communities of interest and/or the efforts and talents of the initial creators—memories fade, bodies fail, and time conspires against everyone. Don't they? You do know Superman/Superwoman are fictional characters, don't you?

Richmond and the state of Virginia have always been considered the heart of the Confederacy. Virginia's influence is seen in its importation of its citizens to other parts of the country, its ways and manners, and the wealth generated by the institution of slavery. John Sydnor and others were not Marvel characters—they were the foundation upon which Galveston's economy relied. And much like the financial barons of New York, these slave merchants and the city benefitted from the heady profits that flowed from these crimes against humanity. Virginia imported more slaves than any other state, and it and South Carolina led other Southern states in the insurrection against the Union. For Richmond to now lead the way in removing the Confederate statues should be instructive to this community. We can no longer ignore the voice circling above us, telling us to correct the previous attempts to rewrite a stained history.[8] This is particularly so when these symbols of hate and insurrection grace the public square.[9] Let us be like Charleston, Richmond, and New Orleans. How about this: be like Fort Bend County.[10] Never telling the truth about genocide proves problematic for a society. We can no longer live the lie.

Be like Los Angeles County and read the record and understand how history and law can be abusive and wrongheaded at times. Taking the land of the disenfranchised and recently freed slaves, designed for the benefit of the colored population, and converting it to land for the sole benefit of Whites is incongruent, and to name the park after a slave owner/slave trader represents a misplaced, abusive historical wrong. Naming the building, which lies on the land, after Robert McGuire's daughter is insufficient. Los Angeles County gave the land back.

In the heart of Dixie and elsewhere, institutions and cities around the country have made policy decisions to start the process. Absolutely there has been and will continue to be pushback. Remember, history repeats itself, with retrenchment in various forms: book banning, legislation, resurrection of the removed statues and names—physical violence, new words, new concepts, new legislation, which are actually old words, old concepts, old law reclothed, while history's persistent drumbeat plays a constant refrain.[11] The names of the insurrectionists are being removed from federal property: army bases,[12] the halls of Congress, etc. However, at the time of the publication of this book, do not be shocked by a movement to change the names back. Isn't this the same struggle we as a society have fought repeatedly, never willing to admit the disease slavery has wrought upon us?[13]

Music, the arts, and history benefit from the creation of a historical district. Be like New Orleans and Los Angeles and cherish even artists of color, welcoming their different and unique offerings, providing venues for their works and day-to-day existence. This will force—here *we* go again—all of *us*, children and adults alike, to rethink *our* understanding of past and present history. This is particularly true when we as a community begin to brag on the architectural wonders, wealth, and contributions Galveston's history gifted us. No, no, no, cotton, cane, corn, nor rice were king: slavery was. And the mentality and disease bequeathed by the institution remain ever present and deadly, unless we act.

EPILOGUE

We Must Talk, Tell Stories, and Then Do More

The earth has completed it journey for today, rotating counterclockwise, permitting life to continue. The sun was now settling in the west, only to return less than ten hours later. The walkers who normally occupied the sidewalk across the street were no more. The streetlights etched a mental note to pull the water hose up to the second floor and clean the front windows. The top of each window appeared dusty, a film of sand and the incoming fog creating a strange glare. I made another mental note, now a predictable behavior on my part. In fact, my behavior was a tad worse—I am now attaching one mental note onto another, much like a sticky pad. Somewhere buried under each note are other reminders, each yet to be done. This was now an established practice. This was okay with me.

Oh, I could have recorded the note in a variety of places, but I didn't. I have struggled to maintain this acquired practice. If challenged, I was ready to attest the mental notes were designed to maintain mental acuity, with a determined intent not to tell on myself—it was a personal protest, rebelling against the years of a well-regulated life: time slotted in increments, assignments placed in a variety of different apps, flashing reminders, verbal and written demands, beeps, buzzers, memorandums, emails from the court, letters, texts, calls from clients. Reminders coming in waves, conjoining, pleading, demanding of one's time, reaching out and touching anyplace and anytime—thoughts, dreams, movement—with nary a moment where time was exclusively yours. A metaphorically owned soul was I, this is what technology had brought us, and since 2014 (year of my retirement from the practice of law), the mental notes were my futile attempt to achieve a less regulated life, coming from a previously well-regulated chaos. Of course, none of this means I handwrote this book and took my unintelligible script to a scribe.

My protestation had nothing to do with social media and/or my use of this medium. It surely has made our lives more connected. Now, of course, this last statement is with limitations. It had made our lives worse in another sense. I, like most of my generatation, rant and rave about what is told (too much), shown (same), and how it is said. C'est la vie, indeed.

Four years had now passed since I stood on the vacant lot, being attacked relentlessly while my mind wandered. As I was nearing the submission date for this work, I was not excessively tired. Yes, anguish and worry made their predictable return. I was not to the point of counting hours and minutes. I was counting the number of days, though. Her—the sun's—return would mean the days were one less. I would start again, with the honorable goals of stabbing my way to completion.

I traditionally check social media twice a day: when I turn on the computer in the morning and at night prior to shutting down. When checkng Facebook, I noticed a message from a Starita Smith. The message said, "I hope you remember me." I laughed.

I have known only one Starita in my life and she was a reporter who contacted me to do a story on my representation of the Ku Klux Klan and the Grand Dragon. When I initially talked to her years ago on the phone, the pitch, tenor, and resonance of her voice told me she was an African American reporter. She was not the first to cover the story and by the time of her contact, hundred of stories had been placed worldwide about the African American lawyer from Galveston, Texas, who elected to represent the Klan and their Grand Dragon. These events occurred in 1993/1994 and the world's reaction ranged from shock and disbelief to appreciation and pride. The historian John Hope Franklin was then asked about the representation and responded rather nonchalantly, speaking rhetorically, saying: "Isn't that something lawyers are supposed to do?" He identified the representation to be progress.[1] Others were not so kind.[2]

I say this to say, I knew who Starita Smith was and I remember vividly our visit. She talked as I demurred (not wanting another story), complained about previous reporting of the subject, and wondered out loud why reporters felt compelled to tell it as a race story. Absolutely, I understood the representation was an anomaly, but I also understood the reporters and I were caught in a racial milieu that had long been established before the Grand Dragon walked through the front door with his girlfriend. Michael Lowe was able to step out of his box and ask for help, even after he discovered his lawyer was Black. His girlfriend never was able to do so, refusing to look at me or extend her hand. When I entered the conference room, my race insulted her. She fled the room. Lowe explained, "She wanted to give us our privacy." A lie I didn't readily expose.

The girlfriend's behavior existed even though the man she was with understood the importance of protecting his First Amendment rights, willing to let race be damned for the moment. I understood this too and wanted so badly for the reporters to understand race had nothing to do with my work as a lawyer and how I wanted to help them try to step out of their boxes and report what the case was about or even perhaps tell the public I was one of the best lawyers in the country (who happens to have more than a little melanin in his skin). No creative lying, whitewashing, or mistatement of the truth. Doing what I did for a living, this seemed to me just as important for boys and girls who looked like me. I remember imploring Starita to step out of the box. I recogized I had little or no control over her story. I don't remember ever talking to her about her story when it appeared in *Emerge* magazine. It appeared thirty years before her Facebook message and her call.

Emerge is no more; it ceased publication in 2000, some twenty-three years before our recent contacts. I stepped away from the practice in 2014, when I decided to just stop. I learned later time had indeed marched, and Starita Smith was no longer a reporter. I responded to the Facebook message by assuring her I indeed remembered her and would make contact in a couple of days. I turned the computer off, gathered my thoughts, and counted—not sheep, but the number of days remaining until this work's submission.

When Starita and I finally did talk, she told me her family intended to visit Galveston in June for a family reunion. She wanted information and to talk about their plans. I promised to think about suggestions and would get back with her after my submission date. I never did give her my recommendations of what she and her family could do in Galveston on Juneteenth. I hope she understands.

Starita asked what I was doing with myself. I stared at the ceiling, rolled in the bed, cleared my throat, and gave her a brief abbreviated CliffsNotes version—I mentioned this book and other works. In hearing about this work, Starita was prompted to share her family's story. After she told me her family's history, I was somewhat embarrassed for flying off the handle. I ranted when I was supposed to have been asking questions. Nor did I do a good job in writing down the facts as she patiently explained. She was not offering her time to listen to me give a speech.

I was happy when we talked again later. I was happy she agreed to reverse our previous involvement with each other and allow me to ask more questions. Starita Smith's family story is no different than others and represents how insidious the transatlantic slave trade and the enslavement of a people was and how it affected even the way we refer to our veritable rainbow of colors.

The slave ads in the newspaper reflected "about" ages, odd names/no names, and the colors of our skin to identify the enslaved. These colors were never meant to be compliments—words that have been passed down, generation after generation, words that have defended how we are treated and how we treat each other

Figure 37: Joyce Finch Landry. The photograph overlooks the land a block away from the federal courthouse parking lot which was part of previous eminent domain proceedings. (Contributed by Matlene Finch. Anthony P. Griffin Collection.)

(i.e., red bone/blue black/shade/lighte/prettier/good hair/kinky/"he dark"/nothing darker than a paper sack), words to draw a distinction, words of favor/disfavor. Standing by the water as teeth and eyes are examined, private parts poked, squeezed, and caressed—marking on paper skin colors and identifiable markings. Did I mention this dehumanizing process was a well-practiced and honed process by the time the City of Galveston was established? Sadly, these descriptive words and names remain today.

W. E. B. Dubois's color line, even if viewed through different prisms, remains in place. A people who are the lighest of light to the darkest of dark, trapped in history's constant refrain. The suggestions found in this chapter are designed to address the need—in these former slave societies—to collect data, pictures, stories, and artifacts, seemingly meaningless, in order to provide an opportunity for the historians/academicians, poets, musicians to make sense of the senseless. The artist india.arie sang, "Brown skin, you know I love your brown skin."[3] Her song was more than a love song. Doing through music that which we should all be willing to do, even when addressing a subject as fraught as hate imposed by the color line. "Where are your people from, maybe

EPILOGUE

Mississippi or an island."[4] So she sang! So we should all sing, question, and search for a greater truth and meaning.

One last point and I will be quiet. Yes, there is hope, but it will take each of us—individually and collectively, pulling and pushing. It will take concerted planning and the creation of museums to help collect and document history and store the data. The previous chapter addressed the creation of a historical district to aid in this process. These suggestions are something different—the collection of data, artifacts, and things. Absolutely, artifical intelligence is wonderful, mindblowing. However, artificial intelligence is actually rather limited—the creation of stories and things based upon a programmer's talents can never have been deemed more valuable than the creativeness of the human mind. I hope I am making sense.

The data should be collected and stored in various museums—some established, others not—around the country (e.g., Washington, DC, New York, Charleston, Atlanta, Chicago, Memphis, Little Rock, Tulsa, New Orleans, Galveston, Los Angeles), with the Central Depository located in Washington, DC (national museum).

Similar arrangements should be made in every country where the enslaved were deposited: Jamaica, Brazil (and throughout South America), Cuba, the greater Carribean, and the shores of Africa. DNA data should be collected for each person of African descent and this data should be used to identify kin, families. There is an absolutely palpable fear in compelling mandatory DNA submission, in the context of civil liberties/civil rights concerns. This author has the same fear; however, the author has an equal concern that our not knowing and the failure to draw the connections will continue the disconnect, prolonging the absence of familiar relationships and preventing the adequate tracking of what the transatlantic slave trade has wrought. We as a society, a community, as those affected by this history will have to make a policy decision on which is worse, testing and all its implications, or the continuation of the rot caused by the absence of adequate information. Once the data, stories, documents, and things are collected, the data should be shared and made available to writers, historians, artists, and scientists.

I fully understand and appreciate why reconciliation commissions were established in South Africa and Rwanda. This country, too, should establish a reconciliation commission. The commissions, if done right, permit further data collection. The data collected in each community should be documented in reports and inventoried, then remitted to a truth and reconciliation commission for well-documented reports.

None of these suggestions are impossible. If we can accomplish one thing—starting—we are winning. A greater truth is necessary to neutralize the poison slavery bequeathed onto us and which continues to course through our veins and communities.

NOTES

Chapter 1

1. Robbins postulated, "The African slave trade in Texas formed part of the Atlantic slave trade that began in the sixteenth century and flourished during the seventeenth and eighteenth centuries. Because the Texas portion of the trade lasted less than fifty years, 1836–1860, Texas did not experience a large nor profound influx of Africans. During the Atlantic slave trade, more than ten million Black Africans were transferred from Africa to the New World. Texas's share of this number only reached as many as one thousand." Robbins' position is consistent with mythology, a post hoc academic paper limiting Texas's involvement in the slave trade, even if other evidence reveals the number was far greater. His is an academic exercise imposing differing conditions and qualifiers, permitting the asserted number to seem normative, if the trafficking of other human beings could ever be considered normative. Fred Robbins, "The Origin and Development of the African Slave Trade in Galveston, Texas, and Surrounding Areas from 1816 to 1836," *East Texas Historical Journal* 9, no. 2 (1971): Article 7, 153, http://scholarworks.sfasu.edu/ethj/vol9/iss2/7.

2. See "Virginia Humanities: Slave Sales," *Encyclopedia Virginia*, accessed March 21, 2021, https://encyclopediavirginia.org/entries/slave-sales/#:~:text=Between%201790%20and%201860%2C%20more,such%20as%20Richmond%20and%20; "Enslavement," National Humanities Center Toolbox Library: Primary Resources in U.S. History & Literature, accessed March 21, 2021, http://nationalhumanitiescenter.org/pds/maai/enslavement/enslavement.htm; "The Story of the Largest Slave Auction in American History Proves This," The History Network, The University of Richmond, accessed March 21, 2021, http://hnn.us/article/168736; "Auction: What Is an Auction?," Corporate Finance Institute, accessed March 21, 2021, https://corporatefinanceinstitute.com/resources/knowledge/finance/auction/.

3. "John 20:24–29 is the source of an unfortunate nickname 'Doubting

Thomas.' Thomas was not present when Jesus came through a locked door and proved to the other disciples that He was alive. He makes an exaggerated demand for proof before he will believe, insisting on more evidence than is reasonable." BibleRef.com, accessed November 16, 2024, https://www.bibleref.com/John/20/John-20-27.html#:~:text=John%20 20%3A24%E2%80%9329%20is,more%20evidence%20than%20is%20 reasonable.

4. *Merriam-Webster.com Dictionary*, s.v. "myth," accessed February 11, 2023, https://www.merriam-webster.com/dictionary/myth.

Chapter 2

1. Anne C. Bailey, "They Sold Human Beings Here. The 1619 Project Examines the Legacy of Slavery in America: The 1619 Project," *New York Times*, February 20, 2020, https://www.nytimes.com/interactive/2020/02/12/magazine/1619-project-slave-auction-sites.html. See also *The 1619 Project*, spearheaded by Nikole Hannah-Jones and *The New York Times Magazine*: *The New York Times, The 1619 Project*, Nikole Hannah-Jones, Caitlin Roper, Ilena Silverman, and Jake Silverstein, eds. (New York: One World, 2021).

2. Iain Burns, "Humans on Sale: Haunting Photographs Show the Commonplace Auctions Held Across America Where Businessmen Fought Bidding Wars Over Black Slaves," *Daily Mail* (UK), November 22, 2017, https://www.dailymail.co.uk/news/article-5106967/Haunting-photographs-reveal-American-slave-auctions.html.

3. "Dickens on the Strand: December 3–5, 2021," Galvestson.com, accessed March 21, 2021, https://www.galveston.com/whattodo/festivals/dickensonthestrand/.

4. "Transatlantic Slave Trade," *Encyclopedia Brittannica.com*, https://www.britannica.com/topic/transatlantic-slave-trade.

5. Dalya Alberge, "Charles Dickens Railed Against 'Atrocity' of Slave Trade in Previously Unpublished Letter," *The Telegraph*, June 25, 2022, accessed February 12, 2023, https://www.telegraph.co.uk/news/2022/06/25/charles-dickens-condemned-inhuman-slave-trade-previously-unpublished.

6. "Charles Dickens and American Slavery," Delanceyplace.com, accessed March 21, 2021, https://delanceyplace.com/view-archives.php?p=3572.

7. W. E. B. Du Bois, *The Souls of Black Folks* (Chicago: A. C. McClung & Co., 1903).

Chapter 3

1. Jonathan Daniel Wells, *The Kidnapping Club: Wall Street, Slavery and Resistance on the Eve of the Civil War* (New York: Bold Type Books, 2020), 81–82.
2. Galveston Historical Foundation, "In 2017, GHF installed the Middle Passage marker outside the Galveston Historic Seaport. The marker commemorates enslaved Africans in Galveston." Facebook photo, January 31, 2022, https://www.facebook.com/permalink.php?story_fbid=4833886366657784&id=103131356399999&_rdr.
3. James M. Schmidt, *Galveston and the Civil War: An Island City in the Maelstrom* (Charleston: The History Press, 2012), 17. With respect to John S. Sydnor: Sydnor served as an alderman for the City of Galveston from 1839 to 1841, as mayor 1846–1847 (two terms). John O. Trueheart also had a relationship with the city government. "The office of Surveyor has been filled by John O. Trueheart, John DeYoung, S. P. Brown, and others": Morrison and Fourmy, *Morrison & Fourmy's General Directory of the City of Galveston: 1859* (Houston, TX: n.p., 1859), 35, https://texashistory.unt.edu/ark:/67531/metapth908994/.
4. Earl Wesley Fornell, *The Galveston Era: The Texas Crescent on the Eve of Secession* (Austin: University of Texas Press, 1961), 15.
5. Fornell, *The Galveston Era*, 115–16.
6. Fornell, *The Galveston Era*, 116.
7. Fornell, *The Galveston Era*, 117.
8. *Civilian and Gazette Weekly* (Galveston), April 20, 1858, 3.
9. *Galveston Daily Civilian*, December 8, 1860, 4.
10. *Galveston Daily Civilian*, December 3, 1860, 4. See also *Civilian and Gazette Weekly* (Galveston), December 25, 1860, 3.
11. Harold M. Hyman, *Oleander Odyssey: The Kempners of Galveston, Texas, 1854–1980s* (College Station: Texas A&M University Press, 1990), 41.
12. "Despite the numerous works on the black Atlantic world and maritime slavery, however, few historians have examined slavery in the Texas port of Galveston, owing, no doubt, to the City's youth (incorporated in 1838) and size (only about 7,000 residents by 1860) relative to the other Gulf and Atlantic ports in the United States": Robert S. Shelton, "Slavery in a Texas Seaport: The Peculiar Institution in Galveston, Slavery and Abolition," *A Journal of Slave and Post-Slave Studies* 28, no. 2 (2007): 155–68, https://doi.org/10.1080/01440390701427990.
13. Martin Kohn, "South to Freedom: The Underground Railroad also led to Mexico," *Humanities: The Magazine of the National Endowment for*

the Humanities 34, no. 2 (March/April 2013), https://www.neh.gov/humanities/2013/marchapril/statement/south-freedom.
14. Wells, *The Kidnapping Club*, 31. See also Solomon Northup, *12 Years a Slave* (New York: Penguin Books, 2012), 117.
15. Wells, *The Kidnapping Club*, 56.
16. Wells, *The Kidnapping Club*, 31.
17. Wells, *The Kidnapping Club*, 56.
18. Wilson Armistead, *Five Hundred Thousand Strokes for Freedom* (London: W. & F. Cash, 1900; reprinted New York: Negro Universities Press, 1969), Leeds Anti-slavery Series, No. 1, Brief Definition of Negro Slavery, 1–2.
19. *Merriam-Webster.com Dictionary*, s.v. "prism," https://www.merriam-webster.com/dictionary/prism.
20. Northup, *12 Years a Slave*; Wells, *The Kidnapping Club*.
21. Fornell, *The Galveston Era*, 116.

Chapter 4

1. "In Texas during the eighteen-fifties, the demand for Negro labor often forced the prevailing selling price for slaves as high as $1500 for men and $1250 for women. Since a 'likely' Negro could be hired out for $250 to $300 per season, with the cost of his upkeep paid by the person employing him, many non-planters acquired slaves merely as income investment. In four to five years, even the most expensive Negro would, by his own labor, pay for his original purchase price." Earl Wesley Fornell, *The Galveston Era: The Texas Crescent on the Eve of Secession* (Austin: University of Texas Press, 1961), 230.
2. Galveston County Office of County Clerk, 1840000227, 410–11.
3. Galveston County Office of County Clerk, 1840000353 (top of page), 536.
4. Galveston County Office of County Clerk, 1840000353, 537–38.
5. Galveston County Office of County Clerk, 1840000398, 595–96.
6. Galveston County Office of County Clerk, 1841000073, 515–16. See also Ephraim Douglass Adams, ed., "Correspondence from the British Archives Concerning Texas, 1837–1846," letter, William Kennedy British Consulate to Earl of Aberdeen, September 5, 1843, *The Southwestern Historical Quarterly* XVII, no. 2 (1913): 188–206.
7. Adams, "Correspondence from the British Archives Concerning Texas, 1837–1846," 198: "No Census of the Republic of Texas having yet been taken, it is impossible to state, with accuracy, the amount of its population, or the respective Number of whites and of colored people forming that population. According to election and other returns, the White population

may be estimated at 80,000 (eighty thousand) souls, the Indians at 12,000 (twelve thousand) and the Slaves at 16,000 (sixteen thousand). The free persons of Colour are extremely few." Consul Kennedy further explained the population was embraced "within the limits that designated Texas as a department of the Republican Mexico" and that the additional territory claimed since the Revolution was neither occupied by "her Settlers, nor held by her troops, contains a considerable Mexican and Indian population, for estimating whose numbers, there are no reliable data. By far the greater portion of this territory is waste."

The correspondence went on to explain that "An Act of Congress 'to raise a Revenue by direct taxation,' imposed a tax upon Slaves and the Assessors appointed under the Act gave in returns for the year 1840," which produced the following results:

Negro Slaves under 15 years of age......4,992
Over 15 and under 50..........................5,899
Over 50..33
Total ....11,223 [sic]

The Consul explained that there were no returns for nine counties. Allowing for the omitted and imperfect returns, the whole estimate for the slave population in the year 1840 was 12,000. Adams, "Correspondence from the British Archives Concerning Texas, 1837–1846."

8. Galveston County Office of District Clerk, District Clerk Minutes, Republic of Texas 1844–1859, vol. 1, 77.
9. Galveston County Office of District Clerk, District Clerk Minutes, Republic of Texas 1849, vol. 2, 181.
10. Galveston County Office of District Clerk, District Clerk Minutes, Republic of Texas 1844–1859, vol. 1, 80.
11. *Dred Scott v. Sandford*, 60 U.S. 393 (1856).
12. *Dred Scott v. Sandford*, 60 U.S. 393, 397.
13. *Dred Scott v. Sandford*, 60 U.S. 393, 396.
14. *Dred Scott v. Sandford*, 60 U.S. 393, 400.
15. The author makes clear that being accorded the status of free meant little. "The position of the free Negro in Galveston was completely untenable, in both legal and social terms. Newspapers often complained about the 'free Negro nuisance' and deplored the threat to the Texas institution presented by the fact that the neighboring states of Louisiana and Arkansas took a lenient view in regard to free Negroes." Texas law didn't differ from *Dred Scott*: "A free Negro could not legally reside within the state of Texas unless special permission had been granted in each case by an act of the

legislature. The testimony of a Negro, of whatever status, was not admissible in a court of law in any case where a white person was a party in the issue. Consequently, a free Negro brought into court as a defendant on a charge by a white man could not testify in his own behalf. The same circumstances prevailed in cases where a free Negro appeared in court to determine whether or not a particular set of circumstances permitted his sale into temporary or permanent slavery. Such cases were decided on the basis of ex parte testimony unless some white person chose to come forward to testify on the Negro's behalf." Fornell, *The Galveston Era*, 232–33.

16. Jonathan Daniel Wells, *The Kidnapping Club: Wall Street, Slavery and Resistance on the Eve of the Civil War* (New York: Bold Type Books, 2020), 5. Much of the city's (New York's) growth had been built on the backs of Southern slaves who picked cotton for hundreds of thousands of cotton bales every year, a crop that was financed by Wall Street banks and exported to New England and British textile mills via New York brokers, businesses, and financiers. Slave masters depended on New York insurance companies to protect their investments in bondage and embraced the credit extended by the city's banks.

17. Samuel May Williams papers, 1795–1858, MS23-0002, Rosenberg Library, Galveston, Texas.

18. Samuel May Williams papers, 1795–1858, MS23-0002, Rosenberg Library, Galveston, Texas. See also *Galveston Daily News*, January 2, 1882, 1; wherein the taxable miscellaneous property is set out, excluding real estate, assessed in the City in 1847:

    Slaves..........................$150,000
    Horses............................8,500
    Cattle..............................7,150
    Money at Interest..........48,000
    Merchandise................107,000

19. Samuel May Williams papers, 1795–1858, MS23-0002, Rosenberg Library, Galveston, Texas.

20. "$5,000,000 in 1838 → 2024 | Inflation Calculator," Alioth Finance, Official Inflation Data, accessed February 9, 2023, https://www.official-data.org/us/inflation/1838?amount=5000000.

21. Fornell, *The Galveston Era*, 247.

22. Fornell, *The Galveston Era*, 247.

23. The source of the authority? Fornell references R. B. Kingsbury Papers, TS, *New York Herald*, August 5, 1860; *Galveston Civilian*, March 23, 1858. Fornell identifies Kingsbury as the friend of Gordon Bennett, publisher of

the *New York Herald*, who was at various times ad editor of small newspapers in the Texas Gulf Coast and postmaster handling the mails at several seaport towns. Fornell, *The Galveston Era*, 248, 179; "$11,000,000 in 1850 → 2024 | Inflation Calculator," Alioth Finance, Official Inflation Data, https://www.officialdata.org/us/inflation/1850?amount=11000000.

24. See *Civilian and Galveston City Gazette*, April 8, 1843, 1. Advertisement in same paper, "Buggy for sale," H. A. Cobb.
25. *Civilian and Galveston City Gazette*, January 28, 1843, 4; *Civilian and Galveston City Gazette*, April 8, 1843, 1.
26. *Civilian and Galveston City Gazette*, March 4, 1843, 1. Note the reference to Custom House Street is Post Office. The location, 23rd, in today's idiom would be Tremont. See Diana J. Kleiner, "Galveston Custom House," Texas State Historical Association Online, accessed March 22, 2021, https://www.tshaonline.org/handbook/entries/galveston-custom-house. See also "Sanborn Maps," University of Texas at Austin: University of Texas Libraries, accessed March 22, 2021, http://legacy.lib.utexas.edu/maps/sanborn/g-i-txu-sanborn-galveston-1877.jpg.
27. *Civilian and Galveston City Gazette*, January 28, 1843, 8.
28. *Civilian and Galveston City Gazette*, January 6, 1844, 4; similar advertisements are found in *Civilian and Galveston City Gazette*, February 1, 1843, 4. These advertisements are provided to show the pervasiveness of the institution on the economy. If not understood by now, think about the sale of any product (e.g., pork belly, cattle, chickens) and how those transactions affect the nation's economy.
29. *Galveston County Sheriff broadside*, July 30, 1851, MS76-00231, Rosenberg Library, Galveston & Texas History Center: "[T]his collection contains a broadside signed by William N. Sparks, Galveston County Sheriff, announcing the sale of six enslaved . . . [souls] at the Galveston County Courthouse on August 1, 1851. Their names were Frances (aged about 27 years), her son Henry (aged about 8 years), Dorcas (aged about 56 years), Charlotte (aged about 19 years) and her two children Sarah (aged about 2.5 years) and Charles (aged about 5 months)." See also *Legal Document Regarding Slaves – Front*, April 16, 1847, Special Collections, University of Houston Libraries, University of Houston Digital Library, accessed February 22, 2021, https://digital.lib.uh.edu/collection/earlytex/item/4108/show/4106 (additional documentation of court ordering execution with respect to the debt).
30. See Wells, *The Kidnapping Club*, 259: "At the same time, the transatlantic slave trade persisted as well. According to one estimate, about one hundred

slavers set sail from New York between early 1859 and the summer of 1860. Initially engaged in the legal business in commodities like ivory and palm oil, ship owners and captains were lured by the tremendous profits to be gained in slaving. Investors were drawn from all quarters of New York and Brooklyn; two female investors netted astonishing profits of nearly $40,000 on the initial outlay, with a cost of only about $35,000, successful slavers could garner a half million dollars' profit. And by paying only about one hundred dollars each for African men, women, and children who could be sold across the Atlantic for as much as $2,000 each, there is little wonder that the trade continued unabated even as the nation began preparing for the 1860 presidential election."

See also Robert S. Shelton, "Slavery in a Texas Seaport: The Peculiar Institution in Galveston, Slavery and Abolition," *A Journal of Slave and Post-Slave Studies* 28, no. 2 (2007): 155–68, accessed March 22, 2021, https://doi.org/10.1080/01440390701427990, wherein Shelton related the plight of a free Black sailor entering the port of Galveston. In November 1856, by trick and device, Charles A. Kleiber advised Charles Thomas, a Black sailor, "that he risked enslavement or worse if he did not sign an indenture and take a white man as master. Thomas signed an indenture document, drawn up by respected local judge Henry M. Trueheart, binding him to Kleiber for fifty years in return for $5 and some clothes at the end of his term." I am not sure whether Shelton's reference to Trueheart as "respected" should be deemed in error, particularly with Trueheart being conflicted. Trueheart was a slave trader and was in the business of auctioning slaves with his father, J. O. Trueheart. Shelton, "Slavery in a Texas Seaport," 162; *Civilian and Gazette*, April 20, 1858, 3.

31. Charles H. Thomas's perils were also recounted in Fornell's *The Galveston Era*. Dr. Fornell does not reference Trueheart as respected: "The indenture document was drawn up by Judge Henry M. Trueheart and attested by "respectable witnesses." Fornell referencing the "respectful" invites the same criticism: both authors fail to reveal H. M. Trueheart's involvement in the slave trade. Fornell, *The Galveston Era*, 247.

In January 1852, a Galveston slave named Frank attempted an escape by secreting himself onto the *Billow*, a brig calling at the port from Boston, Massachusetts. Frank was the property of George Delesdernier, a city alderman. Delesdernier contacted the harbor master and others and tracked Frank to the ship, where he was found hiding. The district court's records reveal three Black crew members aided Frank in his attempt at freedom. The seamen were arrested, tried, and convicted of threatening servile insurrection. They were fined $850, to be paid within five days at risk of enslavement. The sailors were not able to pay and were sold at auction for the sum of $1,570.00. Frank was returned to Delesdernier. Shelton, "Slavery in a Texas Seaport," 162. See also Galveston County District Court, Minutes III, 5, 6, 7, January 8, 1852; Galveston County District Clerk's office, Case Papers, Case 30.

"Delesdernier served as an alderman from 1848–1852." Morrison and Fourmy, *Morrison & Fourmy's General Directory of the City of Galveston: 1859* (Houston, TX: n.p., 1859), 35, https://texashistory.unt.edu/ark:/67531/metapth908994/; *W. & D. Richardson, Galveston Directory for 1859–60* (Galveston, Texas, 1859), 5, https://texashistory.unt.edu/ark:/67531/metapth636854/m1/5/; The 1850 U S. Federal Census identifies George Delesdernier as a slave-owner, owning three slaves, ages 45, 23, 8. "All 1850 U.S. Federal Census–Schedules Results," Ancestry.com, accessed January 29, 2023, https://www.ancestry.com/search/collections/8055/?count=50&residence=_galveston-galveston-texas-usa-77069&residence-x=_1-0.

32. Morrison and Fourmy, *General Directory 1859*, 36.
33. Morrison and Fourmy, *General Directory 1859*, 37.
34. Morrison and Fourmy, *General Directory 1859*, 38, 40.
35. Morrison and Fourmy, *General Directory 1859*, 40.
36. Peter Carlson, "When Signs Said 'Get out' in 'Sundown Towns,' Racism in the Rearview Mirror," *Washington Post*, February 21, 2006, https://www.washingtonpost.com/archive/lifestyle/2006/02/21/when-signs-said-get-out-span-classbankheadin-sundown-towns-racism-in-the-rearview-mirrorspan/0e80ab6c-51a7-4412-a320-168315ced22b/. See also Claudia Kolker, "Unabashed Texas Town Takes Issue with Its Bad Reputation," *Los Angeles Times*, August 24, 2000, https://www.latimes.com/archives/la-xpm-2000-aug-24-mn-9499-story.html#:~:text=That%20passion%2C%20many%20locals%20say,unashamed%20of%20old%2Dfashioned%20values.
37. In the 1859 city directory, the rates of the sales on merchandise at auction and the commissions on sales due and owing to the city were set out. The foregoing rates to be exclusive of brokerage and charges actually incurred:

SALES OF MERCHANDISE AT AUCTION
Per cent.
Sums under One Hundred Dollars..................................10
Sums over One Hundred and under Three Hundred......7

>   Sums over Three Hundred and under One Thousand.....5
>   Sums over One Thousand Dollars..............................2 1/2
>   On Real Estate and Negroes..5
>   Morrison and Fourmy, *General Directory 1859*, 52.

38. "What is the Masculine of Negress?" Answer.com, accessed May 1, 2021, https://www.answers.com/Q/What_is_masculine_gender_for_negress.
39. "Płaszow," Holocaust Encyclopedia, accessed November 22, 2024.
40. Angela Charlton and Jade Le Deley, "Holocaust Survivors Mark 80 Years Since Mass Paris Roundup," *Los Angeles Times*, July 17, 2022, https://www.latimes.com/world-nation/story/2022-07-17/holocaust-survivors-mark-80-years-since-mass-paris-roundup.
41. Democracy Now!, "'What to the Slave is the 4th of July?': James Earl Jones Reads Frederick Douglass's Historic Speech," Youtube video, July 4, 2019, https://www.youtube.com/watch?v=O0baE_CtU08.
42. NPR, "'What to the Slave Is the Fourth of July?': Descendants Read Frederick Douglass's Speech | NPR," YouTube video, July 3, 2020, https://www.npr.org/2020/07/03/884832594/video-frederick-douglass-descendants-read-his-fourth-of-july-speech.

Chapter 5

1. Morrison and Fourmy, *Morrison & Fourmy's General Directory of the City of Galveston: 1859* (Houston, TX: n.p., 1859), 42, https://texashistory.unt.edu/ark:/67531/metapth908994/.
2. Morrison and Fourmy, *General Directory 1859*, 43.
3. Morrison and Fourmy, *General Directory 1859*, 43.
4. Morrison and Fourmy, *General Directory 1859*, 43.
5. *Civilian and Galveston City Gazette*, January 4, 1943, 3.
6. Texas State Historical Association, "Sydnor, John Seabrook," https://www.tshaonline.org/handbook/entries/sydnor-john-seabrook, published 1952, updated November 17, 2021.
7. National Gallery, "About the National Gallery," National Gallery of Art, accessed March 22, 2021, https://www.nga.gov/about.html.
8. National Gallery, "The Early Decades: 1840s–1850s," accessed March 22, 2021, https://www.nga.gov/features/east-of-the-mississippi-nineteenth-century-american-landscape/early-decades.html.
9. See also Erin Mulvaney, "A Lofty Future in Store for Historic Galveston Building," *Houston Chronicle*, January 15, 2016.
10. Juneteenth Plaque put in place by the Texas Historical Commission. The plaque identifies General Gordon's headquarters as being located in the

Osterman building, across from Ufford and Sydnor's Auction Houses.

11. "By 1860, over 80 percent of the free adult males in the South did not own slaves. Only 0.11 percent owned more than 100. The Total Estate for those in the upper tail of the distribution was enormous. It should be emphasized that this is not a small elite; as a group, slave owners were sizeable and wealthy. Those with more than 500 slaves were essentially millionaires in the *current dollars* of 1860. Some of these slaveowners were women." Samuel H. Williamson, Louis P. Cain, "Measuring Slavery in 2016 Dollars," Measuring Worth, accessed February 12, 2023, https://www.measuringworth.com/slavery.php; *Civilian and Galveston City Gazette*, February 1, 1843, 5. Recently, scholars have had to reassess the role White women played in the slave trade. See Rachel L. Swarns, "Scholars Thought White Women Were Passive Enslavers. They Were Wrong," *New York Times*, November 22, 2024, https://www.nytimes.com/2024/11/22/us/white-women-american-slave-trade.html#:~:text=Between%201856%20and%201861%2C%20white,Economic%20Research%20earlier%20this%20year. "Between 1856 and 1861, white women engaged in nearly a third of the sales and purchases of enslaved people in New Orleans, which was home to the nation's largest slave market at the time, according to the working paper released by the National Bureau of Economic Research earlier this year."

12. *Civilian and Galveston Gazette*, March 2, 1844.
13. *Civilian and Galveston Gazette*, March 2, 1844, 4.
14. *Civilian and Galveston Gazette*, October 7, 1843, 3.
15. *Civilian and Galveston City Gazette*, January 25, 1843, 3. The month before, an identical advertisement was published. See also *Civilian and Galveston City Gazette*, January 13, 1857, 3. With respect to advertising for wet nurses: "The slave owners believed that feeding their babies with milk from their native slaves would provide them natural immunity towards Malaria. This had a trickle-down impact on not only racial but also the psychological, financial, and political fabric of the society throughout the Black community": Kamna Kirti, "The Tragic Plight of the Enslaved Wet Nurse, Lessons from History," *Medium*, August 2, 2020, accessed February 12, 2023, https://medium.com/lessons-from-history/the-tragic-plight-of-enslaved-wet-nurses-b1c80b73f290.
16. Michael W. Twitty, *The Cooking Gene: A Journey Through American Culinary History in the Old South* (New York: HarperCollins, 2018), 83.
17. "We analyzed the European genetic contribution to 10 populations of African descent in the United States (Maywood, Illinois; Detroit; New York; Philadelphia; Pittsburgh; Baltimore; Charleston, South Carolina;

New Orleans; and Houston) and in Jamaica, using nine autosomal DNA markers. These markers either are population-specific or show frequency differences 145% between the parental populations and are thus especially informative for admixture. European genetic ancestry ranged from 6.8% (Jamaica) to 22.5% (New Orleans). The unique utility of these markers is reflected in the low variance associated with these admixture estimates (SEM 1.3%–2.7%)." Esteban J. Parra, et al., "Estimating African American Admixture Proportions by Use of Population-Specific Alleles," *American Journal of Human Genetics* 63 (1998): 1839–51, https://www.ncbi.nlm.nih.gov/pmc/articles/PMC1377655/pdf/9837836.pdf.

18. "Sally Hemings," History.com, updated June 7, 2019, original: January 28, 2010, https://www.history.com/topics/slavery/sally-hemings.

19. Amanda Holpuch, "Aaron Burr, Vice-president Who Killed Hamilton, Had Children of Color," *The Guardian* (US News), August 24, 2019, accessed March 21, 2021, https://www.theguardian.com/us-news/2019/aug/24/aaron-burr-vice-president-who-killed-hamilton-had-children-of-color.

20. Mary C. Curtis, "Strom Thurmond's Black Daughter a Symbol of America's Complicated Racial History," *Washington Post*, February 3, 2013, https://www.maryccurtis.com/strom-thurmonds-black-daughter-a-symbol-of-americas-complicated-racial-history/.

21. Robert S. Shelton, "On Empire's Shore: Free and Unfree Workers in Galveston, Texas, 1840–1860," *Journal of Social History* 40, no. 3 (2007): 723, http://engagedscholarship.csuohio.edu/clhist_facpub/2.

22. David A. Hollinger, "The One Drop Rule & the One Hate Rule," *Daedalus* 134, no. 1, On Race (Winter 2005): 18–28, https://www.jstor.org/stable/20027957.

23. Earl Wesley Fornell, *The Galveston Era: The Texas Crescent on the Eve of Secession* (Austin: University of Texas Press, 1961), 67.

24. Encyclopedia.com, "William Pitt Ballinger," accessed January 28, 2023, https://www.encyclopedia.com/law/encyclopedias-almanacs-transcripts-and-maps/ballinger-william-pitt. The 1850 U.S. federal census identifies William Pitt Ballinger as owning seven slaves, ages 40, 2[6], 21, 1[6], 7, 5, 3. "All 1850 U.S. Federal Census–Schedules Results," Ancestry.com, accessed January 29, 2023, https://www.ancestry.com/search/collections/8055/?count=50&residence=_galveston-galveston-texas-usa-77069&residence-x=_1-0. In 1860, U.S. Federal Census, William Pitt Ballinger is identified as owning six enslaved persons, ages, 30 (male), 30 (female), 16 (male), 14 (male), 12 (male), 10 (male), all except for the 30-year-old male, who is identified as Black, are listed as being Mulatto. "All 1860 U.S.

NOTES

Federal Census–Schedules Results," Ancestry.com, accessed January 29, 2023, https://www.ancestry.com/search/collections/8055/?count=50&residence=_galveston-galveston-texas-usa-77069&residence-x=_1-, https://www.ancestry.com/search/collections/7668/?event=Galveston-Texas&count=50&event-x=-1-0&f-80100003=ballinger&f-80100003-x=1.

25. Penny L. Pope, interview by the author, April 20, 2021.
26. Pope interview.
27. "The Galveston firm of R. & D. G. Mills & Company, the largest private bank in Texas during the fifties, was a partnership consisting of Robert Mills, David G. Mills, and John W. Jockusch. Robert Mills also held partnerships with the firm of Mills, McDowell & Company of New York City and in McDowell, Mills & Company in New Orleans. . . . In addition to his banking and trading enterprises, Robert Mills owned and operated several large plantations in Texas. He was not only the largest slaveholder in Texas during the fifties, but also one of the richest men in the state": Fornell, *The Galveston Era*, 14–15.
28. Fornell, *The Galveston Era*, 18.
29. "Bynum Plantation: Brazosport Archaeology Society," LifeontheBrazosRiver.com, Appendix A, Mills Family Genealogy, 18, accessed March 21, 2022, http://lifeonthebrazosriver.com/Bynum-Plantation.pdf.
30. "Bynum Plantation," Brazos.com, 1818.
31. "Bynum Plantation," Brazos.com, 18. See also Benjamin Tumlinson, "The Mills Brothers in Brazoria County," Columbia Historical Museum, October 10, 2022, accessed February 1, 2024, https://columbiahistoricalmuseum.org/mills-brothers/.
32. "Bynum Plantation," Brazos.com, 18.
33. "Bynum Plantation," Brazos.com, 18.
34. "Bynum Plantation," Brazos.com, 6.
35. "Bynum Plantation," Brazos.com, 11.
36. "Bynum Plantation," Brazos.com, 12.
37. "William H. Jones in the 1940 Census," Ancestry.com, accessed April 21, 2021, https://www.ancestry.com/1940-census/usa/Texas/William-H-Jones_5llpjf.
38. "William H. Jones," Ancestry.com.
39. "William H. Jones," Ancestry.com.
40. Obituary, *Galveston Daily News*, September 14, 1980, 4. See also "Anita Elizabeth Jones Barksdale," Ancestry.com, accessed April 21, 2021, https://www.ancestry.com/1940-census/usa/Texas/Anita-L-Barksdale_5llpjj.
41. Obituary, *Galveston Daily News*, September 14, 1980, 4.

42. Obituary, *Galveston Daily News*, March 8, 1983, 4.
43. Obituary, *Galveston Daily News*, March 8, 1983, 4.
44. *Galveston Daily News*, March 29, 1983, 6.
45. *Galveston Daily News*, March 29, 1983, 6.
46. C. Anthony Brown, "GC Canvasses Vote, Swears-in 2," *Galveston Daily News*, April 17, 1980, 2.
47. Brown, "GC Canvasses Vote," *Galveston Daily News*.
48. "1976–1977 Catalog," Galveston College.edu, archives, 6, accessed May 1, 2021, https://gc.edu/wp-content/uploads/2016/09/1976_1977-Catalog.pdf.
49. Dan Bradford, "Stanton Named GC Regent," *Galveston Daily News*, April 14, 1983, 2.
50. Obituary, *Galveston Daily News*, January 29, 1997, 4.
51. Obituary, *Galveston Daily News*, January 29, 1997, 4.
52. "*Roots*, in Full Roots: The Saga of an American Family, Book Combining History and Fiction, by Alex Haley, published in 1976 and awarded a special Pulitzer Prize": "Roots: Work by Haley," Britannica.com, accessed November 20, 2021, https://www.britannica.com/topic/Roots-by-Haley.
53. "Lucy was among the 100 most popular names in 1900 and remained a very common choice each year until 1924, after which it fell into relative obscurity. Its popularity troughed in 1979, when it was the 537th most popular girl's name. The number of babies named Lucy has risen each year since 1998, and in 2010 Lucy returned to the top 100. Last year, 4,257 newborns were named Lucy, or 0.22% of female births, making it the 62nd most popular girl's name in the country": "9 Old Fashioned Baby Names Making a Huge Comeback," Microsoft News, accessed May 1, 2021, https://www.msn.com/en-us/lifestyle/family/9-old-fashioned-baby-names-making-a-huge-comeback/ss-AAcW8Fa.
54. "Bynum Plantation," Brazos.com, 22. See Social Security Administration, "FAQ," SSA.com, accessed February 1, 2024, https://www.ssa.gov/history/hfaq.html#:~:text=Q1%3A%20When%20did%20Social%20Security,benefits%20started%20in%20January%201940. Social Security's first payment of monthly benefits was January 1940. The Social Security Act was signed on August 14, 1935.
55. "Sally Hemings: Daughter, Mother, Sister, Aunt. Inherited as property. Seamstress, World traveler. Enslaved woman. Concubine. Negotiator. Liberator. Mystery," Monticello.org., accessed February 14, 2023, https://www.monticello.org/sallyhemings/.
56. "John Brown's Raid," National Park Service, accessed November 22, 2024,

https://www.nps.gov/articles/john-browns-raid.htm.

57. "John Brown: 1800–1859," PBS, accessed February 19, 2023, https://www.pbs.org/wgbh/aia/part4/4p1550.html; "John Brown," History.com, published October 27, 2009; last updated January 10, 2023, https://www.history.com/topics/slavery/john-brown.

58. Mary Frances Berry, *Black Resistance: White Law: A History of Constitutional Racism in America* (New York: Allen Lane, 1994), 60.

59. "Henry A. Wise," Hollywood Cemetery, accessed February 19, 2023, https://www.hollywoodcemetery.org/henry-a-wise.

60. Starita Smith, interview by author, February 18, 2023. See also "DC Emancipation Day," D.C.gov., accessed February 19, 2023, https://emancipation.dc.gov/page/ending-slavery-district-columbia: "Through the introduction of laws known as 'Black Codes,' they sought to solidify slavery as an institution and to strengthen the concept of racial segregation in the city. They also restricted the meaning and practice of legal freedom for free Black people. The mayor and aldermen legislated the first set of Black Codes in 1808. These codes made it unlawful for 'Negroes' or 'loose, idle, disorderly persons' to be on the streets after 10 p.m. Free Black people who violated this curfew could be fined five dollars (equal to $65 in 2007). Enslaved African Americans had to rely on their owners to pay the fine. The punishment for nonpayment of fines was whipping. The mayor and aldermen enacted a harsher set of Black Codes in 1812. Free Black people could be fined $20 if they violated the curfew and jailed for six months if the fine went unpaid. Enslaved people received the same fine but the punishment for nonpayment was forty lashes. In addition, free African Americans had to register with the local government and carry their certificates of freedom at all times."

61. "William H. Grey," Arkansas Black Lawyers, accessed November 22, 2024, https://arkansasblacklawyers.uark.edu/lawyers/whgrey.html.

62. Starita Smith interview.

63. "William Henry Grey (1829–1888)," Encyclopedia of Arkansas, last updated November 11, 2021, https://encyclopediaofarkansas.net/entries/william-henry-grey-5696/.

64. "William Henry Grey," Encyclopedia of Arkansas. See also "William Henry Grey," My Delta World, accessed February 19, 2023, https://mydeltaworld.com/2020/01/11/william-henry-grey/. "The other children of William and Henrietta are provided. 'They would have nine children together. Their names were Nancy, Nathaniel, William, Edward, Oliver, Ulysses, Charles, Susan and Anna.'"

65. Starita Smith interview; "William Henry Grey," Encyclopedia of Arkansas.

NOTES

66. Henry Watson, *Narrative of Henry Watson, A Fugitive Slave, 1848*, "Negroes for Sale, Slave Auctions: Selections from 19th-century Narratives of Formerly Enslaved African Americans," National Humanities Center, 2007, nationalhumanitiescenter.org/pds/. Full text of narratives online in documenting the American South (University of North Carolina Library), accessed January 4, 2022, https://docsouth.unc.edu/neh/watson/watson.html, 6–9.
67. "Juneteenth and General Order No. 3," Galveston History.org, accessed March 22, 2021, https://www.galvestonhistory.org/news/juneteenth-and-general-order-no-3; Galveston Historical Foundation, "Osterman Building at 22nd and Strand, from where the General Order Number 3 was read, declaring all slaves freed." Facebook post, June 19, 2016, https://www.facebook.com/galvestonhistory/photos/osterman-building-at-22nd-and-strand-from-where-the-general-order-number-3-was-r/10157038546570594/. See also Maturin Murray Ballou (1820–1895), "Article about the State of Texas, with engraved illustrations of the cities of Galveston and Houston - Page 2, Front," November 17, 1855, Special Collections, University of Houston Libraries, University of Houston Digital Library, February 22, 2021, https://digital.lib.uh.edu/collection/earlytex/item/3473/show/3469 (image of Strand, 1855).
68. *Galveston Daily News*, January 2, 1883, 7.
69. *Galveston Flakes Daily Bulletin*, February 13, 1870, 3.
70. "Labadie, Dr. Nicholas, D.," Texas Genealogy Trails, accessed February 10, 2023, http://genealogytrails.com/tex/gulfcoast/galveston/bios_l.htm.
71. *Galveston Flakes Daily Bulletin*, February 13, 1870, 3.
72. The book *Without Sanctuary: Lynching Photographs in America* provides a glimpse of the practice of lynching in the United States. The differences: the advent of cameras, documenting the practice continued during Reconstruction into the twentieth century. The practice was deemed justified, a rough form of justice. The late Congressman John Lewis in the book's foreword explained, "Many people today, despite the evidence, will not believe—don't want to believe—that such atrocities happened in America not so very long ago. These photographs bear witness to the hangings, burnings, castrations, and torture of an American holocaust. Despite all I witnessed during the height of the civil rights movement and all I experienced of bigotry and hate during my lifetime; these photographs shocked me." James Allen, et al., *Without Sanctuary: Lynching Photographs in America* (Hong Kong: Twin Palms Publishers, 2000).
73. Fornell, *The Galveston Era*, 117.

74. *Galveston Daily News*, August 23, 1879, 1. Of the other five executions, three were brothers during the war, one a Negro after the war, and two men accused of robbery and murder.
75. *Galveston Daily News*, August 23, 1879, 1.
76. *Galveston Daily News*, December 28, 1990, 17.
77. *Galveston Daily News*, July 16, 1997, 9.
78. *Galveston Daily News*, February 12, 1890, 17.
79. Ancestry.com/US Bureau of the Census 1860 U.S. Federal Census - Slave Schedules Database (Joseph Osterman; John S. Sydnor), accessed January 29, 2023, https://www.ancestry.com/search/collections/7668/.
80. An Inventory of Galveston County Clerk's Office Records at the Texas State Archives 1838–1982, undated, bulk 1920–1982, Galveston County (Tex.) County Clerk's Office Records, Texas State Library and Archives Commission, accessed March 22, 2022, https://txarchives.org/tslac/finding_aids/90018.xml. "Between 1836 and 1869, the county clerk's duties as recorder for the county included recording all deeds, mortgages, conveyances, other liens, judgments and abstracts of judgments, and all other written instruments concerning goods and movable property required by law to be recorded. In addition, the clerk issued marriage and occupational licenses (Acts 1836, 1st Congress of the Republic of Texas, 20 December 1836, 155–57; Acts 1836, 1st Congress of the Republic of Texas, 5 June 1837, 233–35; Acts 1846, 1st Legislature, Regular Session, 12 May 1846, 236–41). During that time, regardless of the configuration of the county's administrative body, the county clerk's duties as administrative clerk of that body included creating and maintaining a record of its proceedings (Acts 1836, 1st Congress of the Republic of Texas, 20 December 1836, 150–53; and Acts 1846, 1st Legislature, Regular Session, 13 May 1846, 337–38).
81. Mortgage: document number 1844000214, Real Property Records, Galveston County Clerk, Galveston, Texas. See also "$5,795 in 1844 → 2021 | Inflation Calculator," Official Inflation Data, Alioth Finance, accessed February 1, 2023, https://www.officialdata.org/us/inflation/1844?endYear=2021&amount=5795.
82. Release: document number 1845000278, May 14, 1845, Real Property Records, Galveston County Clerk, Galveston, TX.
83. *Civilian and Galveston Gazette*, June 9, 1848, 5, wherein it is clear that auctioneers from other cities also advertised in the Galveston papers during this period. See also *Semi Weekly Journal*, February 9, 1852, 3. (Advertisement announcing the arrival of twenty-six slaves at the Palmetto House: merchant, J. Berloucher, Strand).

NOTES

84. *Galveston Daily Civilian*, August 28, 1857, 7, an advertisement on the corner of Strand and Market, opposite the Brick Wharf.
85. Morrison and Fourmy, *Morrison & Fourmy's General Directory of the City of Galveston: 1859* (Houston, TX: n.p.: 1859), 44, https://texashistory.unt.edu/ark:/67531/metapth908994/.
86. *Galveston Weekly News*, September 27, 1859, 2. The deed records of Galveston County reflect that Charles H. Leonard owned parcels of property on Church Street, which he purchased on September 21, 1854, to wit: Lots 4, 5, 6, block 384. Deed: document 1854000601, Real Property Records, Galveston County Clerk, Galveston, TX. This location is also identified as 2415 Church Street and comprises lots 4, 5 & E-7-10 ft of lot 3 & W 11-6 ft of lot 6, Blk 384. Street address 2405 Church Street is Lot 6. This location is across the street from the current location of the United States Post Office and federal building (which houses the federal courthouse), the courthouse sitting on 25th Street and Leonard's Hall located at 24th and Church. The current federal courthouse building was not built until 1937. U.S. General Services Administration, Location 501 25th Street, Galveston, Texas 77550, accessed November 16, 2024, https://www.gsa.gov/real-estate/historic-preservation/explore-historic-buildings/find-a-building/all-historic-buildings/us-post-office-and-courthouse-galveston-tx.
87. "Grand Lodge I.O.O.F., C. H. Leonard," Grand Lodge I.O.O.F of Texas, accessed March 22, 2021, https://ioof-grand-lodge-texas-pgm.weebly.com/c-h-leonard.html; Deed of Trust between George E. Konig, party in the first part, and Charles H. Leonard and Murray & Winstead, parties in the second, wherein Leonard served as the Trustee on the transaction to assure the payment by Konig for the slave (Harriet, about 28 years of age and brown color and her child). See Deed of Trust, record number 1859000808, Galveston County Clerk Records, Galveston, Texas.
88. "Leonard, Hon. Charles Henry," Genealogytrails, accessed March 22, 2021, http://genealogytrails.com/tex/gulfcoast/galveston/bios_l.htm.
89. "Agenda Center," 3–4, Galvestontx.org, accessed March 22, 2021, https://www.galvestontx.gov/AgendaCenter/ViewFile/Item/8057?fileID=24380.
90. Judicial order - Page 1, June 7, 1848. Special Collections, University of Houston Libraries. University of Houston Digital Library. Accessed February 22, 2021, https://digital.lib.uh.edu/collection/earlytex/item/3588/show/3584.
91. Land Transfer of "Sydnor's Wharf" for E. Martin and Henry A. Cobb, 1, front. 1848, Special Collections, University of Houston Libraries, University of Houston Digital Library, accessed February 22, 2021, https://

digital.lib.uh.edu/collection/earlytex/item/4466/show/4463.
92. "The Liberty Bell," US History.org, accessed February 6, 2023, https://www.ushistory.org/libertybell/; "Liberty Bell," Britannica.com, accessed February 23, 2023, https://www.britannica.com/topic/Liberty-Bell.
93. Morrison and Fourmy, *General Directory 1859*, 40.
94. *Galveston Daily News*, March 19, 1967, 7.
95. The current plaque in place does not identify where the house was moved after the 1900 storm.
96. *Galveston Daily News*, September 21, 1972, 36. See also "Cordray Drug to Install Historic Landmark Plaque," *Galveston Daily News*, March 19, 1967, 7.

Chapter 6

1. Poem by author.
2. Morrison and Fourmy, *Morrison & Fourmy's General Directory of the City of Galveston: 1859* (Houston, TX: n.p., 1859), 29, https://texashistory.unt.edu/ark:/67531/metapth908994/.
3. Morrison and Fourmy, *General Directory 1859*. See also "Commission Merchants and Factors," Encyclopedia.com, accessed March 16, 2021, https://www.encyclopedia.com/history/dictionaries-thesauruses-pictures-and-press-releases/commission-merchants-and-factors.
 COMMISSION MERCHANTS AND FACTORS. "The factor or commission merchant was one of the significant figures in the early commercial life of the country. These merchants were responsible for all facets of exchange and took responsibility for transporting and disposing of goods themselves, as well as providing credit to their customers. The factorage system was known through the colonial and early national periods but was of most importance from 1815 to 1860. During these years cotton, tobacco, sugar, and rice from southern plantations were sent to urban centers in the Northeast and in Europe. Southern planters then purchased manufactured goods and supplies from these cities. Commission merchants advanced money to planters and manufacturers; in return, the products of farm and factory were consigned to them for sale."
4. Referencing an additional source is helpful. See "Categorization of occupations," Census.gov, accessed March 22, 2021, https://www2.census.gov/library/publications/decennial/1900/occupations/occupations-part-5.pdf: Call no man a "commissioner," a "collector," an "agent," an "artist," an "overseer," a "professor," a "treasurer," a "contractor," or a "speculator," without further explanation.

Whenever merchants or traders can be reported under a single word expressive of their special line, as "grocer," it should be done. Otherwise, say dry goods merchant, coal dealer, etc.

You are under no obligation to give any man's occupation just as he expresses it. If he cannot tell intelligently what he is, find out what he does, and characterize his profession accordingly.

5. Reference also, Iain Burns, "Humans on Sale: Haunting Photographs Show the Commonplace Auctions Held Across America Where Businessmen Fought Bidding Wars Over Black Slaves," *Daily Mail* (UK), November 22, 2017, https://www.dailymail.co.uk/news/article-5106967/Haunting-photographs-reveal-American-slave-auctions.html.
6. William Wells Brown, *The American Fugitive in Europe, Sketches of Places and People Abroad, With Memoir of the Author* (Boston: John P. Jewett and Company; Cleveland, OH: Jewett, Proctor & Worthington; New York: Sheldon, Lamport, & Blakeman, 1855), 13–14, https://docsouth.unc.edu/neh/brown55/brown55.html.
7. Bath Street references 25th Street; the location would be between 24th and 25th Street on the Strand. Reference: Silk Stocking Residential Historic District, Application to United States Department of Interior, National Park Service, October 1990, Sec. 7, 5, accessed March 22, 2021, https://www.thc.texas.gov/public/upload/preserve/survey/highway/Silk%20Stocking%20Historic%20District%20Galveston.pdf.
8. McCarty's advertisement identified him as being "Auctioneer, Real Estate and Negro Broker" (in context of Negro trade, "Negroes, their capacity, character, color, age, price, cash or city acceptance"). See *Galveston Daily Civilian*, March 1, 1860, 4.
9. See the advertisement of Jones and Ufford for the sale of "3 likely Negro boys from 18–22." *Civilian and Galveston Gazette*, May 27, 1851, 3.
10. Morrison and Fourmy, *General Directory of the City of Galveston 1859*.
11. E. L. Ufford served as the president pro tem for the City of Galveston in 1843. *Civilian and Galveston City Gazette*, May 17, 1843, 3. The 1850 U.S. federal census identifies E. L. Ufford as owning three (3) slaves, ages 45, 35, 3. Ancestry.com/US Bureau of the Census 1850 U.S. Federal Census - Slave Schedules Database (E. L. Ufford, accessed January 29, 2023), https://www.ancestry.com/search/collections/8055/?count=50&residence=_galveston-galveston-texas-usa-77069&residence-x=_1-0. An Architectural Data Form, identified as a historic American building survey, completed for the United States Department of Interior states the Ufford building was initially built in the 1840s, and rebuilt after a wall partially

collapsed in the 1860s (between October 23, 1860, and February 22, 1861). The building was "probably demolished" in February 1978. The address is identified as 301-309 23rd Street and stated the building was initially built by John Brown for Edmund L. Ufford. Library of Congress, Strand Historic District, Ufford Building HABS-TX 3296, accessed November 25, 2024, https://tile.loc.gov/storage-services/master/pnp/habshaer/tx/tx0000/tx0056/data/tx0056data.pdf; see photos of building taken, https://www.loc.gov/item/tx0056/.

12. *Galveston Daily Civilian*, December 8, 1860, 1. See also an advertisement found at *Galveston Daily Civilian*, April 5, 1860, 2: "No. 1, Negro boy for sale."

13. *Galveston Semi Weekly Journal*, March 22, 1852, 3.

14. See the newspaper advertisement taken out by J. L. Darragh, *Civilian and Galveston Gazette*, August 19, 1851, 3: the sale of "four likely Negroes, a woman about 30 years old, a good cook, washer and ironer, and three boys, the oldest about 13, the second is 9 years old, the third 7 years old, all first-rate negroes." See the advertisements in the April 5, 1860 edition of *Galveston Daily Civilian*, April 5, 1860, 1 & 3: J. O. and H. M. Trueheart: "to hire out Negro woman, in addition to general advertisement with respect to auction business"; E. L. Ufford: "sale of Negro man, likely 30 years of age"; A. S. Ruthven: for sale, "No. 1 Negro woman"; C. L. McCarty: sale of six Negroes, "six in one family," and his additional advertisement, with respect to business of auctioning Negroes.

15. Michael W. Twitty raises the question: "What's in a name? Certainly something of a face but not really a full identity. Cudjo and Phibba, names based on names of Akan origin from what is now Ghana, tell us a narrative of persistence or resistance, or even of white accommodation to the folkways of the enslaved. If you are enslaved, your name can change at any point in time. You must be whoever you're told to be, and you must also be your true self—all at once. Slavery was not ripe with opportunities to build rugged individualism and live a free and industrious life as a unique person with a destiny. It was the erasure of that. Not having much more than a name on paper to testify to your existence, or none at all, is painful for the genealogical seeker who wants more." Michael W. Twitty, *The Cooking Gene: A Journey Through American Culinary History in the Old South* (New York: HarperCollins, 2018), 83.

16. Henry Bibb, *Narrative of the Life and Adventures of Henry Bibb, An American Slave, Written by Himself, 1849*, National Humanities Center, 2007, nationalhumanitiescenter.org/pds/. Full text of narratives online

in documenting the American South (University of North Carolina Library), visited January 4, 2022, https://docsouth.unc.edu/neh/bibb/bibb.html, 101–2.

17. Heartman Collection Texas Slave Trade Documents, Rice.edu, accessed March 22, 2021, https://scholarship.rice.edu/bitstream/handle/1911/36841/USTSOUTSTD-.
18. John H. Heller, *Heller's Galveston City Directory, 1876–1877* (Galveston, TX, 1876), 36.
19. See Texas Historic Commission, Galveston Historical Foundation's Application for Historic District [Galveston-East End Historic District], Nomination Form, National Register of Historic Places, May 11, 1976, 142, 143, accessed March 22, 2021, https://www.thc.texas.gov/public/upload/preserve/survey/highway/NHL%20East%20End%20Historic%20District%20Galveston.pdf.
20. *Civilian and Galveston Gazette*, January 24, 1851, 4.
21. *Galveston Flakes Daily Bulletin*, September 20, 1868, 16.
22. "According to the 1850 census there were 58,161 Negroes in Texas at the time; by 1860 their number had risen to 182,566, or an increase of 124,405." Fornell, *The Galveston Era*, 241. See advertisement, *Galveston Daily Civilian*, August 28, 1857, 3.
23. *Civilian and Galveston Gazette*, January 24, 1851, 3. The R. & D. G. Mills and Company of Galveston is representative of the statement, Galveston being the largest slave port west of New Orleans. This activity included supplying human bodies to the interior of Texas, the maintenance and service of plantations, and other related industries. The Mills' enterprises had interests in firms located in New Orleans, New York, Liverpool, and Havana and ownership in sailing vessels, and large sugar and cotton plantations in Texas. "During the fifties" the Mills had four large plantations and other holdings comprised of 3,300 acres under cultivation and 100,000 of unimproved land. They were reported to be the largest slaveholders in Texas. Fornell, *The Galveston Era*, 14–15, 45–46; *Robert Mills v. Alexander S. Johnston and David Dewbury*, District Court of Galveston, January 12, 1857. For additional reference, see also "Mills, David Graham (ca. 1814–1865)," Texas State Historical Association, accessed March 22, 2021, https://www.tshaonline.org/handbook/entries/mills-david-graham: "David Graham Mills and his brother Robert had 800 slaves and were thus the largest slaveholders in the state."
24. *Galveston Daily Civilian*, August 28, 1857, 3.
25. "Manifest Destiny," History.com, accessed January 24, 2023, https://www.

26. "Archibald Rowland Campbell [1841–1920]," Wood & Torbert Families, accessed January 27, 2023, https://www.woodvorwerk.com/wood/g2/p2504.htm.
27. "Archibald Rowland Campbell [1841–1920]," Wood & Torbert Families.
28. "Archibald Rowland Campbell [1841–1920]," Wood & Torbert Families.
29. See "John William Campbell [1866–1940]," Wood & Torbert Families, accessed January 27, 2023, https://www.woodvorwerk.com/wood/g7/p7756.htm. See also "John William Campbell," Legislative Reference Library of Texas, accessed January 27, 2021, https://lrl.texas.gov/index.cfm.
30. "Archibald Rowland Campbell [1888–1985]," Wood & Torbert Families; *Galveston Daily News*, December 16, 1985; "Find a Grave: Archibald Rowland Campbell," Find a Grave, accessed January 27, 2023, https://www.findagrave.com/memorial/105366402/archibald-rowland-campbell.
31. "Archibald Rowland Campbell, Jr. [1917–1994]," Wood & Torbert Families, accessed January 27, 2023, https://woodvorwerk.com/wood/g2/p2670.htm.
32. "John William Campbell [1888–1985]," Wood & Torbert Families.
33. "Archibald Rowland Campbell, Jr.," *Galveston Daily News*, December 10, 1994.
34. It should be noted that the names appear off in context of sequence for Archibald Rowland Campbell. Where brackets appear, the author places what he believes the proper order and sequence. By way of example, the *Galveston Daily News* identified Archibald III as Jr. and his son as III. The answer, of course, may be one of the newspaper accounts is correct or the person listed in this book may not be in the line of succession. Of course, the proper line of succession is not the author's point anyway, it is the benefit of society engrafted in the well-regulated society of slavery—wealth, land, and prestige—before 1865 and after.
35. "Archibald Rowland Campbell, Jr.," *Galveston Daily News*, December 10, 1994.
36. "John Harris Campbell," Justia Lawyers, accessed January 24, 2023, https://lawyers.justia.com/lawyer/john-harris-campbell-291174.
37. "Archibald R. Campbell III Mineral Rights," Mineral Holders, accessed January 24, 2023, https://www.mineralholders.com/texas/pearsall/archibald-r-campbell-iii/6060281.
38. "John William Campbell [1866–1940]," Wood & Torbert Families, accessed January 29, 2023, https://www.woodvorwerk.com/wood/g7/p7756.htm.
39. "Additional Regulations Concerning the Transportation of Cotton in

Bond," in *Galveston City Directory, 1859–1860* (Galveston, TX, 1859), 29, https://texashistory.unt.edu/ark:/67531/metapth636854/m1/113/.

40. Ancestry.com/US Bureau of the Census 1850 U.S. Federal Census - Slave Schedules Database (William Pitt Ballinger; James P. Cole; Benjamin C. Franklin; John Jones; Hugh McLeod, accessed January 29, 2023), https://www.ancestry.com/search/collections/8055/; Original data: United States of America Bureau of the Census, *Seventh Census of the United States, 1850*, M432, Washington, DC: National Archives and Records Administration. James P. Cole is the same person who represented the enslaved person who was carried out of a slave auction house on the Strand—by a mob—and lynched in 1844. Pope was born in Beaufort, South Carolina, in 1814 and died in Galveston, Texas, in 1886. Pope arrived in Galveston in 1839. He was sworn in as the Chief Justice of the County Commissioner's Court on August 16, 1856, and served in that capacity until July 18, 1864. "James Pope Cole," Find a Grave, accessed November 24, 2023, https://www.findagrave.com/memorial/125876768/james-pope-cole.

41. Ancestry.com/US Bureau of the Census 1850 U.S. Federal Census - Slave Schedules Database (John C. Campbell, accessed January 29, 2023), https://www.ancestry.com/search/collections/7668/; Original data: United States of America Bureau of the Census, *Eighth Census of the United States, 1860*, M653, Washington, DC: National Archives and Records Administration.

42. "John C. Campbell [1824–1907]," Wood & Torbert Families, https://www.woodvorwerk.com/wood/g2/p2499.htm accessed January 30, 2023.

43. "Who We Are: Our History," Descendants Truth and Reconciliation Foundation, accessed January 27, 2023, https://www.descendants.org/who-we-are/history#::text=In%20the%2016th%2C%2017th%20and,profits%20earned%20on%20their%20plantations; Loyola University Maryland recently acknowledged "that it had ties to a 19th-century sale of enslaved people." The sale of 272 men, women and children in 1838, orchestrated by two Jesuit priests connected to Georgetown University, was never before acknowledged by Loyola. See Susan Svrluga, "Loyola University Maryland Says It Had Ties to the 1838 Sale of Slaves," *Washington Post*, January 18, 2024.

44. "Who We Are: Our History," Descendants Truth and Reconciliation Foundation.

45. John Coulter, *The Complete Story of the Galveston Horror* (Atlanta, GA: United Publishers of America, 1900), 283–84.

46. "Mills Shirley: A Historic Law Firm with a Modern Approach," Millsshirley.com, accessed March 22, 2021, https://www.millsshirley.com/about/. See

also "William Pitt Ballinger: Texas Lawyer, Southern Statesman (1825–1888)," Texas State Historical Foundation, accessed March 22, 2021, https://www.tshaonline.org/handbook/entries/ballinger-william-pitt.

47. *William Pitt Ballinger Papers, 1832–1947*, MSS 50-001, MSS-68-0081, MSS 71-0329, Box 1 of 1, Rosenberg Library, Galveston, Texas.
48. Fornell, *The Galveston Era*, 120.
49. Fornell, *The Galveston Era*, 120–21.
50. "[Coffee] personally owned twenty-five slaves, and the plantation he managed, Halcyon had 132." "Coffee, Aaron (1832–1912)," Texas State Historical Association, accessed November 20, 2021, https://www.tshaonline.org/handbook/entries/coffee-aaron. The name Halcyon was also the name of Andrew Jackson's plantation. "Stormy Weather at Andrew Jackson's Halcyon Plantation in Coahoma County, Mississippi, 1838–1845," Cairn, accessed March 21, 2021, https://www.cairn.info/revue-francaise-d-etudes-americaines-2003-4-page-32.htm.
51. *William Pitt Ballinger Papers 1832–1947*, MSS 50-001, MSS-68-0081, MSS 71-0351, Box 1 of 1, Rosenberg Library, Galveston, Texas.
52. Fornell, *The Galveston Era*, 123–24.
53. "Ballinger, William Pitt (1825–1888)," Texas State Historical Association, accessed April 16, 2021, https://www.tshaonline.org/handbook/entries/ballinger-william-pitt.
54. "Ballinger, William Pitt (1825–1888)," Texas State Historical Association.
55. "William Pitt Ballinger: Texas Lawyer, Southern Statesman (1825–1888)," Texas A&M University Press, accessed April 29, 2021, https://www.tamupress.com/book/9780876111994/william-pitt-ballinger/.
56. John Moretta, *William Pitt Ballinger: Texas Lawyer, Southern Statesman (1825–1888)*, Texas: Texas State Historical Association, January 26, 2004, 37–38, https://www.tamupress.com/book/9780876111994/william-pitt-ballinger/.
57. Kenneth R. Stevens, "William Pitt Ballinger: Galveston's Reluctant Rebel," *East Texas Historical Journal* 40, no. 1 (2002), Article 9. Contrast with Paula Bose, "Flashback: Dallas, How Lincoln's Assassination Was Reported in Dallas – 1865," accessed November 24, 2024, https://flashbackdallas.com/2014/04/14/lincoln-assassination/.
58. See George Wallace's inaugural address on January 14, 1963, particularly as related to the tyranny of others who opposed segregation:
"Let us send this message back to Washington, via the representatives who are here with us today," Wallace told the crowd. "From this day, we are standing up, and the heel of tyranny does not fit the neck of an upright man.

"Let us rise to the call of freedom-loving blood that is in us and send our answer to the tyranny that clanks its chains upon the South," Wallace declared from the podium. "In the name of the greatest people that have ever trod this earth, I draw a line in the dust and toss the gauntlet before the feet of tyranny, and I say, segregation now, segregation tomorrow and segregation forever." National Public Radio, "'Segregation Forever': A Fiery Pledge Forgiven, but Not Forgotten," in *All Things Considered*, January 10, 2013, accessed April 16, 2021, https://www.npr.org/2013/01/14/169080969/segregation-forever-a-fiery-pledge-forgiven-but-not-forgotten.

59. Kathryn Pickney, "Ballinger, Texas," Texas Historical Association, accessed March 22, 2021, https://www.tshaonline.org/handbook/entries/ballinger-tx#:~:text=The%20town%20was%20originally%20called,Gulf%2C%20Colorado%20and%20Santa%20Fe.
60. *Civilian and Gazette*, January 13, 1857, 3.
61. *Galveston Daily Civilian*, February 22, 1861, 8.
62. *Galveston Daily Civilian*, February 22, 1861, 8.
63. *Galveston Daily Civilian*, February 22, 1861, 8.
64. James R. Preston in the *Galveston Daily Civilian* identified his business as custom house broker, "Will Make Entries of Merchandise, enter and clear vessels, Slaves . . . Office of F. Gonzales, Kuhn's Building, Strand, Galveston." In the same newspaper, T. B. Stubbs and J. S. Sydnor advertised their business of T. B. Stubbs & Co., located next to Sydnor's Auction House. Ball, Hutchins & Co.—an entity consisting of G. Ball, J. H. Hutchins, and John Sealy—identified itself as being cotton factors and commission merchants, with the appearance it too was in same location. Stubbs identified Mondays, Wednesdays, Thursdays, and Saturdays as the days in which private sales of Negroes and real estate always occur, with 15–20 Negroes available, (again, this is a separate advertisement from the previous one mentioned above; in this he lists J. B. Sydnor and J. S. Sydnor (father and son) as being next door). *Galveston Daily Civilian*, February 22, 1861, 8.
65. Historic American Buildings Survey, Creator, Trueheart-Adriance Building, 212 Twenty-second Street, Galveston, Galveston County, TX, Compiled after 1993, Texas Galveston County Galveston, Photograph, https://www.loc.gov/resource/hhh.tx0091.photos/?sp=1; also reference historic marker application: Trueheart-Adriance Building, September 22, 1972, Recorded Texas Historic Landmark Files, University of North Texas Libraries, The Portal to Texas History, https://texashistory.unt.edu/ark:67531/metapth477772/m1/1/.
66. Bill Moyers, "The Big Story: A Journalist Looks at Texas History,"

NOTES

Southwestern Historical Quarterly 101, no. 1 (July 1977): 4–6.

67. Deed of Trust, record number 1853000433.
68. Deed of Trust, record number 1859000808, Galveston County Clerk Records.
69. Deed of Trust, record number 1859000808, Galveston County Clerk Records.
70. The Galveston Garden Club's discussion of slavery in Galveston is contradictory at best, explaining, "Sydnor's slave market was said to have been the largest slave auction block west of New Orleans," while in the same breath posturing the Texas farmers didn't have the funds to buy slaves, and "Galveston slave auctions likely occurred occasionally, rather than on a daily basis." "1847 Powhatan House," Galvestongardenclub.org, accessed April 29, 2021, https://www.galvestongardenclub.org/1847-powhatan-house.
71. In 1967, three years after the passage of the Civil Rights Act, the Texas Historical Commission placed a marker at the Powhatan House, now located at 3427 Avenue O in Galveston. The marker reads "Early Galveston hotel; built 1847 by John Seabrook Sydnor, Galveston mayor 1846–1847." "Powhatan House, Historical Markers," Galveston.com, accessed March 22, 2021, https://www.galveston.com/whattodo/tours/self-guided-tours/historical-markers/powhatan-house/.
72. Fornell, *The Galveston Era*, 293.
73. Fornell, *The Galveston Era*, 293.
74. "South Carolina Secession," National Park Service, accessed March 22, 2021; https://www.nps.gov/articles/000/south-carolina-secession.htm#:~:text=South%20Carolina%20became%20the%20first,disunion%20across%20the%20slaveholding%20South.
75. "South Carolina Secession," National Park Service.
76. James M. Schmidt, *Galveston and the Civil War: An Island City in the Maelstrom* (Mt. Pleasant, SC: The History Press, September 4, 2012), 21. See also newspaper advertisements by the father and son: [*Auction Sale!* Tuesday, 14th July, at 10 a.m., J. S. and J. B. Sydnor]. "A gang of the likeliest and most desirable NEGROES ever exhibited for sale in Houston—*all of black complexion.*" The auction sale involved 32 persons: [Susan (24), Fanny (21), Susan (50), Elvira (15), Tamer (16), Eliza (16), Lucy Ann (18), Winnie (18), Isiah (6 months), Rueben (21), George (20), Bennett (21), Mason (18), William (21), Henry (10), Charles (16), Sam (16), Jack (15), Harrison (17), Nathan (17), Robert (13), Rachael (14), Charles (31), Jacob (30); Toney and Family: Toney (48), Mary (28), Alfred (12), Eliza (10), Ann (7), Rufus (3), Melinda (5 months)—all auctioned in conjunction

with 7 or 8 large American Mules, two horses and wagons)] [Houston] *Tri Weekly News*, June 20, 1863, 1; ["*Auction Sale*, By J. S. and J. B. Sydnor on Tuesday, 18th August, at 10 a.m., 25 to 35 NEGROES, mostly men . . . "] [Houston] *Tri Weekly News*, August 7, 1863, 3; ["Auction Sale by J. S. & J. B. Sydnor on Friday, Aug. 7th, at 10 a.m. 25 NEGROES, assorted, mostly single Negroes only one family . . . Will be added to Friday's Sale–MATILDA, about 28 years old, and her two daughters, 10 and 12 years old. Matilda is one of the most accomplished house servants in the Southern country, cook, washer and ironer, and her daughters are well grown, **very likely**, and promise to follow the example of the mother. We want a high price for them, will take before the sale $12,000 from any party who will satisfy Matilda, and if not sold privately, will be sold at auction on Friday. CALOMINE, another house servant, about 25 years of age, not quite so likely as Matilda, but also accomplished, and has been well raised. ELVIRA, a girl about 12 years old, unusually likely and well trained in the home." (Emphasis added.) [Houston] *Tri Weekly News*, August 7, 1863, 3.

77. Ancestry.com/US Bureau of the Census 1850 U.S. Federal Census - Slave Schedules Database (John S. Sydnor, accessed January 29, 2023); Original data: United States of America Bureau of the Census. *Eighth Census of the United States, 1860*, Washington, DC: National Archives and Records Administration M653, 1,438 rolls, accessed January 29, 2023, https://www.ancestry.com/search/collections/7668/. It should be remembered Galvestonians were some of the largest land and slave owners in the state. The numbers for enslaved cited for John S. Sydnor and others represent their holdings in Galveston only.
Additional caveats:
General Collection Information
During the 1850 and 1860 United States Federal Censuses, enslaved individuals were recorded separately in what were called slave schedules. This database provides details about those persons, including age, sex, and color, but unfortunately, most schedules omit personal names. Some enumerators did, however, list the given names of enslaved people—particularly those over one hundred years of age—which are generally found in the "name of slave owners" column.
Additional slave schedule fields that are not indexed include:
"Fugitive from the State" (meaning they were a freedom seeker)
"Number manumitted" (or freed)
"Deaf & dumb, blind, insane, or idiotic"
Using this Collection

Sometimes the listings of enslaved persons on large estates or plantations appear to take the form of family groupings, but in most cases, enslaved individuals are listed from oldest to youngest, with no evident attempt to account for family structure or units.

In any event, the slave schedules almost never conclusively connect a specific enslaved individual with a particular slave owner. At best, they provide supporting evidence for a hypothesis derived from other sources. When researching enslaved individuals, the slave schedules are most helpful when used in conjunction with the 1870 U.S. federal census, the US Census mortality schedules from 1850–1885, wills, and probate documents.

Researchers seeking information about slave owners may find slave schedules useful because of the specific information they provide about slave owners' holdings. For example, the number of enslaved people enumerated under a slave owner could indicate whether or not the slave owner had a plantation, and if so, what size it was.

History of the Collection

The official enumeration day of the 1860 census was June 1, 1860. The 1860 slave schedule was used in the following states: Alabama, Arkansas, Delaware, District of Columbia, Florida, Georgia, Kentucky, Louisiana, Maryland, Mississippi, Missouri, North Carolina, South Carolina, Tennessee, Texas, Utah Territory and Virginia. Loretto Dennis, "Research in Census Records," in *The Source: A Guidebook of American Genealogy*, Loretto Dennis Szucs and Sandra Hargreaves Luebking, eds. (Salt Lake City: Ancestry, 1997); William Dollarhide, *The Census Book: A Genealogist's Guide to Federal Census Facts, Schedules and Indexes* (Bountiful, UT: Heritage Quest, 2000).

78. "Civil War Begins," United States Senate, accessed August 9, 2022, https://www.senate.gov/artandhistory/history/minute/Civil_War_Begins.htm.
79. Document number 855000542, August 1, 1954: 47, Property Records, Galveston County Clerk Records; Sale of Lucy, 22 and her son, Doctor, age 4; a release of lien, property, and slaves: John Sydnor to Elizabeth Waring, 1858, document number 1858000039, Property Records, Galveston County Clerk Records, Galveston, Texas; Document number 1859000689, July 14, 1859, Property Records, Galveston County Clerk Records, Galveston, Texas; Document number 1859000690, 1859, Property Records, Galveston County Clerk Records, Galveston, Texas; Document number 1860000340, 1860, Property Records, Galveston County Clerk Records, Galveston, Texas; John B. Sydnor and John S. Sydnor to William Hawley (bill of sale); Galveston County Clerk Records, Property Records;

deed of sale between Henry B. Andrews and John S. Sydnor, John B. Sydnor and T. B. Stubbs dated April 11, 1860; Document number 1861000278, Property Records, Galveston County Clerk Records, Galveston, Texas Transaction between Henry Holmes and Thaddeus Armstrong, William Armstrong, John S. Sydnor.

80. *Galveston Daily Civilian*, December 8, 1860, 2. The location noted was "Strand Street, Galveston, Texas."
81. See also Vicki Betts, "[Houston] *Tri-Weekly Telegraph*, 1863," University of Texas at Tyler: Scholar Works at UT Tyler: Civil War Newspapers, 13, accessed March 22, 2021, https://core.ac.uk/download/pdf/235238624.pdf.
82. Donated items to be sold by "Col. Sydnor to benefit the 2d Texas Regiment." *Galveston Weekly News*, March 25, 1863, 2; "Sydnor lent principal assistance to 'General' Thomas Walker, who proposed to invade Nicaragua and found a colony which would import slaves for Texas and the southwest. Although this expedition proved to be a failure, Sydnor's support of such extreme measures to protect the slave trade was cogent proof of his ardent devotion to the cause of slavery and the 'Southern System.'" "Sydnor was commissioned as a colonel in the Galveston militia at the outbreak of the war. He was charged with the fortification of Galveston against Northern attack. Col. Sydnor was dispatched to Richmond to acquire cannons for the Galveston waterfront and upon completion of his mission, resigned his commission. For the duration of the war, he engaged in blockade running, carrying Texas cotton between Union gunboats to Caribbean ports." "Powhatan House–Galveston, Texas," Waymarking.com, accessed March 22, 2021, https://www.waymarking.com/waymarks/WM8FZ1_Powhatan_House_Galveston_Texas. See also Fornell, *The Galveston Era*, 12–13. "Galvestonians such as William Pitt Ballinger purchased rifled cannon to defend their city."
83. *Sydnor v. Texas Sav. Real Estate Inv.*, 94 S.W. 451 (Tex. App. 1906).
84. *Galveston Daily News,* January 9, 1867, 4. In some documents, John S. Sydnor is referred to as Colonel, other times by name only. The Texas General Land Office explains the benefits the Anglo colonizers received for moving to Texas, fighting against the Mexican government, or just being White in a race-based society (see below).

Colonization Laws of the Republic of Texas

Four empresario colonies were established under contracts with the Republic of Texas: Peters' Colony (1841), Fisher and Miller's Colony (1842), Mercer's Colony (1844), and Castro's Colony (1842). Heads of families were eligible for 640 acres of land, **while single men were eligible** for **320 acres**. The land had to be located within the confines of the colony and settlers were required to cultivate at least 15 acres in order to receive a patent.

Preemption Grants, Republic and State of Texas

From 1845 to 1854, individuals could claim 320 acres of land from the unappropriated public domain. The amount was reduced to 160 acres in 1854 and the grant program was cancelled in 1856. Preemption grants of 160 acres were reinstituted in 1866 and continued until 1898. To qualify for a preemption grant, settlers were required to live on the land for three years and make improvements.

Military Land Grants, Republic and State of Texas

The Republic and State of Texas both issued land grants as **additional compensation for those who served Texas in the military**. The government of Texas, for most of the 19th century, had very little cash with which to pay soldiers, so our most abundant resource—land—was used to supplement the meager military pay.

Bounty grants for military service were issued by the Republic of Texas to soldiers who served in the Texas Revolution and to those who enlisted in the army before October 1, 1837. **The amount of land granted varied depending on length of service. Each three months of service provided 320 acres, up to a maximum of 1280 acres.** Often the heirs of a soldier who died in battle would be granted the full 1280 acres on the assumption that the fallen soldier would have served for the duration of the war. Under a separate law, the Republic of Texas extended bounty grants from 1838 to 1842 to soldiers guarding the frontier. [Emphasis added.] "Categories of Land Grants (revised January 2015)," Texas General Land Office, accessed March 20, 2021, https://www.glo.texas.gov/history/archives/forms/files/categories-of-land-grants.pdf.

85. *Galveston Flakes Daily Bulletin*, May 12, 1867, 3.
86. *Galveston Flakes Daily Bulletin*, May 12, 1867, 3.
87. Galveston County Clerk's Office, Part 2, Book 1, 88–89, June 28, 1869.
88. "History of Seabrook," Seabrooktx.gov, accessed March 22, 2021, https://www.seabrooktx.gov/96/History-of-Seabrook. See also "Letter of Seabrook Town Lot and Improvement Company," in Annual report of the chief of engineers to the secretary of war (Washington, DC: GPO, 1876–1906), accessed March 22, 2021, https://www.google.com/books/edition/Annual_Report_of_the_Chief_of_Engineers/kWZNAAAAYAAJ?hl=en&gbpv=1&dq=who+developed+sydnor+bayou+estates&pg=PA2396&printsec=frontcover.

NOTES

89. See map, including street and body of water, "Elevation of Sydnor Ln., Galveston, TX, USA," Maplogs.com, accessed March 22, 2021, https://www.google.com/search?rlz=1C1CHHM_enUS751US751&sxsrf=ALeKk01FxdmuBb0TMizF6oxhNvHYzoMCtQ%3A1614093235106&ei=sxs1YIr3BYfWtAab4pOICQ&q=sydnor+lane%2C+galveston%2C+tx&oq=syd&gs_lcp=Cgdnd3Mtd2l6EAEYATIECCMQJzIECCMQJzIECAAQQzIECAAQQzIECC4QQzIECAAQQzIKCC4QxwEQrwEQQzIECC4QQzICCC4yBAguEEM6CAgAELEDEIMBOgUIABCxA1DoFViiKmCgPWgAcAJ4AIABkAGIAYcEkgEDMC40mAEAoAEBqgEHZ3dzLXdpesABAQ&sclient=gws-wiz. See also Sydnor Bayou Estates, "Sydnor Estates," Nextdoor.com, accessed March 22, 2021, https://nextdoor.com/neighborhood/sydnorbayouestates--galveston--tx/.

90. Galveston County Clerk's Records, Book F, page 36, #1846000283, Sandusky's Map of Sydnor's Subdivision in Section 4, Galveston Island.

91. Seabrook Sydnor brought a lawsuit seeking to recover block 29 of the Holman addition to the City of Houston. A jury decided against Seabrook Sydnor. *Seabrook W. Sydnor v. Texas Savings & Real Estate Investments Ass'n*, 42 Tex. Civ. App. 138, 94 S.W. 451 (1908).

92. John Nova Lomax, "OLD WEIRD HOUSTON: Five Historic Houston Spots That Need Markers" *Houstonian Magazine*, August 27, 2013, accessed March 22, 2021, https://www.houstoniamag.com/travel-and-outdoors/2013/08/five-historic-houston-spots-that-need-markers-august-2013.

    Place: Congress Avenue between Fannin and Main

    What Happened There: For about the last 15 years leading up to and including the Civil War, former Galveston mayor John Seabrook Sydnor bought and sold slaves on the site. We should never forget this.

    • • •

    Quote: Taken from *The City of Houston from Wilderness to Wonder*, by O. F. Allen: "I have seen that eloquent auctioneer sell many slaves. He was an expert as an orator in the description he gave of the qualities and abilities of the slaves he offered for sale; and often attracted large crowds at his place by his eloquence and voice."

    The Houston auction house's location, as identified by the author (John Nova Lomax), sat in what is now the downtown commercial district of Houston (1098 Congress).

    Sydnor's considerable slave trading wealth also influenced the development of the city of Waco. See "Waco History," Waco: Heart of Texas, accessed March 22, 2021, https://wacoheartoftexas.com/wp-content/uploads/2017/05/Waco-History-2017.pdf.

In 1848 Gen. Thomas J. Chambers sold a two-league grant of land, including the old Waco village site, to John S. Sydnor of Galveston. Sydnor struck a deal with land agent Jacob De Cordova to divide the property and dispose of it at a dollar an acre. George B. Erath, who had first visited the area as one of the rangers stationed at the old 1837 outpost, was one of De Cordova's surveyors, and he urged that the new townsite be placed at the former Indian village. In 1848 the tract was sold to Nathaniel A. Ware and Jonas Butler of Galveston; they became De Cordova's partners in the venture. See also Sharon Bracken, ed., *Historic McLennan County: An Illustrated History* (San Antonio, Texas: Historical Publishing Network 2010), 7.

Chapter 7

1. "John Henry Brown," Legislative Reference Library of Texas, accessed November 16, 2024, https://lrl.texas.gov/legeleaders/members/memberdisplay.cfm?memberID=5056.
2. *Civilian and* [Galveston] *Gazette*, December 15, 1857, 2.
3. Ancestry.com/US Bureau of the Census 1860 U.S. Federal Census - Slave Schedules Database (John Henry Brown, accessed January 29, 2023). Original data: United States of America Bureau of the Census, *Eighth Census of the United States, 1860*, (Washington, DC: National Archives and Records Administration, 1860), M653, 1,438 rolls, accessed January 29, 2023, https://www.ancestry.com/search/collections/7668/.
4. "John Henry Brown (1820–1895)," Texas State Historical Association, https://www.tshaonline.org/handbook/entries/brown-john-henry; Robert Wilonsky, "As Dallas Prepares to Revisit Its Confederate Past," *Dallas Morning News*, March 15, 2018; "John Henry Brown," Dallas Jewish Historical Society, accessed November 16, 2024, https://virtualtour.djhs.org/dallas-historical-places/south-dallas/brown-middle-school/; "John Henry Brown," Texas A&M University Libraries, Library Catalog, accessed November 16, 2024, https://catalog.library.tamu.edu/Author/Home?author=Brown%2C+John+Henry%2C+1820-1895&.
5. The author disagrees with the anticipated argument that Brown's views were the exception to the rule. His were not the exception, they were the rule—stating what needed to be said to protect the status quo. Brown was honored with positions of power in both Galveston and Dallas, with his name bestowed on public places to remind others that *our people's* brilliance

is the reason the country exists. Brown's preaching White superiority was part of the continued rot and, unless excised, will continue to infect our views of history. Brown did not name the streets in his and others' honor, nor place his name and others on numerous public institutions. The statues scattered across the South and the mythical figures set out in literature were not put in place by these figures but their heirs and others who followed— to tell a story, a tale, the fatal lie. This is the importance of recognizing the hallowed places in which human beings were picked and culled like peas, peaches, apples—strange fruit, as we were deemed. See Wilonsky, "As Dallas Prepares to Revisit Its Confederate Past."

Another example is in order. In referencing TSHA's website, any historian, student, or member of the public would never know of John Henry Brown's views by reading the site only; one learns Brown was a newspaperman, working for the *Austin Sentinel* and the *Victoria Advocate* and, after his move to Galveston in 1854, as the associate editor of the *Civilian and Galveston Gazette*. See "John Henry Brown (1820–1895)," Texas State Historical Association, published 1852, updated July 4, 2019, https://www.tshaonline.org/handbook/entries/brown-john-henry. Little is mentioned of his work supporting the institution of slavery in both Galveston and Dallas. The slant is probably a wise decision on TSHA's part—if the intent is not to retell the virulent and poisonous justification for slavery.

6. Michael Davis, "National Archives Safeguards Original 'Juneteenth' Order," June 19, 2020, National Archives News, accessed April 6, 2021, https://www.archives.gov/news/articles/juneteenth-original-document?_ga=2.3014704.1824694626.1617714739-555184832.1614703097. See also Robert C. Conner, *General Gordon Granger: The Savior of Chickamauga and the Man Behind 'Juneteenth'* (Philadelphia & Oxford: Casemate Publishers 2013), 177.

7. Conner, *General Gordon Granger*, 177.

8. Edward Alexander, "Granger's Juneteenth Orders and the Limiting of Freedom," June 23, 2020, Emerging Civil War, accessed March 21, 2021, https://emergingcivilwar.com/2020/06/23/grangers-juneteenth-orders-and-the-limiting-of-freedom/.

9. Alexander, "Granger's Juneteenth Orders and the Limiting of Freedom."

10. After Abraham Lincoln's assassination, the Southern insurrectionists had a more sympathetic president. By way of example, John S. Sydnor's pardon was issued on October 12, 1865, a mere four months after the reading of General Granger's order. "U.S., Pardons under Amnesty Proclamations, 1865–1869," Ancestry.com, accessed April 8, 2021, https://www.ancestry.

NOTES

11. *Brown v. Board of Education of Topeka*, 347 U.S. 483 (1954).
12. Conner, *General Gordon Granger*, 177.
13. "'I can't tell a lie, Pa,' George Washington and the Cherry Tree Myth," George Washington Mount Vernon, accessed March 21, 2021, https://www.mountvernon.org/george-washington/facts/myths/george-washington-and-the-cherry-tree-myth/.
14. Alexander, "Granger's Juneteenth Orders and the Limiting of Freedom."
15. U.S. Bureau of the Census, *Negro Population in the United States, 1790–1915* (Washington, DC, Government Printing Office, 1918), 17–18, 44; U.S. Bureau of the Census, *Statistics of the Population of the United States, 1870* (Washington, DC: Government Printing Office, 1872), 3.
16. Quintard Taylor, *In Search of the Racial Frontier: African Americans in the American West, 1528–1990* (New York: Norton, 1998), 104–6.
17. Lawrence D. Rice, *The Negro in Texas: 1874–1900* (Baton Rouge: Louisiana State University Press, 1971), 152.
18. "Cotton Gin Rites Conducted for 99-Year-Old Man," Newspapers.com, accessed March 21, 2021, https://www.newspapers.com/clip/58941344/obituary-for-james-albert-wright-aged/.
19. "Funeral Set for Resident of Mexia, 104," Newspapers.com, accessed March 21, 2021, https://img4.newspapers.com/clip/58942065/obituary-for-lillie-ann-wright-aged/.
20. "Grandma's Hands," Bill Withers, *Just as I Am*, SUX227, 1971.
21. "Couple Fete Their 75th Wedding Day," *Waco News Tribune*, November 19, 1961.

Chapter 8

1. Dana Burke, "Yarbrough Wins Galveston Race," *The Houston Chronicle*, November 8, 2006.
2. "George P. Mitchell Society," Texas A&M University at Galveston, accessed May 1, 2021, https://www.tamug.edu/develop/campaigns/mitchellsociety.html.
3. Latonia Wilson, interview by author on November 28, 2021; interview notes in possession of author.
4. Ancestry.com New Orleans, Louisiana, U.S. Slave Manifests, 1807–1860 Database (accessed January 24, 2023). This collection was indexed by Ancestry World Archives Project contributors. Original data: "Slave Manifests of Coastwise Vessels Filed at New Orleans, Louisiana, 1807–1860," NAID: 5573655, microfilm publication, M1895, 30 rolls, Records

of the U.S. Customs Service, 1745–1997, Record Group 36, The National Archives in Washington, DC, accessed January 24, 2023, https://www.ancestry.com/search/collections/1562.

5. Ancestry.com New Orleans, Louisiana, U.S. Slave Manifests, 1807–1860 Database (accessed January 24, 2023), https://www.ancestry.com/search/collections/1562/?f-Self-Arrival-Destination=Galveston.

6. Ancestry.com New Orleans, Louisiana, U.S. Slave Manifests, 1807–1860 Database (accessed January 24, 2023), https://www.ancestry.com/search/collections/1562/?departure=_galveston-galveston-texas-usa_77069.

7. Ancestry.com New Orleans, Louisiana, U.S. Slave Manifests, 1807–1860 Database (accessed January 24, 2023), https://www.ancestry.com/search/collections/1562/?departure=_galveston-galveston-texas-usa_77069.

8. The facsimile of a manifest is from Rice University: "Facing the Gulf: Learning Stories of Slavery in Galveston, 1816–1865", FILE #40: 31204_189187-00447.JPG, accessed February 12, 2023, https://digitalprojects.rice.edu/facingthegulf/files/show/40.

9. "Louisiana 210th Anniversary of Statehood (1812): April 20, 2022," Census.gov, accessed August 4, 2022, https://www.census.gov/newsroom/stories/louisiana-admission-anniversary.html#:~:text=Louisiana%20was%20admitted%20to%20the,the%20present%2Dday%20state%20boundary.

10. Ancestry.com New Orleans, Louisiana, U.S. Slave Manifests, 1807–1860 Database (accessed January 24, 2023), https://www.ancestry.com/search/collections/1562/?f-Self-Arrival-Destination=Galveston.

11. Ancestry.com New Orleans, Louisiana, U.S. Slave Manifests, 1807–1860 Database (accessed January 24, 2023), https://www.ancestry.com/search/collections/1562/?f-Self-Arrival-Destination=Galveston.

12. Ancestry.com New Orleans, Louisiana, U.S. Slave Manifests, 1807–1860 Database (accessed January 24, 2023), https://www.ancestry.com/search/collections/1562/?f-Self-Arrival-Destination=Galveston.

13. Solomon Northup, *12 Years a Slave* (New York: Penguin Books, 2012), 16.

14. Northup, *12 Years a Slave*, 16.

15. Northup, *12 Years a Slave*, 35–36. The number to be shipped is always a concern—or an economic concern. In the book, *Barracoon: The Story of the Last "Black Cargo,"* Cudjo Lewis, the formerly enslaved, conveyed to Zora Neale Hurston the starkness of the trade: "When we dere three weeks a white man come in wo men of de Dahomen. One man, he is chief of Dahomey and de udder one his word-changer. Dey make everybody stand in a ring—'bout ten folks in each ring—De men by dey self, de women by dey self. Den de white man lookee and lookee. He lookee hard at de skin and

de feet and de legs and in de mouth. Den he choose. Every time he choose a man he choose a woman. Every time take a woman he take a man, too. Derefore, you unnerstand me, he take one hunnard and thirty. Sixty-five men wid a woman for each man. Dass right." Zora Neale Hurston, edited by Debora G. Plant, *Barracoon: The Story of the Last "Black Cargo"* (New York: Amistad, 2018), 53.

16. "About New Orleans, Louisiana, U.S., Slave Manifests, 1807–1860," Ancestry.com, accessed April 24, 2021, https://www.ancestry.com/search/collections/1562 (Slave Manifest dated April 21, 1840).

Chapter 9

1. John Coulter, *The Complete Story of the Galveston Horror* (Atlanta, GA: United Publishers of America, 1923 / Sacramento: Franklin Classic Trade Press), 57. The author, Coulter, was a journalist, formerly with the *New York Herald*, who travelled to Galveston to document and collect the stories which were the byproduct of the 1900 storm. Coulter, in this documentation, reveals Galvestonians demonized the Negro. This was normally done in context of pleas to the outside world for money and supplies.

    "Tuesday night ninety negro looters were shot in their tracks by citizen guards, one of them was searched and $700 found, together with four diamond rings and two water-soaked gold watches. The finger of a white woman with a gold band around it was clutched in his hands.

    Over 100 ghouls were shot Wednesday afternoon and evening, and no mercy was shown vandals. If they were not killed at the first volley the troops—regulars of the United States army and those of the Texas National Guard—saw that the coup de grace was administered.

    Most of the robbers were negroes, and when executed were found loaded with spoil—jewelry wrenched from the bodies of women, money and watches and silverware and other articles taken from residences and business houses." Coulter, *The Complete Story of the Galveston Horror*, 85. This quote was from a section titled "A City Official's Version of the Reign of Terror."

    After the 1900 storm an estimated 8,000 people perished. The actual number of deaths remains unknown, with estimates between 6,000 and 12,000 people. "The Great Galveston Storm came ashore the night of Sept 8, 1900, with an estimated strength of a Category 4. It remains the deadliest natural disaster and the worst hurricane in US history." John Burnett, "The Tempest at Galveston: 'We Knew There Was a Storm Coming, But We Had No Idea,'" NPR, November 30, 2017, accessed January 21, 2023, https://

www.npr.org/2017/11/30/566950355/the-tempest-at-galveston-we-knew-there-was-a-storm-coming-but-we-had-no-idea. Even with massive destruction and death, race mattered in all respects: "Great difficulty was experienced in securing men to transport bodies to the wharves where the barges lay, and it was practically an impossibility to get anyone to touch the bodies of the negro victims, decomposition having set in earlier than in the cases of whites, and had it not been that the members of the fire department volunteered their services the remains of the negros would have remained unburied for a longer time then they were." Coulter, *The Complete Story of the Galveston Horror*, 47. See also "Lynching of Chester Sawyer," *Galveston Daily News*, June 25, 1917. Sawyer's case accords with other cases recounted that the jailer was overwhelmed by a mob.

2. National Register of Historic Places, Texas, Galveston County, accessed November 16, 2024, https://nationalregisterofhistoricplaces.com/tx/galveston/state.html#google_vignette; Rosewood Cemetery Listed on National Register of Historic Places, Galveston Historic Foundation, accessed November 16, 2024, https://www.galvestonhistory.org/news/rosewood-cemetery-listed-on-national-register-of-historic-places.

3. "95 Down South (All the Places We've Been)," Gil Scott-Heron and Brian Jackson, track 9 on *Bridges*, 1977, https://www.lyricsondemand.com/g/gilscottheronandbrianjacksonlyrics/95southalloftheplaceswevebeen-lyrics.html.

4. Ellen Beasley, *The Alleys and Back Buildings of Galveston: An Architectural and Social History* (Houston: Rice University Press, 1996).

5. Beasley, *The Alleys and Back Buildings of Galveston*, 7.

6. Howard Barnstone, *The Galveston That Was* (Houston: Rice University Press, 1966/1993).

7. Fig. 10 from the author's collection. The picture was taken during the construction of the Galveston Seawall after the 1900 storm. Photograph by Ed Worthy, city engineer for the City of Galveston. What was the races of the laborers? The race of the supervisors? It seems the workers' faces are obscured while the supervisor's faces were not. See also "Raising Galveston Above the Gulf," The Story of Texas.com, accessed April 29, 2021, https://www.thestoryoftexas.com/discovery/texas-story-project/raising-galveston-above-the-gulf.

8. Barnstone, *The Galveston That Was*, 211.

9. City of Galveston, Old Central & Carver Park Neighborhood Plan, prepared by the Department of Planning and Transportation, undated report, 2. See also acknowledgements page. The report was issued during Barbara

Crews' administration (report in possession of author). Crews served as mayor from 1990 to 1996. "The History of Congregation B'nai Israel," Congregation B'nai Israel, accessed May 1, 2021, https://www.cbigalveston.org/our-history.

10. As additional foundation for the concept of destruction and the layering over this history under the rubric of urban renewal, see the Texas Historical Commission links, accessed April 29, 2021; Properties located between 26th and 27th, running north/south between Market to Winnie and running east/west represent five blocks of the land/housing that were taken by eminent domain and replaced with a parking lot for the post office and federal courthouse (between Winnie and Church, 27th and 26th Street) and a physical plant for the utility company and the light company (running from Winnie to Market, 27th Street and 26th Street). See photographs taken by Texas Historical Commission: [Photograph THC_14-0740, 2601 Church; https://bit.ly/373bknL]; [Photograph THC_14-0552; https://bit.ly/3frkK06, 2723 Sealy]; [Photograph THC_14-0884; https://bit.ly/35Reprx; 2820 Post Office]; [Photograph THC_14-0739; https://bit.ly/2USLnl3; 2601 Church]; [Photograph THC_14-0657; https://bit.ly/3nN20Ld; 2827 Winnie]; [Photograph THC_14-0661; https://bit.ly/2J0xz5c; 2818 Ball]; [Photograph THC_14-0742; https://bit.ly/2HvxjLi; 2727 Church]; [Photograph THC_14-0659; https://bit.ly/3pSsVHC; 2818 Ball]; [Photograph THC_14-0654; https://bit.ly/3pRlxM2; 2708 Ball]; [Photograph THC_14-0734; https://bit.ly/3nTauAN; 2609 Church]; [Photograph THC_14-0737; https://bit.ly/3lWVh0H; 2603 Church]; [Photograph THC_14-0736; https://bit.ly/3kRN4JX; 2603 Church]; [Photograph THC_14-0655; https://bit.ly/33afARb; 2821, 2823, 2827 Winnie Street]; [Photograph THC_14-0879; https://bit.ly/2KsY3gp; 2710 Post Office]; [Photograph THC_14-0563; https://bit.ly/3737BXj; 2801 Ball]; [Photograph THC_14-0662; https://bit.ly/3frWieP; 2818 Ball]; [Photograph THC_14-0982; https://bit.ly/35U6Lgb; 2717 Post Office]; [Photograph THC_14-0738; https://bit.ly/2KoYZlW; 2601 Church]; [Photograph THC_14-0256; https://bit.ly/35W129E; 2815 Sealy]; [Photograph THC_14-0546; https://bit.ly/3pRerYq; 2627 Ball]; [Photograph THC_14-0983; https://bit.ly/3kUXtEH; 2705 Postoffice]; [Photograph THC_14-0653; https://bit.ly/2KsVvil; 2620 Ball]; [Photograph THC_14-0735; https://bit.ly/2IR4z0h; 2609 Church]; [Photograph THC_14-0988; https://bit.ly/2KAoykl; 515 27th Street]; [Photograph THC_14-0984; https://bit.ly/2IUQY7D; 2705 Postoffice]; [Photograph THC_14-0660; https://bit.ly/3fm6420; 2818

Ball]; [Photograph THC_14-0554https://bit.ly/2HtGSua; 811 27th Street];[Photograph THC_14-0658; https://bit.ly/35UqcWc; 2818 Ball]; [Photograph THC_14-0986; https://bit.ly/3kXUueG; 2705 Postoffice]; [Photograph THC_14-0555; https://bit.ly/392HNNv; 811 27th Street]; [Photograph THC_14-0743; https://bit.ly/3fmGpGB; 612 28th Street]; [Photograph THC_14-0741; https://bit.ly/3lVA1sp; 2601 Church [Centerpoint's location, note bulldozers]; [Photograph THC_14-0549; https://bit.ly/2IXQcH9; 2619 Ball]; [Photograph THC_14-0567; https://bit.ly/2UMXUX4; 811 28th Street]; [Photograph THC_14-0987; https://bit.ly/3fnvYT3; 2705 Postoffice Street]; [Photograph THC_14-0656; https://bit.ly/36XV1Zg; 2821, 2823, 2827 Winnie Street]; [Photograph THC_14-0564;https://bit.ly/3pUhG15; 2801 Ball]; [Photograph THC_14-0258; https://bit.ly/3kU8Eh1; 2815 Sealy].

11. Arnold J. Toynbee, *The Disintegrations of Civilizations, Vol. V* (Oxford: Oxford University Press, 1939). See also Amoz JY Hor, "NATO Was Founded to Protect 'Civilized' People. That Means White," April 12, 2022, *Washington Post*, wherein the writer aptly describes Toynbee's influence on defining history in a racial construct:

This was not an isolated sentiment. Fifty years before Samuel Huntington's book *Clash of Civilizations*, the term "Western civilization" was the title of history courses. The most famous was Arnold Toynbee's bestseller *A Study of History*, in which he represents "Western Civilization" as the only civilization exclusively made up of the three White "races"—Nordic, Alpine, and Mediterranean. (By contrast, he states that Black "races" have not contributed to any civilization.)

Because "Western Civilization" was (or is) understood to be exclusively made of White "races," the term could function as a surrogate term for "Whiteness," including in the preamble of the North Atlantic Treaty: "The Parties to this Treaty ... are determined to safeguard the freedom, *common heritage and civilization* of their peoples." (Note: emphasis is the author's.)

12. In the book *The Galveston That Was*, the only instance where an African American appears in conjunction with a structure is a bordello on Post Office Street, West of 25th Street, with a Black man sitting in the doorway. The address above the doorway was 2526 Post Office. From a historical standpoint, the same logic applies: Are we to believe the heritage of people who look like me on this island is so insignificant or so unworthy of recognition that omissions from the annals of history are acceptable and appropriate? I would posit the opposite is true; our contributions were fundamental in the structured and regulated society. The persistent failure

of inclusion poisons the well of historical integrity.

13. Rosanna Xia, "Manhattan Was Once Home to Black Beachgoers, but the City Ran Them Out. Now it Faces a Reckoning," *Los Angeles Times*, August 20, 2020; Jacey Fortin, "A Fight for Justice on the Sands of a California Beach," *New York Times*, March 13, 2021, A14.

14. Fig. 11 excerpted from NPR's story about the Bruce family.

15. Izola Ethel Fedford Collins, *Island of Color: Where Juneteenth Started* (Bloomington: AuthorHouse, 2004), 19.

16. Collins, *Island of Color*, 19. Permit me to state the obvious: water has the same effect on all of us. It has been used as symbolism in literature, religion, and daily life; dare I say, it is an essential element of our existence—without it we do not survive. In the same context, people of color are as attracted to the water as others. The segregation of beaches and swimming pools is all part of our Southern heritage. Without citing the academic research on these policies—permit me the privilege this one time—this is one of the reasons African Americans' death rates from drowning exceeds those of other racial and ethnic groups, and it follows the percentage of African Americans able to swim is lower than that of other racial/ethnic groups.

17. *Galveston Daily News*, December 23, 1910. See also *Galveston Daily News*, September 27, 2010, B1, B6. McGuire's partners were W. D. Lewis and Peter Antone. The co-partnership was entered on December 20, 1910, "to be known as: 'The McGuire Park Company.'" The purpose of the agreement was quite clear: "... is for the entertainment of colored People." Document number 1003610, Real Property Record, Galveston County Clerk's Office, Book 242, 696–97. McGuire purchased at least part of the tract of the land in 1904. *Galveston Daily News*, November 8, 1904, 12 (a transaction between Wolfe W. Wenk to Robert McGuire, lot 3, northeast one quarter outlot 149).

What do we know about McGuire's business partners? Reference to the newspapers reveal they, too, were active in business and politics in the city. Peter Antone was a member of the Lone Star Cotton Jammers Association, Local 851, and the International Longshoremen's Association (ILA)—he was chairman of the organization. *City Times*, July 14, 1917, 3. Antone's residence was located at 2820 Avenue M. *Galveston Daily News*, August 18, 1936, 7. Peter Antone Jr. died May 15, 1935, at the age of 24. He is also listed as a "negro longshoremen." *Galveston Daily News*, May 16, 1937, 18. After the city's exercise of eminent domain, Peter Antone started doing business with T. P. Pope in construction ("house repair, carpentry, raising and moving"). *City Times*, November 6, 1915, 8. Their business address was located at 35th and Avenue M 1/2. W. D. Lewis was the proprietor of Lone Star Restaurant and Lodging House located at 2507 Strand, opposite the Union Depot. *City Times*, May 18, 1901, 4. Lewis was a delegate to the State Convention in Dallas for the Republican Party. *Galveston Daily News*, March 13, 1904, 5. Lewis and others sued in 1904, seeking an injunction against W. R. Carruthers, in county court, Judge Lewis Fisher's court. The request for the injunction was denied. *Galveston Daily News*, April 8, 1904, 4. Lewis also bought property off the island in Dickinson in 1904. *Galveston Daily News*, May 31, 1904, 10. He was elected to represent Galveston's local branch of the National Negro Business League in 1904. *Galveston Daily News*, August 30, 1904, 10. He was also on the executive board for the State Farmers Union. *Galveston Daily News*, February 17, 1905, 5. Lewis lived at 2802 Avenue M. *Galveston Daily News*, July 24, 1907, 12.

18. *Galveston Tribune*, April 20, 1911, 4.
19. "Dent, Jessie Mae (1891–1948)," Texas State Historical Association, accessed March 27, 2021, https://www.tshaonline.org/handbook/entries/dent-jessie-may-mcguire.
20. Ancestry.com U.S. City Directories 1822–1995 of Galveston, Texas Database (city directory of 1913, Robert McGuire; accessed December 30, 2023), https://www.ancestry.com/search/collections/2469/.
21. Ancestry.com U.S. City Directories 1822–1995 of Galveston Texas Database (city directory of 1913, Robert McGuire; accessed December 30, 2023), https://www.ancestry.com/search/collections/2469/. Suemedha Sood, "The Origins of Public Bathhouse Cultures Around the World," BBC, November 29, 2012, accessed November 16, 2024, https://www.bbc.com/travel/article/20121129-the-origins-of-bathhouse-culture-around-the-world.
22. "Taxicab Stand," Meriam Webster Dictionary, accessed November 16, 2024, https://www.merriam-webster.com/dictionary/taxi%20standApril 8, 2021; "Hack Stand," Real Estate Definition, accessed November 16, 2024, https://www.realestatedefinition.com/hack-stand.
23. Ancestry.com U.S. City Directories 1822–1995 Galveston, Texas Database (city directory of 1914, Robert McGuire; accessed April 8, 2021), https://www.ancestry.com/search/collections/2469/.
24. William D. Angel Jr., "Controlling the Workers: The Galveston Dock Workers' Strike of 1920 and its Impact on Labor Relations in Texas," *East Texas Historical Journal* 23, no. 2 (1985), Article 6; 15, http://scholar works.sfasu.edu/ethj/vol23/iss2/6.
25. Ancestry.com. City Directories 1822–1995, Galveston, Texas Database (city directory of 1916, Robert McGuire; accessed April 8, 2021), https://www.

NOTES

ancestry.com/search/collections/2469/.

26. In context of identifying the location of other African American businesses, see *City Times*, January 2, 1915: Joseph Cuney, Attorney at Law, is listed at 1519 Mechanic. Dr. William Willis, "the dentist," was at 426 25th Street and Postoffice; office addresses for the physician and surgeon's office were in the Office of the Lone Star Screwman Hall, 2710 Market Street and No. 3505 Avenue L for Dr. L. M. Wilkins; Sons of Ham Brass Band, D. M. J. Sanders, manager, was listed at 314 26th Street; and developer F. E. Stewart at 2722 Market Street (advertising the sale of land in La Marque, Texas, "controlled by colored men").

27. In 1937, Robert McGuire moved his residence and family to La Marque: see *Galveston Daily News*, May 26, 1937, 3. What would the heirs of Robert McGuire say today? Would his daughter say her daddy's name should be the name on the land? Would not the heirs of Robert McGuire—like the Bruce family—demand the land be deeded back by the City of Galveston?

28. Jacey Fortin, "This Black Family Ran a Thriving Beach Resort 100 Years Ago. They Want Their Land Back," *The New York Times*, March 11, 2021.

29. *City Times* (Galveston) [hereafter *City Times*], January 2, 1915, 1. *City Times* was published from 1900 to 1927. The *City Times* office was located at 1925 Mechanic Street. *City Times*, January 2, 1915, 4.

30. Jacey Fortin, "A Fight for Justice on the Sands of a California Beach," *New York Times*, March 13, 2021; Collins, *Island of Color*, 16–18.

31. *City Times*, January 2, 1915, 1.

32. Fortin, "A Fight for Justice on the Sands of a California Beach"; Collins, *Island of Color*, 16–18.

33. *Galveston Daily News*, July 5, 1915, 10. See also "Give a Concert in Menard Park," *Galveston Tribune*, July 5, 1915, 2; "Work at Exposition Grounds," *Galveston Daily News*, May 27, 1916, 10 (detailing work underway at Menard Park).

34. The *Galveston Daily News* reported the city undertaking repairs on the center. The article provided a May 1, 1945, formal opening date for the center. *Galveston Daily News*, May 15, 1978, 36. See also "Community Center to Open May 1," *Galveston Daily News*, April 20, 1945, 31. The center was occupied by (White) troops during World War II. The announcement read: "Menard Park will become Galveston's first community recreational center at the formal opening, May 1, Charles C. Bunnenberg, park and recreation director, announced yesterday following completion of negotiations with the federal security agency. The city is now in complete possession of both the Wright Cuney [where colored troops were housed] and

Menard Park building, formerly occupied by USO. Opening date for the Cuney recreation center will be announced soon, he said." The *Galveston Tribune* announced the band concerts at Menard Park, "usually Saturday and Sunday night." *Galveston Tribune*, August 12, 1916, 5. A "modern band shell" was constructed in 1950 for crowds to listen to bands on the lawn. *Galveston Daily News*, September 3, 1950, 13. Galveston did not cease segregation of public facilities until the 1960s.

35. Ancestry.com 1850 U.S. Federal Census Database (Michael B. Menard; accessed January 30, 2023). Original data: United States of America Bureau of the Census, *Seventh Census of the United States, 1850* (Washington, DC: National Archives and Records Administration, 1850) M432, 1,009 rolls, accessed January 30, 2023, https://www.ancestry.com/search/collections/8055/.

36. Menard County, Eden, Texas, accessed November 16, 2024, https://www.edentexas.com/community/page/menard-county#:~:text=In%20 1858%2C%20Menard%20County%20was,of%20Galveston%2C%20 Michel%20Branamour%20Menard. In the 1860 U.S. federal census of slave schedules, R. H. Menard, M. Menard's fourth wife, is shown as owning ten enslaved; eight out of the ten are listed as mulatto. Ancestry.com 1860 U.S. Federal Census - Slave Schedules Database (Michael B. Menard). Original data: United States of America Bureau of the Census, *Eighth Census of the United States, 1860* (Washington, DC: National Archives and Records Administration, 1860) M653, 1,438 rolls, accessed January 30, 2023, https://www.ancestry.com/search/collections/7668/. See "Find a Grave: Rebecca Mary Fluker Menard," Find a Grave, accessed December 31, 2023, https://www.findagrave.com/memorial/58977380/rebecca-mary-menard. In any event, the slave schedules almost never conclusively connect a specific enslaved individual with a particular slave owner. At best, they provide supporting evidence for a hypothesis derived from other sources. When researching enslaved individuals, the slave schedules are most helpful when used in conjunction with the 1870 U.S. federal census, the U.S. census mortality schedules from 1850–1885, wills, and probate documents. https://www.ancestry.com/search/collections/7668/.

37. J. L. Darragh is listed in 1850 as owning four enslaved persons and in 1860 owning six. Ancestry.com 1850 U.S. Federal Census - Slave Schedules Database; Original data: United States of America Bureau of the Census, *Seventh Census of the United States, 1850* (Washington, DC: National Archives and Records Administration, 1850) M432, 1,009 roll, accessed January 30, 2023, 475, https://www.ancestry.com/search/collections/8055/;

Ancestry.com 1860 U.S. Federal Census - Slave Schedules Database. Original data: United States of America, Bureau of the Census. *Eighth Census of the United States, 1860.* Washington, DC: National Archives and Records Administration, 1860. M653, 1,438 rolls, accessed January 30, 2023, https://www.ancestry.com/search/collections/7668/.

38. Doswell, Hill & Co. is listed in 1860 as owning two slaves. Ancestry.com 1860 U.S. Federal Census - Slave Schedules Database (Doswell, Hill & Co, accessed January 30, 2023). Original data: United States of America, Bureau of the Census. *Eighth Census of the United States, 1860.* Washington, DC: National Archives and Records Administration, 1860. M653, 1,438 rolls, https://www.ancestry.com/search/collections/7668/.
39. John H. Heller, *Heller's Galveston City Directory, 1876–1877* (Galveston, Texas, 1876), 36.
40. *Galveston Daily News*, August 31, 1999, 6.
41. The DAR's website says: "The George Washington Chapter was organized June 17, 1895, when twenty women met in the home of Mrs. George Seeligson in Galveston, Texas. It was the first Texas chapter and holds the distinction of being older than the Texas State Organization." "George Washington Chapter: The National Society of the Daughters of the American Revolution, Galveston, Texas," Texas DAR, accessed April 23, 2021, https://www.texasdar.org/chapters/GeorgeWashington/#:~:text=George%20Seeligson%20in%20Galveston%2C%20Texas,The%20organizing%20Regent%20was%20Mrs.&text=The%20chapter%20also%20organized%20the,Galveston%20during%20World%20War%20I.
42. Sarah Maslin Nir, "For Daughters of the American Revolution, A New Chapter," *The New York Times*, July 3, 2012.
43. The Mary Moody Northen Endowment website is quite explicit in showing Mrs. Northen's connection to Galveston's society and economy: "At the age of 62 when her father died, Mrs. Northen became president of the American National Insurance Company, Moody National Bank, the News Publishing Company (which owned the *Galveston News* and the *Galveston Tribune*), the Commonwealth Life and Accident Insurance Company of St. Louis, American Printing Company and W. L. Moody and Company, Unincorporated Bankers of Galveston." She also chaired the boards of directors of the Moody Foundation, the W. L. Moody Cotton Company, the Southern Trading Company, the National Hotel Company and nearly 40 hotels owned by Affiliated National Hotels, and Silver Lake Ranches, which owned properties in Texas, Oklahoma, and West Virginia. "About Mrs. Northen," Northenendowment.org, accessed April 23, 2021, https://

www.northenendowment.org/MrsNorthen.asp.

44. John Wayne Ferguson, "In Galveston, a New Monument Honors Korean War Dead," *Galveston County Daily News*, May 27, 2022, 1.
45. *Galveston Daily News*, December 23, 1910. See also *Galveston Daily News*, September 27, 2010, B1, B6.
46. Inflation Calculator, U.S. Inflation Calculator.com, accessed February 14, 2023, http://www.usinflationcalculator.com.
47. "Programs for This Week to Entertain Service Men," *Galveston Daily News*, January 25, 1942, 20.
48. "CPI Inflation Calendar," December 29, 2024, https://www.in2013dollars.com/us/inflation/1915?endYear=2024&amount=18000; see also City Times, January 2, 2015, 1.
49. "Galveston Seawall and Grade Raising," ASCE, accessed February 2, 2023, https://www.asce.org/about-civil-engineering/history-and-heritage/historic-landmarks/galveston-seawall-and-grade-raising#:~:text=Galveston%20Island%20is%20a%20barrier,against%20hurricanes%20and%20tropical%20storms.
50. Rosanna Xia, "Bruce's Beach Can Return to Descendants of Black Family in Landmark Move Signed by Governor Newsom," *Los Angeles Times*, September 30, 2021. See also Rosanna Xia, "Manhattan Was Once Home to Black Beachgoers, but the City Ran Them Out. Now It Faces a Reckoning," *Los Angeles Times*, August 20, 2020; Jaclyn Cosgrove and Rosanna Xia, "Bruce's Beach May Return to Family's Hand," *Los Angeles Times*, April 10, 2021, B-1, accessed April 10, 2021.
51. William Shakespeare, *The Tragicall Historie of Hamlet, Prince of Denmarke*: [...] (Second Quarto), London: [...] I[ames] R[oberts] for N[icholas] L[ing] [...], published 1604, OCLC 760858814, [Act III, scene ii].
52. "Johnson, Eddie Bernice," History, Art, & Archives, United States House of Representatives, accessed December 31, 2023, https://history.house.gov/People/Detail/15852.
53. Congresswoman Johnson, interview by author, February 19, 2020.
54. See also "Raising Galveston Above the Gulf," The Story of Texas, accessed April 29, 2021, https://www.thestoryoftexas.com/discover/texas-story-project/raising-galveston-above-the-gulf.
55. Mindy Thompson Fullilove, MD, "Eminent Domain & African Americans: What Is the Price of Commons?" Institute of Justice, 1, accessed April 1, 2021, https://ij.org/wp-content/uploads/2015/03/Perspectives-Fullilove.pdf.
56. Fullilove, "Eminent Domain & African Americans," 2.

NOTES

Chapter 10

1. Izola Ethel Fedford Collins, *Island of Color: Where Juneteenth Started* (Bloomington: AuthorHouse, 2004), 27.
2. Texas State Library and Archives Commission, "Early African American Senators," accessed April 14, 2021, https://www.tsl.texas.gov/treasures/giants/aalege.html; Texas State Historical Association, "Ruby, George Thompson (1841–1882)," accessed May 1, 2021, https://www.tshaonline.org/handbook/entries/ruby-george-thompson; Texas State Library and Archives Commission, "Did You Know in Texas History: George T. Ruby," accessed March 13, 2022, https://www.tsl.texas.gov/outofthestacks/did-you-know-in-texas-history-george-t-ruby/.
3. *Galveston Daily News*, December 9, 1869, 3; In 1896, DeBruhl testified in the case of Frank Davis, which was called to jury trial in the criminal district court. Davis's lawyers filed a motion to quash the indictment and complained about the lack of persons of African descent.
"John De Bruhl, colored, testified that he had lived in Galveston thirty-seven years, held offices—justice of the peace four years, and alderman one year. The district attorney [Gillaspie] objected to his testimony because there was nothing to predicate it on, nothing having been introduced to show discrimination." *Galveston Daily News*, March 11, 1896, 12; The court [Judge Cavin] overruled defense counsels' motion. The news article also identified two colored lawyers, W. H. Smith and H. H. Swanson. Judge John F. De Bruhl died in 1904; his service was held at Reedy Chapel A.M.E. *Galveston Daily News*, July 18, 1904, 8; "De Bruhl, John (col.), Justice Peace, 105 Tremont Street, residence near Ursuline Covent," Heller, John H., *Galveston City Directory: 1872*, 50; "Reed, Jo[h]nson (col.), District Clerk. Court House, residence cor. Tremont and Avenue Q." Heller, *Galveston City Directory: 1872*, 108; Johnson Reed and John De Bruhl both were members of Reedy Chapel, A.M.E. Heller, *Galveston City Directory: 1870*, 88 (reference to Johnson Reed); Heller, *Galveston City Directory: 1870*, 33 (reference to John DeBruhl); *Galveston Daily News*, November 7, 1895, 16 (reference to De Bruhl).
After the City of Galveston's city council was permitted to resume operations after the Civil War, Governor Edmund J. Davis appointed Johnson Reed and Henry Ballinger as additional members of the city council, removing two other members at the same time. Prior to the new members taking their seats, Mayor McKee challenged their sitting as members. The following exchange took place:
The Mayor asked: "Mr. Johnson Reed, have you taken the oath?"

Mr. Reed: "I have and forwarded it to the Secretary of State."

Mr. Stuart asked: "Have you taken the oath under the charter?"

Mr. Reed answered: "No."

Mr. Patton contended the oath was unnecessary, because there was a law which disqualified persons from leaving the State to avoid service to the Confederacy. If any part of the oath was not law, no part was.

Mr. Stuart then moved that the two-colored appointees to be admitted to seats.

Thereupon the Mayor decided that they should take the charter oath.

Mr. Plumly stated that for two years that oath had been ignored. Judge Austin refused to administer it.

Mr. Frederich thought that if there a charter, the oath that is it is binding. Either the oath is taken or we have no charter.

Col. Stancel thought that the property qualification was ignored by the military, and the Board had no right to revive it.

The friends of Mr. Reed assert that he asked the Mayor the following, which they have given to Secretary, and insisted that it be inserted in the minutes, which believe has been done: "Does the Civil Rights bill settle that question in this, that all men are entitled to the same rights, without regard to color, race, or previous condition?"

They further contend that this was the question decided by Mayor McKee.

The Mayor then repeated his decision and directed the Secretary to call the roll.

Messrs. Frederich and Baker voted to sustain the chair.

Messrs. Stancel, Mosebach, Mason, Ogle, Parker, Plumly, Stuart, and Patton, voted no.

The Chair was not sustained, and Johnson Reed and Henry Ballinger took their seat. Thereupon the Board adjourned until next Monday.

See exchange in *Galveston Flakes Daily Bulletin*, September 6, 1870, 3. Henry Ballinger's information can be found in the 1872 Galveston city directory, with the following listing: "Ballinger Henry. (col) Inspector Custom, residence Church [S]treet, between 8th and 9th Street." Heller, *Galveston City Directory: 1872*, 29.

4. *Dred Scott v. Sandford*, 60 U.S. 393 (1856); Maud Cuney Hare, *Norris Wright Cuney: A Tribune of the Black People* (The Crisis Publishing Company, January 1, 1913), 64.

5. Merline Pitre, "Norris Wright Cuney (1846–1898)," Texas Historical Commission, accessed November 16, 2024, https://www.tshaonline.

org/handbook/entries/cuney-norris-wright; Hare, *Norris Wright Cuney*, 22; Fulton Honorable R. L., "Biographies – Galveston County," Texas Genealogy Trail, accessed November 16, 2026, https://genealogytrails.com/tex/gulfcoast/galveston/bios_f.htm.
6. Hare, *Norris Wright Cuney*, 64–65.
7. Hare, *Norris Wright Cuney*, 66.
8. Hare, *Norris Wright Cuney*, 91.
9. Hare, *Norris Wright Cuney*, 91. See also Leslie Anne Lovette, "The Jaybird-Woodpecker War: Reconstruction and Redemption in Fort Bend County, Texas, 1860–1889," (master's thesis, Rice University, 1994), 9–10, https://scholarship.rice.edu/bitstream/handle/1911/13861/1360073.PDF?sequence=1&isAllowed=y.
10. *Galveston Daily News*, September 7, 1888. See also *Ferguson v. Moore-McCormack Lines, Inc.*, 352 U.S. 521 (1957) (petition filed on August 31, 1889; directed against men responsible for the ouster of six Black elected officials; Ferguson was the district clerk at the time); Lovette, "The Jaybird-Woodpecker War," 73–74. The illegal removal of elected officials in Fort Bend County took place on August 16, 1889. Governor L. S. Ross refused to intervene and permitted the removal of almost all elected officials by violence. Lovette, "The Jaybird-Woodpecker War," 77–80; *Galveston Daily News*, August 19–22, 1889.
11. Hare, *Norris Wright Cuney*, 1.
12. Hare, *Norris Wright Cuney*, 46, 67.
13. C. G. Woodson, "The Cuney Family," *Negro History Bulletin* 11, no. 6 (March 1, 1948): 123. See also Douglas Hales, *The Cuneys of Texas: A Southern Family in Black and White* (College Station: Texas A&M University Press, 2003).
14. Hales, *The Cuneys of Texas*, 6–7.
15. Hales, *The Cuneys of Texas*, 11.
16. Hare, *Norris Wright Cuney*, 3–4.
17. Hare, *Norris Wright Cuney*, 42.
18. Hare, *Norris Wright Cuney*, 42–43.
19. Hare, *Norris Wright Cuney*, 95.
20. "Treasure of the Month, Remembering Galvestonian James B. Stubbs," Rosenberg Library Museum, August 5, 2015, accessed February 2, 2023, https://www.rosenberg-library-museum.org/treasures/james-b-stubbs.
21. Hare, *Norris Wright Cuney*, 121–22.
22. Hare, *Norris Wright Cuney*, 123.
23. Brazosport Archaeological Society has placed on its website a manuscript

entitled *Darrington Plantation*. The manuscript tracks the history of the land, which is now a prison farm known as Darrington and is owned by the State of Texas. The manuscript reveals the influence those original incorporators of Galveston and the State of Texas possessed and how the influence played out during slavery and after emancipation.

"In the northern part of Brazoria County, Texas lands from of a major portion of the David Tally League were purchased to form the Darrington Plantation. Initially owned by David Tally, a member of Stephen F. Austin's Original 300 Families, acreage on the east side of the Brazos River along Oyster Creek was eventually acquired by Attorney John Darrington of Clark County, Alabama. Though Darrington never came to Texas the plantation would forever assume the name. Passing through several owners, including Sterling McNeel, the Darrington Plantation remained in the Abner Jackson Estate through the Civil War. Robert Mills, part owner of R. & D. G. Mills of Galveston, gained control of the property shortly after the Civil War. Convict labor leased from the Texas Prison Commission supplanted the original slave labor and freemen as the plantation continued to produce cotton and sugar under several different owners. . . . Basset and Bonnie Blakely of Fort Bend County acquired the property in 1917 and January 1, 1918, sold 6747 acres to the Texas Prison Commission for $337,340." "Darrington Plantation: Brazosport Archaeology Society," Life on the Brazos.com, accessed July 20, 2021, http://lifeonthebrazosriver.com/DarringtonPlantation.htm. As previously mentioned, R. & D. G. Mills were cotton factors, commission merchants, and exchange brokers. They were also plantation owners and actively involved in the slave trade—buying and selling human souls. After emancipation, the Mills and other large land holders retained their properties and continued to receive support from the State in the tending of fields and crops by using the convict leasing system.

24. Harold M. Hyman, *Oleander Odyssey: The Kempners of Galveston, Texas, 1854–1980s* (College Station: Texas A&M University Press 1990), 222.

25. See also "Award of Honorary Degrees by Year," Howard University, accessed April 2, 2021, https://www.howard.edu/secretary/convocations/recipients-year.htm.

26. The *Dignified Resignation* monument portrays a returning Confederate soldier. It has stood in front of the Galveston County Courthouse since 1911. The Galveston Veuve Jefferson Davis chapter, part of the United Daughters of the Confederacy, is responsible for the statue's placement. "The plaque praises the 'purity of motives, intensity of courage and heroism' of Confederate soldiers and sailors." Brooke A. Lewis, *Houston Chronicle*,

August 24, 2020. The front plaque has been removed; the plaque at the rear of the statue remains in place.

27. The only statue in the city honoring an African American is one of Jack Johnson, located in a park behind Old Central Cultural Center at 2627 Avenue M.
28. Collins, *Island of Color*, 23–25.
29. Heller's *Galveston Directory: 1880–1881*; "Maud Cuney Hare," in *Galveston Directory 1880–1881*, 41; Hare, *Norris Wright Cuney*, 44–46, 62, 79–80.
30. Morrison and Fourmy, *Morrison & Fourmy's General Directory of the City of Galveston: 1859* (Houston, TX: n.p., 1859), 232.
31. The Lone Star State Medical, Dental and Pharmaceutical Association, "Courage & Determination: A Portrait of Pioneering African American Physicians in Texas," SlideShare, accessed March 27, 2021, https://www.slideshare.net/stevelevine/courage-and-determination.
32. Morrison & Fourmy, *Morrison & Fourmy's General Directory of the City of Galveston: 1901–1902* (Houston, TX: n.p., 1902), 64; *City Times*, June 24, 1922, 4.
33. *Galveston Daily News*, June 24, 1886, 8 (confirming the meeting to organize as a medical association and petition the State of Texas for legal formation). See also The Lone Star State Medical, Dental and Pharmaceutical Association, "Courage & Determination: A Portrait of Pioneering African American Physicians in Texas," 7. The *Galveston Daily News* also reported, on the day of the Lone Star State Medical, Dental and Pharmaceutical Association meeting, that colored teachers (statewide) were in their second day of meetings in Galveston, colored editors (statewide) were also meeting in the city. *Galveston Daily News*, June 24, 1886, 8.
34. *Galveston Daily News*, June 24, 1886, 23.
35. *Galveston Daily News*, June 3, 1890, 17. See additional notices: held at St. Charles Garden, "a popular colored people's resort near Woolham's lake." *Galveston Daily News*, June 6, 1890, 24 Banquet; Eighth Annual Meeting; meeting held between 24th and 25th streets, Holmes Building on Market. *Galveston Daily News*, June 27, 1894, 17; Forty-third Annual Conference held at Wesley Tabernacle Church, Twenty-eight and Avenue I. *Galveston Daily News*, June 11, 1929, 14.
36. Galveston (Texas) Screwmen's Benevolent Association Records, 1866–1922, Briscoe Center for American History, University of Texas at Austin, accessed May 2, 2021, https://legacy.lib.utexas.edu/taro/utcah/01517/cah-01517.html.
On November 4, 1916, an advertisement was taken out by the Lone Star

Cotton Jammers' Association, Local No. 851, ILA, announcing its officers: "D. H. Hamilton, president, N. Foots, vice president; F. Banks, financial secretary; R. Richardson, recording secretary." The board of directors included: Edward Jackson, chairman; Henry Warner; A. Ross; H. Choop; R. B. Williams; and John North. In context of political activism, the organization identified both its East End and West End Relief Committee. *City Times*, November 4, 1916, 3.

37. Joseph Anthony Abel, "Opening the Closed Shop: The Galveston Longshoremen's Strike, 1920–1921" (master's thesis, Texas A&M University, 2004), 118, accessed February 25, 2023, https://oaktrust.library.tamu.edu/handle/1969.1/1372.

38. Collins, *Island of Color*, 28. See also *Oliver v. Lone Star Cotton Jammers' L.*, 136 S.W. 508 (Tex. App. 1911), wherein a suit was brought against the Cotton Jammers. The opinion reflects the organization was represented by the Black lawyers practicing in the city at the time. The Cotton Jammers prevailed on appeal.

39. Morrison and Fourmy, "Doc Hamilton," *Morrison & Fourmy's General Directory of the City of Galveston: 1909–1910* (Houston, TX: n.p., 1910), 176.

40. "The Great White Hope [1970]," IMDb, https://www.imdb.com/title/tt0065797/; Will Harris, "The Legacy of the Great White Hope," *Smithsonian Magazine*, February 25, 2021, accessed April 1, 2021, https://www.smithsonianmag.com/history/looking-back-legacy-great-white-hope-180977089/.

41. "Jack Johnson (1878–1946)," BlackPast, accessed April 1, 2021, https://www.blackpast.org/african-american-history/johnson-jack-1878 1946/#:~:text=Jack%20Johnson%2C%20the%20first%20African,His%20parents%20were%20former%20slaves.

42. "Jack Johnson and the Wrench–February 2005," Ferris State University: Jim Crow Museum of Racist Memorabilia, accessed April 1, 2021, https://www.ferris.edu/HTMLS/news/jimcrow/question/2005/february.htm. See also "Negro Battle Royale–May 2014," Ferris State University: Jim Crow Museum of Racist Memorabilia, accessed April 1, 2021, https://www.ferris.edu/HTMLS/news/jimcrow/question/2014/may.htm.

This scene was commonplace at many carnivals, fairs, and boxing matches throughout the American landscape. Blindfolded African American men and boys beat each other senseless for the comedic pleasure of the audience and in the hopes of winning a few dollars. These battle royal matches were held at many types of venues and involved anywhere from four to thirty blindfolded "negroes." While there were a few instances of White participants, the overwhelming majority of fighters were African American males. Advertisements for these events typically promoted them as comic events with "Negro" or "Colored" combatants. See Morrison and Fourmy, *Morrison & Fourmy's General Directory of the City of Galveston: 1909* (Houston, TX: n.p., 1909), 204, 206. See "Soldiers to Scrap in Holiday Cards: Chamber of Commerce Assisting Fort Crockett on July 5, Bouts," *Galveston Daily News*, June 29, 1926, 4; "A battle royal between five husky negroes will start the program." "Leonard and Jackson Top Card Tonight," *Galveston Daily News*, August 29, 1929; "A Battle royal is also carded and the local promoter wants any colored boys who would like to enter it to get in touch with Matchmaker Gaffney at the Turf gymnasium on Market Street." "Hughes in Initial Workout at Turf; Wolfe Expected to make Arrival Here Today," *Galveston Daily News*, November 9, 1922, 4.

43. Reference to a series of articles that appeared in the *Galveston Daily News*: "Counsel Declares White Slave Act does not Forbid Immoral Pursuits," *Galveston Daily News*, December 18, 1912, 4; "Causes Jack Johnson's Arrest: Girls, Claimed Pugilist Abducted, to Go Before Federal Jury," *Galveston Daily News*, October 19, 1212, 4; "Dismissed Jack Johnson's Appeal," *Galveston Daily News*, February 4, 1913, 66; "Three Additional Indictments," *Galveston Daily News*, December 18, 1912, 4. See also as a general reference: *Galveston Daily News*, August 8, 1913, 8, "Jack Johnson Buys Home," *Galveston Daily News*, December 22, 1912, 2.

44. "Three Additional Indictments," *Galveston Daily News*.

45. "Jack Johnson: American Boxer," Britannica, accessed January 21, 2024, https://www.britannica.com/biography/Jack-Johnson. See also "Who Discovered Johnson?" *Galveston Daily News*, March 8, 1910, 4; *Galveston Daily News*, March 2, 1919, 14; "Jack Johnson Will Take Part in Finish Fight at Mexicali," *Galveston Daily News*, April 2, 1920, 9; "Jack Johnson's Taxes," *Galveston Daily News*, July 20, 1910, 9.

46. *New Idea*, June 13, 1908, 4.

47. It was announced the applicants, Thos. Pope, J. Willis Wilkins, and Joseph Pope, made an application to city commissioner for the passage of an ordinance to permit the placement of a bathhouse at 37th Street. *Galveston Daily News*, September 29, 1907, 3,

48. *City Times*, May 1, 1909, 4. The colored newspapers during this period were *The New Idea* and the *City Times*.

49. Advertisement: "East End Café," *City Times*, April 10, 1920, 4.

50. Morrison and Fourmy, "Joseph Cuney," in *Morrison & Fourmy's General*

Directory of the City of Galveston: 1909–1910 (Houston, TX: n.p., 1910), 121, 421: Cuney Joseph (c), attorney, notary, room 6, Mosle bldg), lab, rms rear 2810 N. Curtis Jesse C. (c), r. 2524 M. 2. Cuney Joseph (c), 2125 Mechanic. See also John G. Browning and Chief Justice Carolyn Wright, "Unsung Heroes: The Earliest African-American Lawyers in Texas," *Texas Bar Journal* 77, no. 11 (2014), 960–63.

51. Morrison and Fourmy, "L. M. Wilkins," in *Morrison & Fourmy's General Directory of the City of Galveston: 1909–1910* (Houston, TX: n.p., 1910), 232.

52. The *City Times* advertised the "Colored Undertakers and Funeral Directors." *City Times*, December 4, 1915, 2. See also the advertisement for C. S. Willis, an undertaker and embalmer, who advertised, "Our Morgue and Restroom Free." *City Times*, February 19, 1916, 3. See also "Silas Emeline (c), midwife, r. 2808 N. . . . wks S. P. grain elevator, rms 3601 Postoffice": Morrison and Fourmy, "E. Silas," in *Morrison & Fourmy's General Directory of the City of Galveston: 1909–1910* (Houston, TX: n.p., 1910), 330.

53. See Gregg Andrews, "Black Working-Class Political Activism and Biracial Unionism: Galveston Longshoremen in Jim Crow Texas, 1919–1921," *The Journal of Southern History*, no. 3 (2008): 643, last accessed March 27, 2021, https://doi.org/10.2307/27650231; https://www.jstor.org/stable/27650231.

54. Andrews, "Black Working-Class Political Activism and Biracial Unionism," 643.

55. William D. Angel Jr., "Controlling the Workers: The Galveston Dock Workers' Strike of 1920 and its Impact on Labor Relations in Texas," *East Texas Historical Journal* 23, Article 6 (1985): 14.

56. Angel, "Controlling the Workers," 21.

57. Andrews, "Black Working-Class Political Activism and Biracial Unionism," 646.

58. Andrews, "Black Working-Class Political Activism and Biracial Unionism," 650, 657. See also [Galveston] *New Idea*, April 17, 1920.

59. Angel, "Controlling the Workers," 21.

60. Angel, "Controlling the Workers," 21. Joseph Abel provides the importance of the port to the state in 1920 in his thesis: "Galveston played a major role in bringing about statewide prosperity. Although it ranked as only the sixth largest city in Texas, Galveston was the most important shipping center in the state. In 1920, the port exported $637.5 million in cargo and imported $30.9 [million], up from $464.2 million and $17.7 million the year before. The first year of the decade also saw 400,000 more bales of cotton pass over

the city's docks than in 1919. Out of forty-nine United States ports reporting, Galveston ranked second total tonnage, eight in exports, and eleventh in imports." Abel, "Opening the Closed Shop,) 26–27.

61. Andrews, "Black Working-Class Political Activism and Biracial Unionism," 627.
62. *Galveston Daily News*, September 27, 1898, 10; *Galveston Daily News*, September 28, 1898, 10.
63. Abel, "Opening the Closed Shop," 32–33.
64. Willis Woods was the business agent representing Local 329's Black screwmen at the time. He was involved in Republican Party politics at the county, state, and federal level. Andrews, "Black Working-Class Political Activism and Biracial Unionism," 632, 643.
65. Andrews, "Black Working-Class Political Activism and Biracial Unionism," 632.
66. Andrews, "Black Working-Class Political Activism and Biracial Unionism," 639.
67. Hyman explained Galveston was unlike most of the South, in that it harbored unusually vigorous labor unions and Black voting blocs. At the time there were different labels attached to the political clubs/parties in the city including City Club, City Party, New City Party, Galveston Party, and Popular or People's Party. Hyman, *Oleander Odyssey*, 253,
68. Residence of Willis Wood, 34th and M 1/2:
    … Thomas (c) 3413 Jones H Ira (c) 3415 Woods Willis (c) rear Williams Henry (c) 3416 Rochelle D S (c) 3417… Woods Estelle (c) rear McClain Georgia (c) 3408 LeBird Mary Mrs 3410 Washington Edwd (c) 3411 Davis… Anderson Delia (c) 3419 Pope Maude (c) 3420 Barner Willis (c) 3424 Love T H (c) 3428 Barbour Alfred Rev (c). Morrison & Fourmy, *Morrison & Fourmy's General Directory of the City of Galveston: 1919* (Houston, TX: n.p., 1919), 493.
69. Residence of Thos. Jamison was in the same neighborhood as Willis Woods. Isaiah (c) 3218 Robinson Chas (c) rear Berringer Zion (c) 3223 Stanton S H (c) 3224 Thomas Wm Jr (c) rear. … Holdridge W G 3308 Livingston Freeman (c) 3310 Christian W J (c) 3314 Thomas George (c) 3318 Bailey C A (c)… Thomas (c) 3413 Jones H Ira (c) 3415 Woods Willis (c) rear Williams Henry (c) 3416 Rochelle D S (c) 3417… R Jr 3718 Hantsche F L 3722 Collison Alex 3723 Jamison Thos (c) 3724 Bercaw C L 38th intersects 39th.
    Morrison & Fourmy, *Morrison & Fourmy's General Directory of the City of Galveston: 1919* (Houston, TX: n.p., 1919), 493.
70. Andrews, "Black Working-Class Political Activism and Biracial

Unionism," 639.
71. Andrews, "Black Working-Class Political Activism and Biracial Unionism," 654. On June 2, 1901, it was reported that W. S. Noble announced the appointed representatives for the Southern Negro Congress. Of the Texas appointed members, thirty-six were from Galveston. *Galveston Daily News*, June 2, 1901, 16.
72. Andrews, "Black Working-Class Political Activism and Biracial Unionism."
73. Modification of political system in Galveston, moving away from ward system to an at-large arrangement, race was an issue in 1901. Hyman, *Oleander Odyssey,* 155; Texas's passage of Black Codes in 1866 to control a freed formerly enslaved people—physical violence by Whites directed against Blacks increased from 1865 to 1868—Blacks in Millican and Brazos Counties organized a local militia to defend their community after attacks by Klansmen. County Whites counter-organized with the two groups, breaking out into open warfare in July 1868. Lovette, "The Jaybird-Woodpecker War," 27–29.
74. Lawrence D. Rice, *The Negro in Texas: 1874–1900* (Baton Rouge: Louisiana State University Press, 1971), 120.
75. Rice, *The Negro in Texas*, 122.
76. Lovette, "The Jaybird-Woodpecker War," 58. Dr. Rice identified Henry Ferguson as the older and more prominent of the two brothers. "Henry succeeded Walter Burton as sheriff in 1874 and was destined to be the leader of the Negroes in the county for many years. He had been a slave of a planter named Ferguson in Jasper County. Granted his freedom when he was thirty years of age." Rice, *The Negro in Texas*, 91.
77. Rice, *The Negro in Texas in Texas*, 91.
78. Lovette, "The Jaybird-Woodpecker War," 80. See also Rice, *The Negro in Texas*, 94–130.
79. Lovette, "The Jaybird-Woodpecker War," 58.
80. David F. Krugler, *1919, The Year of Racial Violence: How African Americans Fought Back* (New York: Cambridge University Press, 2015), 58–65.
81. Krugler, *1919, The Year of Racial Violence*, 66–98.
82. Krugler, *1919, The Year of Racial Violence*, 99–130.
83. "The 1917 Houston Riots/Camp Logan Mutiny," Prairie View A&M University, accessed April 30, 2021, https://www.pvamu.edu/tiphc/research-projects/the-1917-houston-riotscamp-logan-mutiny/.
84. Krugler, *1919, The Year of Racial Violence*, 131–64. Texas hostility is well documented. Rice, *The Negro in Texas*, 94–130. See also Robin Young, "In the 1920's 1 in 3 Eligible Men Were KKK Members," WBUR, November 6, 2019, accessed April 16, 2022, https://www.wbur.org/

hereandnow/2019/11/06/ku-klux-klan-dallas-texas; Anabel Burke, "The History of the Ku Klux Klan in Waco," Waco History, accessed April 16, 2022, https://wacohistory.org/items/show/200.

85. Francine Uenuma, "The Massacre of Black Sharecroppers That Led the Supreme Court to Curb the Racial Disparities of the Justice System," *Smithsonian Magazine*, August 2, 2918, accessed February 2, 2023, https://www.smithsonianmag.com/history/death-hundreds-elaine-massacre-led-supreme-court-take-major-step-toward-equal-justice-african-americans-180969863/; Scott Neuman, "In 2 U.S. Cities Haunted by Race Massacres, Facing the Past Is Painful and Divisive," NPR, December 11, 2022, accessed February 3, 2023, https://www.npr.org/2022/12/11/1137090651/elaine-massacre-tulsa-race-riot.

86. "1921 Race Massacre," Tulsa History, accessed February 3, 2023, https://www.tulsahistory.org/exhibit/1921-tulsa-race-massacre/.

87. Dick Smith, "Texas and the Poll Tax," *The Southwestern Social Science Quarterly* 45, no. 2 (1964): 167–73.

88. Andrews, "Black Working-Class Political Activism and Biracial Unionism," 636. See also "White Primary," Texas States Historical Association, accessed April 30, 2021, https://www.tshaonline.org/handbook/entries/white-primary.

89. Mary Frances Berry, *Black Resistance, White Law: A History of Constitutional Racism in America* (New York: Allen Lane/The Penguin Press, 1994), 98.

90. "The 1890's: Black Codes," Texas State Library and Archives Commission, accessed February 4, 2023, https://www.tsl.texas.gov/exhibits/forever/endofanera/page2.html#:~:text=At%20the%201866%20Constitutional%20Convention,their%20earlier%20condition%20as%20slaves.

91. "Excerpts from Texas Black Codes 1866," US History Scene, accessed February 4, 2023, https://ushistoryscene.com/article/excerpts-texas-black-codes-1866/.

92. "Excerpts from Texas Black Codes 1866," US History Scene.

93. "Excerpts from Texas Black Codes 1866," US History Scene.

94. Quintard Taylor, *In Search of the Racial Frontier: African Americans in the American West, 1528–1990* (New York: Norton, 1998), 107–8.

95. *Galveston Tri-Weekly News*, October 30, 1865, 2.

96. *Galveston Tri-Weekly News*, October 30, 1865, 2.

97. Andrews, "Black Working-Class Political Activism and Biracial Unionism," 666.

98. *United States v. International Longshoremen's Association*, 334 F.Supp. 976 (S.D. Texas, Brownsville Division, 1971).

99. *United States v. International Longshoremen's Association*, 334 F.Supp. 976 (S.D. Texas, Brownsville Division, 1971).
100. Woodson, "The Cuney Family," 123.
101. J. Clay Smith Jr., *Emancipation: The Making of the Black Lawyer, 1844–1944* (Philadelphia: University of Pennsylvania Press, 1993), 346.
102. Smith Jr., *Emancipation*, 346.
103. Smith Jr., *Emancipation*, 354. In *Making of the Black Lawyer*, the author, J. Clay Smith, short-changes Smith by not reporting Smith won twice before the United States Supreme Court. *Carter v. State*, 177 U.S. 442, *20 S.Ct. 687*, 44 L.Ed. 839 (*1900*). See *Houston Daily Post*, December 17, 1899, 23 (reporting on *Carter v. State*, documenting Wilford H. Smith's work). See also *Rogers v. Alabama*, 24 S.Ct. 257 (1904).
104. M. Bloomfield, *From Deference to Confrontation: The Early Black Lawyers of Galveston, Texas, 1895–1920, The New High Priest* 151 (G. W. Gawalt ed., 1985).
105. Smith Jr., *Emancipation*, 347.
106. History.com succinctly sets out who Marcus Garvey was and his place in history:
Marcus Garvey was a Jamaican-born Black nationalist and leader of the Pan-Africanism movement, which sought to unify and connect people of African descent worldwide. "In the United States, he was a noted civil rights activist who founded the *Negro World* newspaper, a shipping company called Black Star Line and the Universal Negro Improvement Association, or UNIA, a fraternal organization of Black Nationalists. As a group, they advocated for 'separate but equal' status for persons of African ancestry, and as such they sought to establish independent Black States around the world, notably in Liberia on the west coast of Africa." "Marcus Garvey," History.com, accessed April 23, 2021, https://www.history.com/topics/black-history/marcus-garvey. The contrast with respect to Booker T. Washington is seen by referencing the same website: "Booker T. Washington (1856–1915) was born into slavery and rose to become a leading African American intellectual of the 19th century, founding Tuskegee Normal and Industrial Institute (now Tuskegee University) in 1881 and the National Negro Business League two decades later. Washington advised Presidents Theodore Roosevelt and William Howard Taft. . . . In perhaps his most famous speech, given on September 18, 1895, Washington told a majority white audience in Atlanta that the way forward for African Americans was self-improvement through an attempt to 'dignify and glorify common labor.' He felt it was better to remain separate from Whites than to

attempt desegregation, as long as Whites granted their Black countrymen and women access to economic progress, education, and justice under U.S. courts: 'The wisest of my race understand that the agitation of questions of social equality is the extremest folly and that progress in the enjoyment of all the privileges that will come to us must be the result of severe and constant struggle rather than artificial forcing. The opportunity to earn a dollar in a factory just now is worth infinitely more than to spend a dollar in an opera house.'" "Booker T. Washington," History.com, last updated, December 18, 2023, accessed February 10, 2024, https://www.history.com/topics/black-history/booker-t-washington. See also Steven H. Hobbs, "An Entrepreneurial Perspective on the Business of Being in Our Profession," *Fordham Urban Law Journal* 40 (2012): 397, 414–22, accessed January 31, 2024https://ir.lawnet.fordham.edu/ulj/vol40/iss1/8/.

107. Smith Jr., *Emancipation*, 348.
108. Smith Jr., *Emancipation*, 348.
109. Smith Jr., *Emancipation*, 366n249. On December 12, 1903, the *New York Times* provided information about a new publication, a book in which Wilford H. Smith contributed. *New York Times*, December 12, 1903, 6. The book was *The Negro Problem* by Booker T. Washington, Prof. W. E. B. Du Bois, Charles Chesnutt, Paul Laurence Dunbar, T. Thomas Fortune, Wilford H. Smith, H. T. Kealing. In 1908 a *New York Times* reporter visited Wilford H. Smith in his office to discuss a case wherein Smith agreed to represent a John Tyler, a colored man. Tyler had just been released from the state's insane asylum in Middletown, CT. This after serving 15 years for another crime, while the real criminal was in a cell near his own. *New York Times*, December 8, 1908, 6. On February 13, 1908, the *New York Times* reported on Smith bringing an injunction against Rev. Matthew W. Gilbert to restrain him from continuing to officiate as pastor of Mount Olivet Baptist Church. *New York Times*, February 13, 1908, 6.

As evidence of his connection to both cities: The *City Times*, on April 15, 1922, reported "Attorney Wilford Smith left for New York last week." *City Times*, April 15, 1922, 1. On May 23, 1922, the *Galveston Daily News* reported on a beach resort for Negroes at 28th Street and Avenue R 1/2. Some of the visitors included the Mayor Keenan, Commissioner Norman, Chief of Police James O. Stevenson, and Wilford H. Smith. *Galveston Daily News*, May 23, 1922, 15. On January 1, 1923, the paper reported Smith attended a meeting in Galveston for the permanent advancement of the race. ("Negroes Conduct Get-Together Meeting: Permanent Organization is Formed for Advancement of the Race.") *Galveston Daily News*, January

1, 1923, 3. Smith was reported to have said, "'Forty Acres and an old mule' no longer satisfies the negro." The meeting was held at Loyal Knights of Progress Hall, 2609 Avenue L. Some of the others in attendance were Mrs. A. L. Bradley, H. T. Davis, J. R. Gibson, R. A. Scull, Thomas A. Love, John Clausen, R. Warren, Drs. C. C. McClendon, E. A. Etter, M. J. Mosely, and Henry E. Warner, J. E. Johnson, J. House, E. W. Branch, John L. Lewis, R. F. Dorsey, Rev. W. Burford, L. Phelps, Theo Patrick, C. H. Ferguson, Mrs. Jenkins, Mrs. F. C. [C]lary. Georgie Freeman, and Mrs. J. E. Johnson. "The following committee was appointed by W. H. Noble, Jr., the president, to draw up a constitution and by-laws: L. C. Sholors, J. E. Johnson, Dr. R. H. Stanton, Wilford S. Smith, Rev. J. R. M. Lee, W. F. McCullough, Mrs. Alfred M. Rogers and Mrs. A. L. Bradley." In 1926, the *Port Arthur News* referenced Smith and two other Negro lawyers argued a case before the Texas Supreme Court. *Port Arthur News*, April 6, 1926, 2. Smith was noted as being located in Houston at the time. He argued with two Chicago lawyers. Smith died June 9, 1926, in Manhattan, New York. It was reported Wilford H. Smith grew ill in Houston and was transported to New York by his daughter.

110. Andrews, "Black Working-Class Political Activism and Biracial Unionism," 635.
111. "Old Central Cultural Center," Galveston Old Central Cultural Center, accessed April 26, 2021, https://www.galvestonoldcentral.com/Old_Central_Cultural_Center.asp.
112. Collins, *Island of Color*, 53.
113. See City of Galveston Texas – Government, "The Rosenberg Library Colored Branch: A History of the First Public Library for African Americans in Texas…" Facebook photo, February 5, 2014, https://www.facebook.com/cityofgalveston/posts/the-rosenberg-library-colored-brancha-history-of-the-first-public-library-for-af/646111432117209/; "Integrating Ball High and Central High in Galveston," from Doug Matthews oral history interview, July 21, 2016, Galveston, TX, Civil Rights in Black and Brown Interview Database, https://crbb.tcu.edu/clips/5823/integrating-ball-high-and-central-high-in-galveston.
114. Collins, *Island of Color*, 32.
115. "Jessie McGuire Dent," Find a Grave, accessed on March 31, 2021, https://www.findagrave.com/memorial/79604584/jessie-dent.
116. Renee Hayes, "Jessie McGuire-Dent: 1891–1948," Women's Activism NYC, accessed March 31, 2021, https://www.womensactivism.nyc/stories/4229.

117. *City Times*, March 28, 1914, 1; Morrison & Fourmy, *Morrison & Fourmy's General Directory of the City of Galveston: 1919* (Houston, TX: n.p., 1919), 493.
 . . . Theatre No 1, 2120 Av D Dixie Theatre No 2, 2110 Av D Lincoln Theatre, 413–15 25th Palace Theatre, 2128 Av... bottom lines) & CO, v B Theatres Crystal Vaudeville Theatre, 409–11 23d Grand Opera House, 2018 Av E. . . . Theatres-Motion Pictures Best Theatre, 2111 Av D Cozy Theatre, 2519 Av D Crystal Theatre, 405–7 23d Dixie... D Princess Theatre, 2621 Av D QUEEN THEATRE, 2105–2107 Av D (see right side lines) Rex Theatre..., 2211 Av D STAR THEATRE THE, 2515 Av D *Tile HARTEL FRED, 2221–23 Av F page 32) SCHADT WM, 2801–05.
118. *City Times*, July 17, 1915, 4.
119. *City Times*, July 17, 1915, 4.
120. *City Times*, July 17, 1915, 4.
121. *City Times*, July 17, 1915, 4. See additional advertisement contained therein: "The book, 'Life of Norris Wright Cuney,' by Maud Cuney Hare, his daughter . . . containing 230 pages, with an eloquent introduction by Gen. Jas. S. Clarkson." The first edition was published in 1912. In the same newspaper, Joseph Cuney announced that his office had moved from 300 Twentieth Street to 1925 23rd Street. By 1918, Joseph Cuney moved to 421 24th Street. *City Times*, April 27, 1918, 4. Cuney, at this time, was representing Mrs. J. H. Washington surrounding the Washington Addition in the La Marque Development ("lots for sale"). H. T. Davis, located at 819 Avenue K, took out an advertisement: "West end lots are selling fast and you better get one before they advance in price." Eureka Café identifies its location at 30th and Avenue M, "serving good meals all the time; also supplies for school children can be purchased here." The *City Times*'s office at the time was located at 1925 Mechanic Street—"subscribe to the Times for 20¢ a month; three months 50¢; one year $2. It is a spicy weekly newspaper published in the interest of the colored race."
122. *City Times*, January 14, 1922, 2.
123. *City Times*, January 14, 1922. In the same paper, a Black dentist advertised and identified the location of his business.
124. "Maud Cuney-Hare: Musicologist and Black Activist," *Song of the Lark* (blog), May 30, 2108, accessed March 29, 2021, https://songofthelarkblog.com/2018/05/30/maud-cuney-hare.
125. "Maud Cuney-Hare: Musicologist and Black Activist," *Song of the Lark* (blog).
126. Herb Boyd, "Maud Cuney Hare, an Early Black Musicologist and Musician,"

New York Amsterdam News, October 7, 2021, accessed November 24, 2024, https://amsterdamnews.com/news/2021/10/07/maud-cuney-hare-early-black-musicologist-and-music/.

127. "Maud Cuney-Hare: Musicologist and Black Activist," *Song of the Lark* (blog).
128. Anthony W. Neal, "Maud Cuney Hare: 'Lifting the Race through the Arts,'" *Bay State Banner*, accessed March 29, 2021, https://www.baystatebanner.com/2012/11/07/maud-cuney-hare-lifting-the-race-through-the-arts/.
129. Neal, "Maud Cuney Hare."
130. *Galveston Daily News*, February 18, 1936, 9.
131. Neal, "Maud Cuney Hare."
132. "W. E. B. Du Bois Papers, Series 1A. General Correspondence Letter from Maud Cuney Hare to W. E. B. Du Bois dated May 28, 1930," UMass Amherst, accessed March 29, 2021, https://credo.library.umass.edu/view/full/mums312-b054-i047 (concerning lack of press coverage of the center's production of "Dessalines, Black Emperor of Haiti").
133. See generally "W. E. B. Du Bois Papers, Series 1A. General Correspondence Letter from Maud Cuney Hare to W. E. B. Du Bois dated November 18, 1924," UMass Amherst.
134. Maud Cuney-Hare, *Negro Musicians and Their Music* (Washington, DC: Associated Publishers, Inc., 1936), 15, accessed March 29, 2021, https://digital.library.upenn.edu/women/cuney-hare/musicians/musicians.html. The book was dedicated to her musical partner, William Howard Richardson, Baritone, "In Remembrance of Twenty Years of Musical Partnership."
135. "Camille Howard born 29 March 1914," *From the Vaults* (blog), March 29, 2017, accessed April 7, 2021, https://fromthevaults-boppinbob.blogspot.com/2017/03/camille-howard-born-29 D-march-1914.html.
136. "Camille Howard," *From the Vaults* (blog).
137. "Camille Howard," *From the Vaults* (blog).
138. "Memory of Dr. Frederick C. Tillis: 1930–2020," UMass Amherst Fine Arts Center, accessed April 7, 2021, https://fac.umass.edu/Online/default.asp?BOparam::WScontent::loadArticle::permalink=Tillis.
139. "Frederick C. Willis," American Composers Alliance, accessed April 7, 2021, https://composers.com/frederick-tillis.
140. "Frederick C. Willis," American Composers Alliance.
141. The image of General Gardner, Dr. Tillis's stepfather, can be found on the cover of Marilyn Spievak Brodwick's book containing images of the aged. The author explained her work thusly, "I hope viewers see a new wrinkle in these images and appreciate the wisdom and beauty in the lines the old

possess," 7. The picture was taken in 1992, when General Gardner was 92. The text next to his picture reads: "He grew up in Galveston and doesn't like to hear about 'that old Jim Crow.'" Marilyn Spievak Brodwick, *Faces of Aging* (The University of Texas Medical Branch at Galveston, 2001).

142. Obituaries, *Galveston Daily News*, May 8, 2020.
143. "Works of African-American Composers to be Celebrated Today at Reedy Chapel," *Galveston Daily News*, February 20, 2000, 29.
144. Harvey Rice, "Izola Collins, Galveston Educator Who Wrote Book on Juneteenth, Dies at 87," *Houston Chronicle*, June 16, 2017.
145. Rice, "Izola Collins," *Houston Chronicle*.
146. "Obituary, Izola Collins of Galveston, Texas [1921–2017]," Carnes Funeral Home, accessed April 7, 2021, https://www.carnesbrothers.com/obituary/izola-collins.
147. Rick Cousins, "Galveston Educator Makes a Case for Traditional Hymns," *Galveston County Daily News*, March 29, 2014, 11 & B9.
148. Dolph Tillotson, "The Woman Who Can't Slow Down," *Galveston Daily News*, June 4, 1995, 10.
149. *Galveston Daily News*, March 22, 2002, 8; obituary, *Galveston County Daily News*, June 14, 2017, A1 & A7.
150. *Galveston County Daily News*, June 14, 2017.
151. *Galveston County Daily News*, June 14, 2017.
152. "Esther Phillips, 48, Is Dead; A Rhythm-and-Blues Singer," *New York Times*, August 8, 1984, sec. D, 21.
153. "Esther Phillips," Discogs, accessed April 9, 2021, https://www.discogs.com/artist/86339-Esther-Phillips.
154. "Esther Phillips," Discogs.
155. "Esther Phillips," Soulwalking, accessed November 16, 2024, http://www.soulwalking.co.uk/Esther%20Phillips.html.
156. "Remembering Esther Phillips," Creed Taylor produced, accessed November 16, 2024, https://www.ctproduced.com/remembering-esther-phillips/.
157. "Louis Prince Jones, Jr. [Blues Boy]," Texas State Historical Association, accessed April 20, 2021, https://www.tshaonline.org/handbook/entries/jones-louis-prince-jr-blues-boy.
158. "Louis Prince Jones, Jr. [Blues Boy]," Texas State Historical Association.
159. "Louis Prince Jones, Jr. [Blues Boy]," Texas State Historical Association.
160. "Barry Eugene Carter/Barry White (1944–2003)," Blackpast, accessed April 8, 2021, https://www.blackpast.org/african-american-history/carter-barry-eugene-barry-white-1944-2003/.
161. "Barry Eugene Carter/Barry White (1944–2003)," Blackpast.

162. "Carter, Barry Eugene [Barry White] (1944–2003)," Texas State Historical Association, accessed April 8, 2021, https://www.tshaonline.org/handbook/entries/carter-barry-eugene-barry-white.
163. "Celestine Ann Beyonce," public member profile, Ancestry.com, accessed April 8, 2021, https://www.ancestry.com/search/collections/1093/.
164. Brittany Spanos, "Tina Knowles Announces New Memoir: *Matriarch*," *Rolling Stone*, October 29, 2024, accessed November 16, 2024, https://www.rollingstone.com/music/music-news/tina-knowles-memoir-matriarch-1235146398/.
165. Charles Trepany, "Beyoncé's Mom, Tina, Recalls How a Racist Birth Certificate Change Created the Star's Name," *USA Today*, September 16, 2020, accessed April 8, 2021, https://www.usatoday.com/story/entertainment/celebrities/2020/09/16/beyonce-how-racist-birth-certificate-change-created-stars-mononym/5821942002/.
166. Izola Collins's reference to Dr. Rufus and Janice Stanton aids in identifying the location of this park: "We went to City Party Park on Avenue S, between 37th and 39th Streets. For social life, we went to and had a lot of yard parties." Collins, *Island of Color*, 172. The Park and Pavilion of No. 2 Cotton Jammers located at 37th and Avenue S is possibly the same park as City Party Park. The Cotton Jammers' local was ultimately dissolved, and the union and its members were blended into ILA, Local 851. *City Times*, August 26, 1916, 3 (references location of Cotton Jammers' Park). See also *City Times*, July 14, 1917, 3.
167. "Negro Park Situation Here Discussed" (article written by Benjamin K. Peek, Chairman Statistics, Citizens Committee, Galveston, Texas). *Galveston Daily News*, January 14, 1932, 2.
168. The "Negro Park Situation" map was prepared by Benjamin Peek, chairman of statistics of the citizens committee; the map accompanied the article. In May 1932, an additional article was published setting out Peek's business location and his role in city's politics: *Galveston Daily News*, May 22, 1932, 9.
169. "Local Doctor Shows Great Civic Spirit in Agreeing to Price," *Galveston Voice*, October 17, 1931, 1.
170. Source of information: text exchange between Debbie Allen, daughter of Gus Allen, and the author on April 10, 2021.
171. Part of author's collection, courtesy of Patricia Ann Jackson Tate. See also "John E. Palmer: An Inventory of His Collection in the Photograph Collection at the Harry Ransom Center," Harry Ransom Center, accessed April 6, 2021, https://norman.hrc.utexas.edu/fasearch/findingAid.

cfm?eadid=00280.
172. *City Times*, October 17, 1917, 1. See also "Big Meeting of Colored Businessmen: Staff of Eight Illinois Regiment Invited to Galveston": ("... roll call followed and reading of minutes by Secretary F. E. Stewart and reports by Messrs. Thos. E. Hall, W. Dominick, W. C. Hollinsworth, representing committees on enterprises, etc., among the colored people of Galveston ..."). See similar reporting, *City Times*, December 8, 1917, 1.
173. *City Times*, November 10, 1917, 1.
174. "John E. Palmer," Harry Ransom Center.
175. See also "Galveston History Center," Galveston and Texas History Center, accessed April 26, 2021, https://www.galvestonhistorycenter.org/research/african-american-history.
176. See also "History," Circle-Lets.org, accessed April 20, 2021, https://circleletsinc.wildapricot.org/page-18170.
177. "The Negro Motorist Green Book," Smithsonian Institute Traveling Exhibition Service, accessed November 16, 2024, https://negromotoristgreenbook.si.edu/.
178. Victor H. Green, *Negro Motorist Green Book*, Smithsonian Store, accessed April 30, 2021, https://www.smithsonianstore.com/product/negro-motorist-green-book-compendium-10846.do?code=N2ISGPLA&gclid=Cj0K-CQiA2af-BRDzARIsAIVQUOckGjNvbky-OSm9J1gyLpIC4nv4bqn-y8TRouKKCn26F_rYpLotdTBgaAkr4EALw_wcB, 116; or Victor H. Green, *The Negro Motorist Green Book 1945* (New York: Victor H. Green, 1938).
179. *New Idea*, June 13, 1908, 4.
180. Penny L. Pope, interview by author on April 13, 2021. Penny L. Pope served as a justice of the peace after the redistricting lawsuit was won against the County of Galveston. Judge Pope was elected in 1993 to fulfill a two-year term and was elected thereafter in six different elections (six 4-year terms; twenty-six years of service from January 2, 1993, to December 31, 2018); Pope interview.
181. Pope interview.
182. Pope interview. In an interview of Sheila Roque, Booker T. Washington was identified as the school located near the football stadium on 27th Street, south of Broadway. This interview was conducted on April 14, 2021, by the author.
183. Oral interview by author of Judge Penny Lynne Pope, April 13, 2021.
184. Victor H. Green, *Negro Motorist Green Book*, Smithsonian Store, accessed April 30, 2021, https://www.smithsonianstore.com/product/negro-motoris

t-green-book-compendium-10846.do?code=N2ISGPLA&gclid=Cj0K-CQiA2af-BRDzARIsAIVQUOckGjNvbky-OSm9J1gyLpIC4nv4bqn-y8TRouKKCn26F_rYpLotdTBgaAkr4EALw_wcB, 183; or Victor H. Green, *The Negro Motorist Green Book 1945* (Victor H. Green, New York, 1938).

185. Green, *Negro Motorist Green Book*; or Green, *The Negro Motorist Green Book 1945*.
186. "African American Travel, Gus Allen," Texas Historical Commission, accessed April 26, 2021, https://www.thc.texas.gov/public/upload/preserve/survey/highway/Gus%20Allen%20AfricanAmericanTravel.pdf. See Gus Allen Collection, Special Collections #191, Rosenberg Library, Galveston, Texas.
187. See Richard L. Elam, "Behold the Fields: Texas Baptists and the Problem of Slavery" (PhD diss., University of North Texas, 1992), 83, https://digital.library.unt.edu/ark:/67531/metadc277972/. Although slaves were welcomed into "full fellowship," it was not always clear what this meant. As noted earlier, slaves were required to have permission of their owners before they could join, and then sat in specially designated areas. Moreover, Black Baptists were almost always listed or mentioned by first name only. The owner's last name was sometimes added parenthetically, and most minutes indicated slave/master relationships. The phrases "belonging to," "servant of," or "property of," followed by the owner's name, were common. Slave members were referred to as "property," "servant," "colored," "girl," "boy," or sometimes a combination of these. In some church membership rolls, names of Blacks and Whites were interspersed, approximating the period in which they joined. Other minutes listed Blacks separately. Overall, there seemed to be no standard practice; preferences of the individual congregation or, in most cases, the church clerk, prevailed.
188. Wilson Armistead, *Five Hundred Thousand Strokes for Freedom* (London: W. F. Cash, 1900, reprinted New York: Negro University Press, 1969), 1.
189. Armistead, *Five Hundred Thousand Strokes for Freedom*, 2.
190. Armistead, *Five Hundred Thousand Strokes for Freedom*, 2.
191. Wilson Armistead, "A Tribute for the Negro: Being a Vindication of the Moral, Intellectual, and Religious Capabilities of the Coloured Portion of Mankind; with Particular Reference to the African Race," Academic Affairs Library, University of North Carolina, Chapel Hill 1999, accessed November 16, 2024, https://docsouth.unc.edu/neh/armistead/armistead.html.
192. See "Avenue L Baptist Church," Texas State Historical Association,

NOTES

accessed April 7, 2021, https://www.tshaonline.org/handbook/entries/avenue-l-baptist-church. See also Elam, "Behold the Fields," 91, 92.

193. "What to Do Tours," Galveston.com, accessed April 7, 2021, https://www.galveston.com/whattodo/tours/self-guided-tours/african-american-historic-places/avenuelmissionarybaptistchurch/.
194. Elam, "Behold the Fields," 16–17.
195. Elam, "Behold the Fields," 45.
196. Elam, "Behold the Fields," 92.
197. The first board of trustees included R. E. B. Baylor, A. G. Haynes, A. C. Horton, James Huckins, and Nelson Kavanaugh, all of whom owned bondsmen. In addition, three of the first four presidents (Graves, Burleson, and Baines) were slaveholders. Elam, "Behold the Fields," 131.
198. "10 things we've learned about slavery/racism & Baylor's history from the Conversation Series," Baylor.edu, accessed April 10, 2021, https://www2.baylor.edu/baylorproud/2021/03/10-things-weve-learned-about-slavery-racism-baylors-history-from-the-conversation-series/.
199. Elam, "Behold the Fields," 96–97.
200. Elam, "Behold the Fields," 138.
201. Elam, "Behold the Fields," 131. See also "Baylor University Releases Independent Report of Commission on Historic Campus Representations," Baylor.edu, March 23, 2021, accessed April 10, 2021, https://www.baylor.edu/mediacommunications/news.php?action=story&story=222585.
202. Ancestry.com. 1850 U.S. Federal Census - Slave Schedules Database (Gail Borden, accessed January 29, 2023). Original data: United States of America Bureau of the Census, *Seventh Census of the United States, 1850* (Washington, DC: National Archives and Records Administration, 1850) M432, 1,009 rolls, https://www.ancestry.com/search/collections/8055/?count=50&residence=_galveston-galveston-texas. Ancestry.com 1860 U.S. Federal Census - Slave Schedules Database (Gail Borden, accessed January 29, 2023). Original data: United States of America Bureau of the Census, *Eighth Census of the United States, 1860* (Washington, DC: National Archives and Records Administration, 1860), M653, 1,438 rolls, https://www.ancestry.com/search/collections/7668/.
203. See "Wesley Tabernacle United Methodist Church: Galveston's African American Historic Places & Historical Marker," Galveston.com, accessed April 7, 2021, https://www.galveston.com/whattodo/tours/self-guided-tours/african-american-historic-places/wesleytabernacle/.
204. Sarah Barringer Gordon, "Why the Split in the Methodist Church Should Set Off Alarms for Americans: Methodist Were Divided Before - Over

Slavery," *Washington Post*, January 16, 2020.
205. Gordon, "Why the Split in the Methodist Church Should Set off alarms for Americans."
206. Doug Paul Gleason, "Of Circuit Riders and Circuit Courts: A Case Study of the Methodist Border Conflict in Antebellum Virginia" (thesis, College of William and Mary, 2015), 16.
207. *Smith v. Swormstedt*, 57 U.S. 288, 309 (1853).
208. Collins, *Island of Color*, 144–49. See also "Holy Rosary Catholic Church: Galveston's African American Historic Places & Historical Marker," Galveston.com, https://www.galveston.com/whattodo/tours/self-guided-tours/african-american-historic-places/holyrosarycatholicchurch/.
209. Rachel L. Swarns, "Jesuits Vow to Raise $100 Million to Atone for Role in Slavery," *New York Times*, Tuesday, March 16, 2021, A15.
210. David Paulsen, "Visit to Castle's Dungeon in Ghana Offers ACC Lessons on Church's Complicity in the Trans-Atlantic Slave Trade," Episcopal News Service, February 1, 2023, accessed February 18, 2023, https://www.episcopalnewsservice.org/2023/02/15/visit-to-castles-dungeon-in-ghana-offers-acc-lessons-on-churchs-historic-complicity-in-the-trans-atlantic-slave-trade/.
211. Paulsen, "Visit to Castle's Dungeon in Ghana Offers ACC Lessons on Church's Complicity."
212. Armistead, *Five Hundred Thousand Strokes for Freedom*, 2.
213. Jonathan M. Pitts, "Episcopal Church Established by Baltimore Slave Owners Creates $500,000 Reparations Fund," *Baltimore Sun*, January 29, 2021.
214. Rachel L. Swarns, "272 Slaves Were Sold to Save Georgetown. What Does It Owe Their Descendants?" *New York Times*, April 16, 2016.
215. Ryan Di Corpo, "Georgetown Reparation Plan for Slaves Sold by University Draws Criticism from Students," *America: The Jesuit Review*, November 4, 2019, accessed March 11, 2022, https://www.americamagazine.org/politics-society/2019/11/04/georgetown-reparations-plan-slaves-sold-university-draws-criticism.
216. "The Diocesan Reparations Committee," The Episcopal Diocese of New York, accessed April 10, 2021, https://www.dioceseny.org/mission-and-outreach/social-concerns/reparations-for-slavery/.
217. David Paulsen, "Oldest Episcopal Parish's Past Holds Uncomfortable Truths in City Where African American History Began," Episcopal News Service, January 22, 2020, accessed on April 10, 2021, https://www.episcopalnewsservice.org/2020/01/22/oldest-episcopal-parish-begins-to-confront-d

ifficult-truths-in-city-where-african-american-history-began/.

Chapter 11

1. "The Confederacy would lose the war in April 1865, but in the succeeding decades would win the all-important peace. The Confederates would manage to take hold the public imagination with gauzy portrayals of the Lost Cause. Two of the most influential and popular films of the early twentieth century—*Birth of a Nation* and *Gone with the Wind*—fed the country and the world the Confederate version of the war and portrayed the people of the degraded lowest caste as capable of brute villainy or childlike buffoonery." Isabel Wilkerson, *Caste: The Origins of Our Discontents* (New York: Random House, 2020), 335.
2. Alvin Powell, "Dual Message of Slavery Probe: Harvard's Ties Inseparable from Rise, and Now University Must Act," *The Harvard Gazette*, April 26, 2022, accessed on August 8, 2022. https://news.harvard.edu/gazette/story/2022/04/slavery-probe-harvards-ties-inseparable-from-rise/.
3. "Harvard and the Legacy of Slavery," the Presidential Committee on Harvard & the Legacy of Slavery, 2022, accessed August 8, 2022, https://radcliffe-harvard-edu-prod.s3.amazonaws.com/b2c5a41d-8bfd-4d04-933c-858670839e50/HLS-whole-report_FINAL_2022-04-25FINAL-ua.pdf.
4. Sudhin Thanawala, "Georgia Park with Giant Confederate Carving Proposes Changes," Associated Press News, April 26, 2021, https://apnews.com/article/georgia-race-and-ethnicity-063b603e0113a18b9cbc62086cde3bc0.
5. "America's First Museum," Charleston Museum, accessed April 12, 2021, https://www.charlestonmuseum.org/.
6. Adam Parker and Emily Williams, "One Year after Groundbreaking, Charleston's African American Museum Taking Shape," [Charleston] *Post and Courier*, March 24, 2021.
7. Parker and Williams, "One Year After Groundbreaking."
8. The National Civil Rights Museum is being rehoused, with the public and private funds expenditures to make the project a reality. The private donations, and tax rebates include: "$120 million for the museum building, plus an additional $30 million for the endowment, and $61 million for the park redesign." Arthur Lubow, "In Memphis, a Park and Art Upgrade: Revamping a Waterfront, and Moving a Museum Downtown," *New York Times*, November 7, 2021, AR-22.
9. Makeda Easter, "Seeing Black Heritage Sites: African American History Across L.A. is Focus of a Project to Preserve Landmarks," *Los Angeles Times*, April 12, 2021, E-1.

10. Easter, "Seeing Black Heritage Sites."
11. Easter, "Seeing Black Heritage Sites."
12. "New Orleans Tourism Visitation and Visitor Spending Break Spending Records in 2019 Highlighting Depth of Economic Crisis Still to Unfold," New Orleans (website), May 19, 2020, accessed April 9, 2022, https://www.neworleans.com/articles/post/new-orleans-tourism-visitation-and-visitor-spending-break-records-in-2019/.
13. Tegand Wendland, "With Lee's Statue Removal, Another Battle of New Orleans Comes to a Close," NPR, May 20, 2017, accessed April 12, 2021, https://www.npr.org/2017/05/20/529232823/with-lee-statues-removal-another-battle-of-new-orleans-comes-to-a-close; "See All 4 Confederate Monument Removal in New Orleans in Photo and Video," NOLA.com, July 22, 2019, accessed April 12, 2021, https://www.nola.com/news/politics/article_3a11f27b-bce2-5a2c-98ac-53ab0d67d259.html.
14. The United States Civil Rights Trail's website provides the following information about the Tremé neighborhood: "Tremé, a historic community just north of the French Quarter, is the oldest African American neighborhood in America. In the 18th and early 19th centuries, free persons of color and eventually those African slaves who obtained, bought, or bargained for their freedom were able to acquire and own property in Tremé. The ability to acquire, purchase and own real property during an era when America was still immersed in slavery was remarkable and only in New Orleans did this occur with any regularity and consistency. Today, the neighborhood is viewed by many as ground zero for New Orleans culture. Tremé is home to several museums dedicated to African American life, art, and history, as well as Louis Armstrong Park, a memorial to the great jazz legend Louis Armstrong." "Tremé," Civil Rights Trail, accessed April 12, 2021, https://civilrightstrail.com/attraction/treme/
15. "Tremé," Civil Rights Trail.
16. James McCandless, "San Antonio African American Museum Planning $40 Million Downtown Move," *San Antonio Business Journal*, July 20, 2023. See also Brian Kirkpatrick, "Bexar County Approves Funding for San Antonio African American Community Archive and Museum," Texas Public Radio, January 10, 2024.
17. James Russell, "The Long Road to a Juneteenth Museum: Architects Have Made the Neighborhood's History Part of the Plan," *Texas Observer*, February 1, 2024. See also a press release by the National Juneteenth Museum: "National Juneteenth Museum Visionary Takes the Seat as CEO, Accelerating the Capital Fundraising Process to Reach $70 Million

Goal," National Juneteenth Museum, accessed on February 6, 2024, https://nationaljuneteenthmuseum.org/news-blog/national-juneteenth-museum-announces-ceo.

18. FWTX Staff, "The National Juneteenth Museum is $1 Million Closer to Becoming a Reality," *Fort Worth Magazine*, July 10, 2023.
19. Joe Heim, "Maryland Awards $5 Million in Grants to Help Preserve Black Heritage Sites," *Washington Post*, February 6, 2024.
20. "African American History Month," National Register of Historic Places, accessed April 12, 2021, https://www.nps.gov/subjects/nationalregister/african-american-history-month.htm; State of Mississippi National Register of Historic Places registration for Mound Bayou Historic District form, sec. 6, p. 7, June 15, 2023, accessed February 7, 2024, https://www.apps.mdah.ms.gov/nom/dist/235.pdf.
21. Tracey McManus, "Paine College inducted into National Register of Historic Places," *The Augusta Chronicle*, January 16, 2013.
22. "History of American Beach," National Park Service, accessed February 8, 2024, https://www.nps.gov/timu/learn/historyculture/ambch_history.htm.
23. Dr. Judith Wellman, "The Sherwood Equal Rights Historic District: Cayuga County," *Amsterdam News*, February 1, 2016.
24. "Jackson Ward Historic Ward," Virginia Commonwealth University, accessed April 12, 2021, https://digital.library.vcu.edu/islandora/object/vcu%3Ajwh. See also "127-0237 Jackson Ward Historic District," Virginia Department of Historic Resources, accessed April 12, 2021, https://www.dhr.virginia.gov/historic-registers/127-0237/; "Gentrification: A Mixed Bag in Historic Richmond, Virginia Neighborhood," National Community Reinvestment Coalition, accessed April 12, 2021, https://ncrc.org/gentrification-a-mixed-bag-in-historic-richmond-virginia-neighborhood/.
25. Eric Ortiz, "These Confederate Statues Were Removed. But Where Did They Go?" NBC News, September 20, 2020, accessed April 12, 2021, https://www.nbcnews.com/news/us-news/these-confederate-statues-were-removed-where-did-they-go-n1240268; Sabrina Moreno, "Richmond Has Removed the Most Confederate Symbols in the Country Since the Killing of George Floyd. Here's How It Happened," *Richmond Times-Dispatch*, September 4, 2020.
26. Andrew Limbong, "Emmett Till Funeral Site, Other Black Landmarks Share $3 Million Preservation Grant," NPR, July 15, 2012, accessed on August 6, 2021, https://www.npr.org/2021/07/15/1016352140/emmett-till-funeral-site-other-black-landmarks-share-3-million-preserv

ation-grant.
27. The Civil Rights Act of 1866 (14 Stat. 27–30, enacted April 9, 1866, reenacted 1870).
28. In 1964, Congress passed Public Law 88-352 (78 Stat. 241).
29. Editorial Board, "Palm Springs Bulldozed a Black Neighborhood. Compensate Survivors," *Los Angeles Times,* November 17, 2022.
30. Scott Gold, "A Lesson Born of Intolerance," *Los Angeles Times,* January 12, 2002. See also KESQ News, Channel 3, "Palm Springs to Apologize for Section 14 Destruction," YouTube video, September 20, 2021, accessed on November 20, 2022, 3:09, https://www.youtube.com/watch?v=duYDyNOlexo.
31. Mark Talkington, "Palm Springs Official Move to Apologize for 'City Engineered Holocaust' at Section 14," *Palm Springs Post,* March 18, 2021. See also Rebecca Plevin, "City OKs Payout for Razing Homes in the 1950s," *Los Angeles Times,* November 10, 2024 (Palm Springs approved $5.9 million for Black, Latino families ousted for urban renewal).
32. Wilkerson, *Caste,* 121.
33. Jean Guerrero, "My Family Hid Black Ancestors—I Found Them," *Los Angeles Times,* February 13, 2023, A11; more of Guerrero telling tale:
I'm grateful to my grandmother for showing me a photo of her mother, even if it took time. I believe it was brave, and in a way, an act of resistance against Black erasure. . . .

When I look at my face in the mirror, I can't find my *bisabuelas* at first. I see the jawline of a white cop, my Puerto Rican grandfather's father, who wouldn't recognize his mixed-race son until the boy's mother Pura died. I see the green eyes of the Spanish man who raped my Mexican grandmother Carolina when she was a teenager.

But further down, on my left ribcage under my heart, there's a brown birthmark in the shape of an upside-down Mexico. I like to imagine that my Mexican tatarabuela Juanita, a *curandera,* or healer, descended from Indigenous Caxcans, left it there to say, *"No te olvides, gringa."* Don't you forget, gringa.
34. Guerrero, "My Family Hid Black Ancestors."
35. "Mahalia Jackson Prompts Martin Luther King Jr. to Improvise 'I Have a Dream' Speech," History.com, accessed February 5, 2023, https://www.history.com/this-day-in-history/mahalia-jackson-the-queen-of-gospel-puts-her-stamp-on-the-march-on-washington.
36. *Moore v. Barr,* 718 S.W.2d 925 (Tex. Civ. App.–Houston [14th] 1986).
37. *Price v. Lewis,* 45 S.W.3d 215 (Tex. Civ. App.–Houston [1st] 2001).

38. History tells us the poll tax worked as an impediment to the African American voter. A seemingly neutral tax imposed, surely, could not be deemed discriminatory. The exercise of any such practices today would not occur in Texas or elsewhere. One more example, see *Galveston Daily News*, August 3, 1925, 6. The City of Galveston ran a legal notice related to "AN ORDINANCE prohibiting and making unlawful sexual intercourse between any white person and any negro person, and making it unlawful for any white person to habitually associate with negro prostitutes or with negro women leading an idle, immoral or profligate life, and for any negro person to habitually associate with white prostitutes or with white women leading an idle, immoral or profligate life, and fixing a penalty for the violation hereof." Section 4 of the ordinance defined a negro as "used herein, shall include also a mulatto or colored person, or any other person having one-eighth or more negro blood. All persons not included in the definition of negro shall be deemed white person within the meaning of this ordinance." Remember Representative John Brown. He must have been happy when the ordinance was posted. Remember the news articles posted of a "likely negro girl"? I still scream at the same litany of lynchings/executions because of an accusation of rape directed against those colored/Negro/Black men. A culture, a legal system, a way of life. The ordinance was passed by the City of Galveston's city commissioners on July 23, 1925.
39. Gary Cartwright, *Galveston: A History of the Island* (Fort Worth: TCU Press, 1991), 90.
40. A founding father's assessment of a nonsensical position seems apropos: In 1781, Benjamin Franklin—one of the country's founding fathers and premier scientist of his day—penned a letter to the Royal Academy of Brussels related to a question posed to its members. At the time "[t]here were a number of royal academies of science, in particular, that specialized more in the trivial realms of science than the practical ones. Some of them regularly held contests in which their members were to solve complex theoretical problems, to test their skills and wit." Franklin was none too happy with the question posed that year and proceeded to complain through the use of satire.
"To the Royal Academy of Brussels—
Gentlemen, I have perused your late mathematical Prize Question, proposed in lieu of one in Natural Philosophy, for the ensuing year, viz. . . .
I was glad to find by these following Words—"*l'Académie a jugé que cette découverte, en étendant les bornes de nos connoissances, ne seroit pas sans utilité*" [The academy has judged this discovery, by widening the boundaries

of our knowledge, will not be without utility]—that you esteem *Utility* an essential Point in your Enquiries, which has not always been the case with all Academies; and I conclude therefore that you have given this Question instead of a philosophical, or as the Learned express it, a physical one, because you could not at the time think of a physical one that promised greater *Utility*.

Permit me then humbly to proposed one of that sort for your consideration, and through you, if you approve it, for the serious Enquiry of learned Physicians, Chemists, etc. of this enlightened Age.

It is universally well known, That in digesting our common Food, there is created or produced in the Bowels of human Creatures, a great Quantity of Wind.

That the permitting this Air to escape and mix with the Atmosphere, is usually offensive to the Company, from the fetid Smell that accompanies it.

That all well-bred People therefore, to avoid giving such Offence, forcibly restrain the Efforts of Nature to discharge that Wind."

Before continuing and without any attempt to interpret a founding father at this time, let me provide a self-serving bit of wisdom: do not kill the messenger. I am just recounting what Benjamin Franklin said. I will not bother providing the text of the entire letter—only a bit more—to make Franklin's point. With this explanation, may I continue?

"That so retained contrary to Nature, it not only gives frequently great present Pain, but occasions future Diseases, such as habitual Cholics, Ruptures, Tympanies, &c., often destructive of the Constitution, & sometimes to Life itself.

Were it not for the odiously offensive Smell accompanying such Escapes, polite People would probably be under no more Restraint in discharging such Wind in Company, than they are in spitting, or in blowing their Noses.

My Prize Question therefore should be, *To discover some Drug wholesome and not disagreeable, to be mixed with our common Food, or Sauces, that shall render the Natural Discharges, of Wind from our Bodies, not only inoffensive, but agreeable as Perfumes.*"

Franklin's rant remained consistent while keeping a firm tongue in cheek, "That this is not a chimerical Project, and altogether impossible, may appear from these Considerations. That we already have some Knowledge of Means capable of Varying that Smell. He that dines on stale Flesh, especially with such Addition of Onions, shall be able to afford a Stink that no company can tolerate; while he that has lived for some Time on Vegetables only, shall have that Breath so pure as to be insensible to the most delicate Noses; and if he can manage so as to avoid the Report, he may any where give Vent to his Griefs, unnoticed."

Our founding father then provided suggestions: "a little Powder of Lime (or some equivalent) taken in our Food . . . [a] few Stems of Asparagus eaten, shall give our Urine a disagreeable Odour; and a Pill of Turpentine no bigger than a Pea, shall bestow on it the pleasing Smell of Violets. And why should it be thought more impossible in Nature, to find Means of making a Perfume of our *Wind* than of our *Water*?" Not my words, no, no, not mine—Dr. Franklin did say what he said:

"Are there twenty Men in Europe at this Day, the happier, or even the easier, for any Knowledge they have picked out of Aristotle? What Comfort can the Vortices of Descartes give a Man who has Whirlwinds in his Bowels! The Knowledge of Newton's Mutual *Attraction* of the Particles of Matter, can it afford Ease to him who is racked by their mutual *Repulsion*, and the cruel Distensions it occasions? The Pleasure arising to a few Philosophers, from seeing, a few Times in their Life, the Threads of Light untwisted, and separated by the Newtonian Prism into seven Colours, can it be compared with the Ease and Comfort every Man living might feel seven times a Day, by discharging feely the Wind from his Bowels? Especially if it be converted into a Perfume: For the Pleasures of one Sense being little inferior to those of another, instead of pleasing the *Sight* he might delight the *Smell* of those about him, & make Numbers happy, which to benevolent Mind must afford infinite Satisfaction." See Carl Japikse, comp. and ed., *Fart Proudly: Writings of Benjamin Franklin You Never Read in School* (Columbus: Enthea Press, 1990), 12, 15–16, 17.

Dr. Franklin, in expressing his ultimate displeasure, expressed the view the assigned topic by the Royal Academy was "scarcely worth a FART-HING."

41. "'Amazing Grace'—the Story Behind One of the Best Beloved Songs of All Time," Oregon Catholic Press (OCP), accessed February 7, 2024, https://www.ocp.org/en-us/blog/entry/amazing-grace#:~:text=The%20story%20behind%20the%20hymn%20%22Amazing%20Grace%22&text=Knowing%20the%20story%20of%20John,for%20God's%20truly%20amazing%20grace. See also Amazing Grace, Hymnal.net, https://www.hymnal.net/en/hymn/h/313, accessed June 27, 2024.

Chapter 12

1. City of Galveston, Department of Planning and Transportation: Old Central & Carver Park Neighborhood Plan. The Planning and Transportation Department's report is not dated; however, initial information in the

report provides some indication of when it was issued. "The neighborhood boundaries were established through data provided by the 1980 census. The neighborhood planning process is a directive of both the 1973 and 1988 Comprehensive Plans and in the case of Old Central, this plan supersedes the 1982 Neighborhood Plan." The document uses 1990 Census data, "which indicates that the neighborhoods are predominantly non-white (76%)." City of Galveston, Department of Planning and Transportation: Old Central & Carver Park Neighborhood Plan, 2, 3 (in possession of author). At the time of the report's issuance, Barbara Crews was the mayor; Crews served as mayor from 1990 to 1996. Douglas W. Matthews was the city manager.

2. *City Times*, January 2, 1915, 1.
3. *City Times*, July 17, 1915, 4.
4. "Local Doctor Shows Great Civic Spirit in Agreeing to Price," *Galveston Voice*, October 17, 1931, 1. The reference to eminent domain being threatened on Dr. Stanton's land was also in 1931.
5. *City Times*, October 17, 1917, 1.
6. *City Times*, November 10, 1917, 1.
7. *City Times*, November 10, 1917, 1.
8. There remains a Confederate statue in front of the Galveston County Courthouse located at 722 21st Street.
9. A statue paying tribute to Confederate General Sidney Sherman and Republic of Texas President David G. Burnet is located on Avenue J (Broadway) at 7th Street; Sherman served as "the commandant of Galveston by the Secession Convention." "[His son], Lt. Sidney Sherman, was killed in the battle of Galveston. David Burnet Sherman, the remaining son, died after the family moved to Richmond, and Mrs. Sherman died in 1865. Sherman spent his last years in Galveston. He died there at the home of his daughter, Mrs. J. M. O. Menard, on August 1, 1873. Sherman County and the city of Sherman in Grayson County are named in his honor." Julia Beazley, "Sherman, Sidney (1805–1873)," Texas State Historical Association, accessed April 21, 2021, https://www.tshaonline.org/handbook/entries/sherman-sidney. The ship channel bridge over the port of Houston retains his name. The Galveston statue is in the interstate's esplanade, owned by the State of Texas. "Highway History," Federal Highway Administration, accessed April 21, 2021, https://www.fhwa.dot.gov/interstate/faq.cfm#question5. The statue was erected in 1936. "General Sidney Sherman," HMdb.org, The Historical Marker Database, accessed November 16, 2024, https://www.hmdb.org/m.asp?m=49823.

NOTES

10. Jaybird statue was erected at the Fort Bend County Courthouse in 1896; Fort Bend County Commissioners voted to dismantle and remove it from the public square and relocate it to Hodges Bend Cemetery in Sugar Land. Stefan Modrich, "Contentious Jaybird Monument in Process of Being Relocated," *Fort Bend County Star*, October 27, 2020.

11. Teo Armus, "Alexandria Speeds Up Renaming of its Confederate Streets," *Washington Post*, January 11, 2023; Mark Ballard, "LSU Renames Well-Known Campus Street Named After Confederate Admiral as Part of Modernization Plan," *The Advocate*, March 27, 2017; Anthony Kustura, "Charlotte to Change Streets Named for Confederate Leaders," WSOC-TX, accessed February 6, 2023, https://www.wsoctv.com/news/local/charlotte-change-streets-named-confederate-leaders/T3QHE4NOZ5BHZEMFEQECPMFY6Q/; John H. Glenn, "Montgomery Officials Considering Renaming Streets Named for Confederates, Klansmen," *Alabama Political Reporter*, March 7, 2022, https://www.alreporter.com/2022/03/07/montgomery-officials-considering-renaming-streets-named-for-confederates-klansmen/; Kevin Lewis, "City of Fairfax May Change 14 Street Names Because of Hurtful Ties to Confederacy, Slavery," ABC News, accessed February 6, 2023, https://wjla.com/news/local/fairfax-city-virginia-street-name-change-council-vote-mosby-woods-confederate-slavery-confederate-plantation-lee-ranger-stonewall; "Houston's Dowling Street to Be Renamed Emancipation Avenue," Houston Public Media, January 12, 2017, accessed February 6, 2023, https://www.houstonpublicmedia.org/articles/news/local/2017/01/12/183416/houstons-dowling-street-to-be-renamed-emancipation-avenue/; "Missouri City Council Renames Confederate Court, Confederate South Drive," ABC 13 News, April 19, 2022, accessed February 6, 2023, https://abc13.com/missouri-city-street-name-changes-streets-renamed-confederate-court/11769599/; Daniel Chang and Sujin Shin, "UC Berkeley Students Call for Renaming of Campus Buildings Tied to Confederacy," *The Daily Californian*, accessed February 6, 2023, https://www.dailycal.org/2015/07/09/uc-berkeley-students-call-for-renaming-of-campus-buildings-tied-to-confederacy; Matthew Watkins, "UT-Austin removes Confederate Statues in the Middle of the Night," *The Texas Tribune*, August 21, 2017, accessed February 6, 2021, https://www.texastribune.org/2017/08/20/ut-austin-removing-confederate-statues-middle-night/; Ericka Mellon, "HISD Votes to Rename Schools with Confederate Ties," *Houston Chronicle*, May 12, 2016, https://www.chron.com/news/houston-texas/article/HISD-removes-names-of-8-school

s-with-Confederate-7465929.php; Samantha Ketterer, "Rice Founder's Statue to Be Moved in Courtyard Change," *Houston Chronicle*, February 7, 2023, Section A, 3 (relocation of statue of institution's founder, whose legacy came under scrutiny after the nationwide racial uprising in 2020).

12. "10 Much Better Names for the Army Bases Honoring Confederate Generals," Military.com, accessed February 6, 2023, https://www.military.com/off-duty/10-much-better-names-army-bases-honoring-confederate-generals.html.

13. Barbara Sprunt, "The House Votes to Remove Confederate Statues in the U.S. Capitol," NPR, June 29, 2021, accessed February 6, 2023, https://www.npr.org/2021/06/29/1011303611/the-house-votes-to-remove-confederate-statues-in-the-u-s-capitol.

Epilogue

1. "The Genius of John Hope Franklin," in *Black Issues in Higher Education* (1994), interview conducted by publisher Frank L. Matthews.
2. Brando Simeo Starkey, *In Defense of Uncle Tom: Why Blacks Must Police Racial Loyalty* (Cambridge: Cambridge University Press, 2015), 25–41, wherein the author kindly refers to me as an Uncle Tom; his was not a complimentary assessment.
3. india.arie, *Acoustic Soul*, Motown, 2001, writers Mark Batson, India Arie, and Shannon Sanders.
4. india.arie, *Acoustic Soul*.

INDEX

Note: Entry numbers in italics refer to images.

Allen, Augustus, 135, 158, 163. *See also* Gus Allen Café; Gus Allen Hotel
Antone, Peter, 215–16n17
Armistead, Wilson, 142–43
Arnold, Menard & Co, 67, 102
Atkinson, Jesse (407 25th Street), 115
Atlantic slave trade, 175. *See also* slave trade, transatlantic
auction houses, 13, 22–24, 51, 55, 58, 94, 102, 142, 149, 165
  contemporary evidence places Sydnor's, 52
auctioneers, 33–34, 51, 54, 62, 64–65, 68, 73, 78, 191n83, 206n92
Austin County, 13, 77
Avenue L Baptist Church (2612 Avenue L), 143, 164
Ayred, Charles, *163*
Ayred, Hilda, *163*

Baldridge, Dorothy Corine, *158*
Baldridge, Ellis Bernard, *158*
Ballinger, Henry, 221–22n3
Ballinger, William Pitt, 44, 48, 69–72, 186n24
  slave of, 71
Barbour, John H., 125
Barksdale, Anita Jones, 44, *46*, 46–47
Barksdale, Joan Pendergraff, *46*
Barksdale, Leonard N., II, *46*
Barksdale, Leonard N., III, *46*
Bath Avenue, 63, 65
Baylor University, 144
Beasley, Ellen, 99

Bell, J. V. (FBI agent), 117
Bell, John, 115
Benj. Lockett Hotel (2627 Church), 115
Berry, Mary Frances, 49
Bexar County, 77
Black Codes, 120, 123, 189n60, 230n73
Black lawyers, first, 124, 155
Black newspapers, 101, 118
Bolling & Sayre, 62, 64
Borden, Gail, 143, 145
Bosque County, 78
Bradley, Anna (charter member of the Galveston NAACP), 116
Brazoria County, 45, 72, 77, 224n23
Brazosport Archaeology Society, 222–24n23
Brick Wharf, 55–56, 64, 192n84
Bridge, Allen D., 125
Brink, Peter, 95, 106
Brown, John, 49, 108
Brown, John (Representative), 247n38
Brown, John Henry, 78–79, 97, 108, 207–8n5
Brown v. Board of Education, 13, 84
Broyles, M. H., 125
Bruce, Charles, *98*, 99
Bruce, Willa, *98*, 99
Bruce family, 101, 215n14, 217n27
Bruce's Beach, 99
Bynum Plantation, 48

Campbell, Ann Williamson, 68–69
Campbell, Archibald Rowland, 68–69, 197n34
Campbell, Archibald Rowland, III, 69
Campbell, Archibald Rowland, Jr., 69
Campbell, Archibald Rowland, Sr., 68

INDEX

Campbell, John C., 70
Campbell, John Harris, 69
Campbell, John Wesley, 68, 70
Campbell, John William, 69–70
Campbell, Samuel Williams, 69
Cartwright, Gary, 160
Carver, George Washington, 140
Carver Park Historic District, 167
Causeway Hotel and Café, 115
Cayuga County, 152
Central High School, *125*, 125–26
Charleston Museum, 150
Charleston's International African American Museum, 151
Church Street, 55, 58, 73, 141, 161, 192n86
city bell, 36, 57
City Halls, 56–57, 102
City Marketplace, 73
City of Galveston's Development Services Department, 55
City of Galveston Transportation and Planning Department, 161
City Party, 117–18, 134, 229n67
City Party Park (Avenue S), 238n166
City Times (Galveston), 101, 112, 115, 118, 124, 126, 135–37, 162–64
Civilian and Galveston City Gazette, *33*, *34*, 67
Clark, Ann Williamson, 68, 70
Clouser, John Henry, 166
Coahoma County, 199n50
Cobb, Henry A., 55–56
 advertisements, 33, 42
 auction house, 33
Cole, James P., 52, 70, 198n40
Collins, Izola, 99, 101, 126, 130–32, *130*, *131*, 155, 165, 238n166
Collins, Roy Lester, Sr., *131*
Colored Screwmen's Benevolent Association (CSBA), 113
Colored Women's Clubs, 116
Compton Memorial Church OGIC (2628 Avenue H), 164
Confederacy, 76, 112, 153, 166–67, 222n3, 243n1

Confederate statues, 151, 153, 168, 250nn8, 9
Conner, Robert C., 84
Coolie Negroes, 123
Cordray Drugstore, 58
cotton factors, 62–64, 73, 200n64, 224n23
Cotton Jammers, 113, 117, 226n38, 238n166
Cotton Jammers' Park, 238n166
Coulter, John, 70, 211–12n1
Cuney, Joseph, 116, 124–25, 235n121
Cuney, Maud. *See* Hare, Maud Cuney
Cuney, Norris Wright, 108, 110–13, 116, 119, 123, 126, 157–58, 163

DAR. *See* Daughters of the American Revolution
Darragh, John L., 30, 63, 65, 67–68, 101, 195, 218. *See also* auction house location in 1854,
Darrington Plantation, 224n23
Daughters of the American Revolution (DAR), 102, 219n41
 George Washington Chapter, 102, 219n41
DeBruhl, John F., 107, 221n3
Dedicated Historic District, 161
Delesdernier, George, 182–83n31
Dent, Jessie McGuire, 126, 156
Dent, Thomas, 126
Dent, Thomas H., 125
Dewitt County, 77
Dickens, Charles, 17–18
district, historical, 164, 168, 173
Doswell, Hill and Co., 67, 101, 219n38
Dowdy, Lucy, 44–45, 48
Dred Scott v. Sandford, 30, 83, 108, 179–80n15, 222
Dr. L. D. Davis 2513 1/2 Market Street, 135
Dubois, W. E. B., 172

emancipation, 25, 54, 81, 84, 86, 102, 108–9, 118–19, 123, 142, 145, 224n23

254

INDEX

Emerge magazine, 171
eminent domain, 98–99, 101, 135, 142, 163, 213n10, 215n17, 250n4
Episcopal Diocese of New York, 148
E. T. Chissell, 318 26th Street, 115

federal census, 183n31, 186–87n24, 194n11, 202–3n77, 218n36
of slave schedules, 70, 75, 101
federal census of slave schedules in Galveston, 70, 75
Ferguson, C. M., 108–9, 119, 223n10, 234n109
Ferguson, Henry, 119, 230n76
Five Hundred Thousand Strokes for Freedom (Armistead), 142
Fornell, Earl Wesley, 23, 44, 180–81n23, 182n31
Fort Bend, 109, 118–19
Fort Bend County, 108, 111, 118, 168, 223n10
Frances Rebecca Campbell, 68–69
Franklin, John Hope, 170
Freestone and Limestone Counties, 6
Freestone County, 85
Fullilove, Mindy Thompson, 106

Galveston, TX
founding members, 14
outsize role, 15
seawall, *95*, 103, 212n7
slave auctions, 201n70
Galveston City Company, 39, 68, 145
Galveston City Gazette, 33
Galveston College, 46–47, 158
Board of Regents, *47*
Galveston Colored Men's Business League, 135, 165
Galveston Commercial Association, 101, 116
Galveston County, 24, 29–30, 32, 69, 89, 108, 125
Galveston Daily News, 52, 54, 58, 112
Galveston Directory, 67, 102
Galveston Garden Club, 75
Galveston Heritage Choral Choir, 132

Galveston Historical Foundation (GHF), 17, 40, 96, 166, 177n2
Galveston NAACP, 116, 123
Galveston News, 58, 111
Galveston Standard, 107
Galveston to New Orleans, 90, 92
Galveston Tri-Weekly News, 123
Galveston Wharf Company, 55, 67
Galveston wharves, 44
Galveston's Development Services Department, 55
Galveston's Reedy Chapel, 131
Gardner, General, 129, 236–37n141
Garvey, Marcus, 124, 232n106
Gazette Weekly, 177
Georgetown University, 70, 148
Georgia Paine College Historic District, 152
GHF. *See* Galveston Historical Foundation
Gibson Chapel, 6
Gillespie County, 77
Graham, Jennett, 44
Grand Opera House, 132
Granger, General Gordon, 57, 83
Granger's order, 83–84, 107, 117, 123, 156, 208n10
Green, Alex, 125
Green Front Café, 115
Grey, William Henry, 50
Griffin Collection, Anthony P., 100, 103, 110, 125, 129–31, 133, 135, 142, 158–59, 163–65, 172
Grocers, W. D. Lewis and Geo. W. Williams, 115
Gus Allen Café, 163
Gus Allen Hotel, 141, 163

Hamilton, Doc, 113, 118
Hare, Maud Cuney, 108–9, 126–28, 155
Harmony Club (2111 Postoffice), 115
Harris County, 77–78
Heller, John H., 67
Henrico County, 55
Historic American Buildings Survey, 194n11

INDEX

Hollier, Homer, 115
Holy Rosary (1420 31st Street), 146, 164
Houston, auction house location, 206–7n92
Houston Chronicle, 131
Houston Post, 111
Howard, Camille, 128
Howard University, 126
Huckins, James, 143–44, 241n197
Hurston, Zora Neale, 210–11n15

Ida Bennett, Alamo Café, 115
ILA. *See* International Longshoremen's Association
International African American Museum, 150
International Longshoremen's Association (ILA), 113, 117, 124, 215n17
Island of Color (Collins), 99

J. B. Spiller, 25th and Winnie Street, 115
Jackson Ward Historic District, 153
Jasper County, 77, 119
Jaybird-Woodpecker War, 223n10
Jefferson County, 77
Jerusalem Baptist Church (2717 Avenue H), 164
Jessie McGuire/Menard Park/Robert McGuire's Bath House, 163
John Brown's Raid, 49
John Williams's Restaurant, 115
Johnson, Congresswoman Eddie Bernice, 104
Johnson, Jack, 114, 163, 225n27
Jones, Bessie Scott, *46*
Jones, Charles Scott, 44–47, 158
Jones, Esther Mae, 132
Jones, Harold S., 44–46
Jones, John, 70
Jones, Louis Prince, Jr., 132
Jones, Richard, 115
Jones, William H., 44–46, *46*
Jones, William H., Jr., 48
Jones, William Henry, 48
J. S. Lewis, a Black organizer, 116

Juneteenth Plaque, 40–41, *41*, 84, 184–85n10

Kidnapping Club (Wells), 158
Knowles-Lawson, Celestine Beyoncé, 134
Ku Klux Klan, *120*, 170, 230n73

Landry, Joyce Finch, *172*
Leonard, Charles H. (mayor), 55, 83–84, 123, 192n86, 192n87
Leonard's Hall (Church Street), 55, 58, 192n86
Leon County, 68
Lewis, Congressman John, 190n72
Lewis, J. Vance, 125
Lewis, M. G., 125
Lewis, Sharon Baldridge, *158*
Lewis, W. D., 115
Liberty Bell, 57
Liberty County, 77
Limestone Counties, 6
Lincoln Theatre (Ave D Lincoln Theatre, 413–15 25th), 126
Live Oak Baptist Church (1020 32nd), 164
Local 329, 116
Local 807, 116
Lone Star Cotton Jammers, 113, 215n17
Lone Star Medical Association, 112–13
Lone Star Screwman Hall, 116, 162, 217n26
longshoremen strike, 117
Los Angeles, Department of City Planning, 151
Los Angeles, South Central, 132
Los Angeles County, 99, 103, 168
Los Angeles Times, 98, 151
Louis Blues Boy Jones Day, 132
Louis Blues Boy Jones Street, 132
Loyola University Maryland, 198n43
Lynch, E. O., 34, 68
lynchings, 120, 156, 247n38

Macedonia Missionary Baptist Church (2920 Avenue M 1/2), 164

Madison County, 68
Manhattan Beach, 101
Market Street, 42, 55–56, 115–16, 135, 162, 165, 217n26, 227n42
martial law, 93, 116–17, 119
Mason County, 77
Matagorda County, 118
McCarty, C. L., 22–24, 34, 42, 64, 72, 194n8
McCollough County, 77
McGuire, Jessie, 126
McGuire, Robert, 99, 101–2, 115, 126
  business partners, 215n17
  property, 101
McGuire Park, 99
Mechanic and Church Streets, 161
Mechanic and Market Street, 55
Mechanic Street, 115–16, 136, 165, 217, 235n121
Medina County, 77
Meharry Medical College, 112
Melton, Lewis, 112, 162
Menard, Michel B., 39, 101, 218n36
Menard County, 77, 101
Menard Park, 102, 165
Messrs. Oliver, Young & Porter (2712 Market Street), 115
Middle Passage, 21, *22*, 26, 177n2
Mills, Ballinger, 44–45, 47
Mills, David G., 45, 48, 187n27
Mills, Robert, 45, 187n27, 224n23
Mills and Company of Galveston, 196n23
Mills Brothers, 45, 187n27
Mitchell, George, 90
Morgan and Mallory steamship lines, 116
Mound Bayou Historic District, 152
Moyers, Bill, 150

NAACP, 116, 123, 127
National American Woman Suffrage Association (NAWSA), 126
National Gallery, 40
National Juneteenth Museum, 152, 244n17
National Negro Business League, 216n17, 232n106
National Register of Historic Places, 151, 152, 212n2
National Society of the Daughters of the American Revolution (NSDAR), 102
NAWSA. *See* National American Woman Suffrage Association
Negro boys
  dark-complexioned, 30
  for sale, 194n9
  smart, 72
negro girl, active, 33, 42
Negro Motorist Green Book, 138
Negro Park Situation map, 238n168
negroes and negresses, 23–24, 68
  in Texas, 85, 196n22
  "likely," 42, 68, 178n1, 194n9
New Idea (Galveston), 118, 123
New Orleans, LA
  ports of, 90–91
  status as largest slave auction in the US, 185n11
New Orleans to Galveston, 107
New York and New Orleans, 90
New York and Texas, 125
New York Times, 132
Norris Wright Cuney: A Tribune of the Black People (Hare), 126
Norris Wright Cuney Park, 112
NSDAR. *See* National Society of the Daughters of the American Revolution

OCCPHD. *See* Old Central/Carver Park Historic District
Old Central & Carver Park Neighborhood Plan, 212, 249–50n1
Old Central Carver Park, 4, 115
Old Central / Carver Park, 96, 161
Old Central / Carver Park Historic District (OCCPHD), 166–67
Old Central Cultural Center, 225n27
Oleander Drug Store (417 25th Street), 126
Osterman, Joseph, 30, 41–42, 54–55, 191

Osterman Building, 40, 52, 54, 73, 84, 185n10

Paine College Historic District, 152
Palmer, John E., 135–36
Palm Springs, CA, 153, 246n31
park, segregated city, 102, 163
Pendergraff, Beverly W., *46*
Pendergraff, Lena Verdell, *46*
Perkins, Allen G., 124
Phillips, Esther, 132
Piney, Laura A. (union organizer and leader of the Woman's Progressive), 116
Polk County, 77
Pope, Joe, 138
Pope, Lynne Nita, *46*, 47, 138–39
Pope, Melba, 100, 103
Pope, Penny L., 44, 48, 140, 155, 239n180
Pope, Rachel, 138–39, *139*, 155, 158
Pope, Reginald, 48, 139–40
Pope's Bath House, *114*
Port Arthur News, 234n109
ports of New Orleans and Galveston, 90
Postoffice (Street), 58, 97, 99, 112–13, 115, 162
Powhatan House, 201n71
Prairie View A&M University, 127, 131–32
primaries, White, 119
Pullman's Café for Colored People (507 25th Street), 126
Purdy's Bookstore (217 Market Street), 126

race massacres, 231n35
Reed, Johnson, 221–22n3
Reedy Chapel, 84, 131, *165*, 221n3
Republic of Texas, 25, 39, 97
Rice, Lawrence D., 86
Richardson, W. H., 126
Rochester Ladies Anti-Slavery Society, 37
Roque, Sheila, 141, 239
Rosenberg Library, 14, 69, 125, 163, 166
Ruby, George T., 107–8, 112

Runnels County, 72
Rusk County, 122

Scott, Dred, 30–31
Scott, William H., 112
Scott-Heron, Gil, 94, 155
Scott Restaurant, 115
Sherman County, 250n9
Sherwood Equal Rights Historic District, 152
Shiloh A.M.E. (1310 Martin Luther King Blvd.), 164
Shirley, Mills, 44, 47, 71
Silk Stocking Residential Historic District, 194n7
slave auction
  business, 111
  houses, 11–15, 25, 78, 91, 166, 198n40
  locations, 58
Slave Business District, 55
slave trade, transatlantic, 18, 21, 25, 91, 148, 171, 173, 176, 181–82n30
slave traders, 21, 24, 42, 57, 73, 101, 111, 123
slaveholders, largest, 48, 187n27, 196n23
slaves
  auctioning, 56, 182n30
  freed, 81, 168
  houses, 14, 69, 156
  manifests of, 48, 90, 209–11
  population, 85, 179n7
  records of, 89
Smith, Starita, 49–50, 170–71, 189n60
Smith, Wilford H., 117, 124, 232n104, 233–34n109
South America, 91, 142, 147, 173
Southern Baptist Convention, 144
Southern Trading Company, 219n43
St. John's Baptist Church (2917 Sealy Street), 164
St. John's Church, 69
St. John's Episcopal Church, 148
St. Paul United Methodist Church, 46
Strand
  corner of, 52, 55, 63–64, 192n84

location, TSHA attributes, 40
Street and Bath Avenue, 63, 65
strike of October 1917 and 1898, 119
Stuart, Adeline, 109–10
Stubbs, James B., 11
Stubbs, T. B., 73, 111, 200n64, 204n79
Swanson, Henry H., 125
Sydnor, John, 30, 33, 75, 91, 102, 145, 167, 203n79
Sydnor, John B., 75, 203–4n79
Sydnor, John Seabrook, 29–30, 55, 57–58, 75–76, 78, 143, 177n3, 201n71, 202n77, 204n82, 204n84, 207–8
Sydnor, Seabrook, 78, 206n91
Sydnor's advertisement, 40, 54, 56, 58
Sydnor's Auction House, 40, 52, 58, 73, 185n10, 200n64
   in Houston, 78
   location at Market Place and Strand, 1857, 55
Sydnor's Wharf, transferred, 56

Tate, Patricia Ann, 133, 163
Texas Historical Commission, 41, 56, 97, 108
Texas Medical Association, 112
Texas State Historical Association (TSHA), 40, 144
Thomas, Jennie, 115
Thurmond, Strom, 43, 186n20
Till, Emmett, 153
Tillis, Frederick C., 128, 236–37n141
Tremé (New Orleans neighborhood), 151, 244n14
Tremont House, 53
Tri Weekly News (Houston), 75–76
Tri-Weekly Telegraph, 76
Trueheart, H. M., 23, 42, 64, 65, 71, 73, 74, 182n30, 182n31, 195n14
Trueheart, John O., 64, 73, 177n3, 182n30, 195n14
Trueheart-Adriance Building, 73, 200n65
TSHA. *See* Texas State Historical Association

Tuskegee, Alabama, 124
Twitty, Michael W., 195n15

Ufford, E. L., 52, 53, 58, 64, 185n10, 194–95n11
UNIA. *See* Universal Negro Improvement Association
United States Supreme Court, 13, 30, 124, 146
   Brown v. Board of Education of Topeka, 84
   Dred Scott, 83
Universal Negro Improvement Association (UNIA), 124, 232n106
University of Texas Medical Branch, 106, 156
US Census mortality schedules, 203n77

Washington, Booker T., 124, 140, 232–33n106, 233n109, 239n102
Webb, M. W., 115
Wesley Tabernacle United Methodist Church (902 28th Street), 126, 145, 164, 225n35
West Point (3003 Avenue M), 164
W. H. Brown Café, 2512 Market Street, 115
White, Barry, 132
Wilkins, John Henry, 112
Wilkins, Lewis Melton, 112
Williams, Cornelius J., 124–25
Williams, Samuel May, 31, 69
Willis, William, 162, 217n26
Wilson, Latonia, 89, 91
Wilson, Webster, 125
Winnie Street, 114–15, 213–14n10
Wise, Henry A., 49–50
Women's Business League, 136
Woods, Willis, 118, 229n64
Wright, Albert, 7, 12–13, 84, 86
Wright, Chesterana, 5, 10, 159
Wright, Lillian, 7, 12, 159
Wright, Louis, 86
Wright Cuney building, 217n34
Wright Cuney Park, 102, 112
W. T. Matthews, Sea-wall Hotel, 115

Zollah & Green, No. 415 25th Street (Market), 115

ABOUT THE AUTHOR

Anthony P. Griffin practiced law from 1978 to 2014, trying many high-profile cases, including one where he represented the grand dragon of the Ku Klux Klan. He has contributed work to anthologies of Gulf Coast recipes, a history of Black cowboys in Texas, and a volume of essays edited by Henry Louis Gates Jr.